English Drama: Forms and Development

English Drama:
Forms and Development

ESSAYS IN HONOUR OF
MURIEL CLARA BRADBROOK

EDITED BY
MARIE AXTON AND RAYMOND WILLIAMS
WITH AN INTRODUCTION BY RAYMOND WILLIAMS

CAMBRIDGE UNIVERSITY PRESS

CAMBRIDGE

LONDON · NEW YORK · MELBOURNE

Published by the Syndics of the Cambridge University Press
The Pitt Building, Trumpington Street, Cambridge CB2 IRP
Bentley House, 200 Euston Road, London NWI 2DB
32 East 57th Street, New York, NY 10022, USA
296 Beaconsfield Parade, Middle Park, Melbourne 3206, Australia

© Cambridge University Press 1977

ISBN 0 521 21588 9 hard covers

First published 1977

Printed in Great Britain by
W & J Mackay Limited, Chatham

Library of Congress Cataloguing in Publication Data
Main entry under title:
English drama.
Includes bibliographical references and index.
Contents: Axton, R. Folk play in Tudor interludes. –
Axton, M. The Tudor mask and Elizabethan court drama.–
Salingar, L. Comic form in Ben Jonson. [etc.]
1. English drama – History and criticism – Addresses,
essays, lectures. 2. Bradbrook, Muriel Clara – Bibliography.
I. Bradbrook, Muriel Clara. II. Axton, Marie.
III. Williams, Raymond.
PR627.E48   822'.009   76–57099
ISBN 0 521 21588 9

Contents

Introduction

The problem of form is central to the history and analysis of drama. Yet it is soon clear that even the definition of the problem involves radical differences of theory and method. At one extreme, which can be called formalist, each work has its specific form, though there is then a deep divergence between those who assign the specific form to a specific experience and those who see each form as specifying the formal properties of some more general mode, either the dramatic mode itself or one of its generic variants. At the other extreme, which can be called historical, each work is specific but its form is a variable matter, over a range from pure examples of historically dominant forms, through cases of adaptation and combination of previously known forms, to instances of specific mutations of form, in discoverable historical situations.

The theoretical issues raised in these positions, and in the many intermediate or eclectic positions, are relevant to the whole range of writing and indeed of all imaginative composition. But that they are especially relevant and in one sense inevitable in the history and analysis of drama is due mainly to the extraordinary richness, the extraordinary time-span, and in this sense – though definition is again difficult – the extraordinary persistence of major drama. We bring together, and in one sense are bound to bring together, in what can seem to be a tradition, dramatic works which to the most casual eye are radically different in form yet in which we can see both a community and a range of communities. The study of forms and their development is then necessarily part of the practical work, on whatever theoretical basis or at whatever level of consciousness of the theoretical issues involved, of every student of drama.

This point has a significant relation to the study of drama in the Faculty of English in Cambridge, to which all the contributors to this book belong or have recently belonged. Cambridge English is most widely and influentially known for its emphasis on 'practical criticism', though members of the Faculty know – and with especial acuteness today – how varied and variable that emphasis has been and can be. For while, in the study of almost all drama, there are indeed 'words on pages', in this local and practical sense, it is or ought to be evident, as an inherent and defining fact about them, that they are not intended to be confined to printed pages and indeed, to put it more strongly, that the words on the pages are either a preparation or a record of that more specific composition which is a dramatic performance. Of course the pages vary. Sometimes, as in certain modern texts, the words are not only the words to be spoken in the performance but also detailed descriptions of dramatic scene and movement. Indeed the variability of this relation between 'text' and 'performance' is a central instance of the general and theoretical problems of dramatic form.

There are few who would deliberately deny this, but the study of drama in Cambridge has undoubtedly been affected by the unresolved character of this basic question. There are, of course, many for whom the simple formulation – 'the words on the page' – is simply shorthand for close reading and close analysis of what is actually written, and when this is the case it is not difficult to establish the need, in close reading and analysis of dramatic writing, to discover and understand the notations which indicate what is not always verbally present but is essential to the specific arrangement and composition, and, further, to discover and understand the conventions, those strictly formal elements, which are often not present, as words on the page, but which are essential to any significant or accurate reading of them. Notations and conventions have then undoubtedly also to be read, and in the case of drama this reading of notations and conventions involves study of the conditions of performance, ranging from the physical properties of stages to the nature of the occasion and of the audience, which, though in varying degrees, are inherent elements of the specific composition.

Two tendencies can however be discerned, in Cambridge and elsewhere, in the study of major drama. There are those who, whatever their other differences, take the words on the page as also the words on the stage, and extend their analysis and their history to the development of dramatic forms and to the most general conditions of performance. There are others who, in effect, and especially in relation to the conditions of performance, reject this extension as distraction, or, to put it another way, assimilate dramatic texts to the status of all other printed texts, and indeed to printed texts which were intended from the beginning to be silently read. Everything of real importance, they argue, can be read where it is, on the page. It is a striking fact that these two tendencies have coexisted in Cambridge, both in the study of Shakespeare, where for half a century there has been important but radically variable work, and in the study of Tragedy, which again for half a century has been a major element of the Tripos and which is indeed now the only compulsory reading paper in Part Two of the Tripos, which can itself be identified as the most specific contribution to English studies now represented by Cambridge.

It is inevitable and perhaps even right, in existing circumstances, that a major faculty should include, even in its central work, radical differences of theory and method, though this is only certain to be an educational advantage if it is something more than passive coexistence and includes open and regular clarification and argument. But what has also to be said is that a school of English cannot be reduced, either in popular reputation or in formal account, to any one of its elements. The emphasis on 'practical criticism', as a feature of Cambridge English, is historically just, but there have been at least three other significant features, and it is by no means certain which of the four will eventually be identified as the most fruitful and influential. There has been the striking and persistent correlation of literature and social history, always controversial but always active. There has been the persistent if difficult enquiry into the relations between imaginative literature and moral and philosophical ideas. There has also, and of most immediate importance in the present context, been important and sustained work in the study of dramatic forms and their conditions of performance. Any adequate history of the Cambridge English Faculty has then to include all of these four kinds of work.

In one of these kinds, the history and analysis of dramatic forms and their conditions of performance, the work of Muriel Bradbrook has been defining and pre-eminent. Over her whole working life she has contributed very generally to the work of the Faculty, but the most significant thread is the work which began with *Elizabethan Stage Conditions* in 1931 and was continued with the remarkable *Themes and Conventions of Elizabethan Tragedy* in 1935. The titles of these early works sufficiently indicate the position and interests from which her work on drama was begun. They have influenced successive generations of students and scholars, and beyond this properly academic influence have provoked and helped in defining and sometimes solving more general questions of dramatic form and performance. There has been a lifetime's contribution as a scholar, but there has also been this significant emphasis, most notable in such later works as *The Growth and Structure of Elizabethan Comedy* (1955; revised 1973), *The Rise of the Common Player* (1962) and especially *English Dramatic Form: a history of its development* (1965).

All the contributors to the present volume have been colleagues of Muriel Bradbrook in the Cambridge English Faculty. In coming together to write a book on the occasion of her formal retirement they have been moved by the spirit of *Festschrift* but have also tried to write something more than a *Festschrift*, in the spirit of her own most significant work. The problems of English dramatic forms and their development are of outstanding importance both in the history of all English writing and in the history of world writing. At the same time, from the very richness and variety of the material, every general question and every preliminary historical outline moves into the complexity of local definition and specific variation. It is doubtful how far the contributors would agree in matters of general theory and method; the reader will observe at least implicit differences. But two general features of the book can be affirmed. First, that its emphasis is historical, both in the simple sense that its chapters range from medieval drama through all the centuries of English drama down to our own, and in the more specific sense that the problems of form, however strictly and locally defined, are normally considered in relation to specific historical circumstances, whether social, dramatic or theatrical. Then, second, there is an important continuity of attention, on work widely separated in historical time, to the complex relations between actual audiences, actual styles of drama and those alternative and sometimes conflicting traditions which the simple concept of tradition so often obscures. Much more would need to be done if all the significant material for a history of the making and development of English dramatic forms was to be brought together, in the necessary actuality of detail. Yet the book can be seen as a conscious pointer, in the spirit of Muriel Bradbrook's own work, one of the titles of which it deliberately echoes, towards the definition and development of such work, and to its necessarily collaborative character.

All detailed editorial work on the volume has been done by Marie Axton. I am grateful to her, as co-editor, and to my fellow contributors. Our common gratitude to Muriel Bradbrook is implicit in the book but can also be made explicit in our common pleasure that she is still, in every real sense, our colleague in this developing work.

Cambridge, September 1976   Raymond Williams

Folk play in Tudor interludes

RICHARD AXTON

THE HISTORICAL PROBLEMS OF FOLK PLAY

The early kinds of English folk drama are uncertain; they float formless in a dim region of our dramaturgy visited only by historians and folklorists. The terms, however punctuated, cling uneasily together, looking for mutual support and definition: folk-drama, 'folk' drama, folk 'drama'. Apart from the difficulty of defining folk and drama, the factual problems are substantial ones: at any single place or time the evidence is too thin on the ground to support a solid reconstruction of medieval popular drama comparable with the church's great edifice of 'textual' plays. And by the time texts of popular plays are available, that is, by the time of printing, it is too late: the plays are, as the folklorists would say, 'contaminated' and 'literary'.

Early students of the field, working in a golden Frazerian age, delighted in cultural promiscuity, ranging thousands of miles and years for comparative materials, and did not blush to stand honest English ploughlads, Saint George and 'Bonapurt' in a line with Thracian Dionysos. Such generous syncretism is easily criticised; it is harder to forswear the footnotes which it garnered. The work of E. K. Chambers and C. R. Baskervill half a century ago has left us a rich store of reference.[1] These scholars tackled the historical problem of folk drama from both ends, treating nineteenth-century mummers' plays as survivals of a lost pagan drama whose 'ritual' significance had become obscured. They thus ignored any current function or meaning the plays might have. They also assumed a continuity in popular practices which can sometimes be verified from very early sources. (A prohibition, c. 1250, forbidding Oxford clerks to dance in summer in churches and public places, wearing masks or dressed in leaves and flowers, does not imply innovation but the reverse.[2]) Clearly there was a time before Shakespeare when the hobby-horse was not forgot.

But it is obviously hazardous to assume that folk drama remained unchanged through several centuries. In particular, we are separated from the medieval folk drama by the English Reformation. In the course of the sixteenth century popular culture was eroded precisely at the points where it was attached to official religious ceremonies.[3] The reformation and abolition of many church festivals and practices, the suppression of community religious plays and processions, also struck at the popular dramatics sheltering under the same umbrella. Pressures to conformity in devotional practice, the simultaneous growth of London-based government, the spread of standard English, the publishing of polemic and educational drama for playing by professional troupes – these were some of the factors working to produce a new self-consciousness about popular dramatic culture and the forces implicit in it. Folk play became a point of reference for the new drama in the era of print.

Popular playing was seasonal and festive; it involved disguise, impersonation and boisterous activity, rather than the representation of a story. It was linked with the major feasts of the Roman Catholic year, particularly with night vigils and processions, and often took the form of licensed misrule. During the decades of strong anti-Roman feeling, of iconoclasm and social unrest, popular drama came under a new scrutiny. The same wind blew it in contrary directions, depending on whether it was seen as anti-church or anti-state. At the same parish church the destruction of *tabernacles* (centre-pieces of devotional plays) sometimes coincided with the organising of shooting and wrestling games and the buying of 'interlude books'. Throughout the sixteenth century churches continued to receive 'silver' from *ales*, from processions with the plough, and from *Mays* (the games, plays and dancing associated with leafy bowers built in churchyards or against churches); and sometimes churchwardens paid for bells for Morris dancers. Elsewhere, a dragon was taken away without the consent of the parishioners.[4] Responses to folk drama were deeply ambivalent. Sir Richard Morison, writing a programme of reformatory propaganda for Henry VIII in about 1536, approves the traditional 'hoptide' (i.e. Hocktide) plays of women's rule, 'wherin it is leaful for them to take men, bynde, wasshe them, if they will give them nothing to bankett'. The exemplary expulsion of Danes, which the play is supposed to celebrate, can urge common people to throw the 'bisshop of Rome out of this Realme'. On the other hand, Morison disapproves of Robin Hood plays because of their encouragement to civil licence; he suggests they be replaced by straight propaganda:

In somer comenly upon the holy daies in most places of your realm, ther be playes of Robyn hoode, mayde Marian, freer Tuck, wherin besides the lewdenes and rebawdry that ther is opened to the people, disobedience also to your officers, is tought, whilest these good bloodes go about to take from the shiref of Notyngham one that for offendyng the lawes shulde have suffered execution. Howmoche better is it that those plaies shulde be forbodden and deleted and others dyvysed to set forthe and declare lyvely before the peoples eies the abhomynation and wickednes of the bisshop of Rome, monkes, ffreers, nonnes, and suche like . . .[5]

Both Morison's examples of traditional popular drama are based on the disruption of normal order. A century earlier, in 1439, Peter Venables was accused in Derbyshire of using Robin Hood's disguise for nefarious purposes, 'beyng of his [i.e. Robin Hood's] clothinge, and in maner of insurrection wente into the wodes in that county like it hadde be Robyn Hode and his meynee'. Similar accusations are quite frequent in the 1520s and 1530s.[6] At Wymondham in Norfolk, the traditional play (for which, in 1539, the Kett family helped make a giant, armour, and devil's shoes) provided cover for Kett's rebellion ten years later.[7] On the other hand a Calvinist satirist writing in 1569 thought a penny or two spent 'to see a play of Robin Hood, or a Morisse daunse . . . were a great deal better bestowed [than] upon those apishe toies of these good Priests'.[8]

In this confusion two main drifts are discernible: folk play had become an 'issue'; it was also gradually being choked. A zealous town council deprived Coventry of its traditional plays (including *hocking*) in the 1560s. Chester's religious plays were stopped by the Privy Council in 1575; thereafter successive mayors reformed the Midsummer *Watch* too: the dragon, men in women's apparel, 'naked boys', the devil-in-his-feathers, all disappeared. By the end of the century the loss was strongly felt. In *Albions England* William Warner laments a rhythm and a richness of life broken at the Reformation. His simple Northern spokesman is 'no friend to monke or frier', but mourns a time when,

> At Ewle we wonten gambole, daunce, to carrole, and to sing,
> To have gud spiced Sewe, and Roste, and plum-pies for a king:
> At Fasts-eve pan-puffes: Gang tide gaites did alie Masses bring:
> At Paske begun our morrise: and ere Penticost our May:
> Tho Roben hood, liell Iohn, frier Tucke, and Marian, deftly play . . .
> At Baptis-day with Ale and cakes bout bon-fires neighbors stood:
> At Martelmasse we turnde a crabbe, thilke tolde of Roben hood.

> (3rd edition 1592, Book v, ch. 24)

By Warner's time many grosser aspects of folk 'playing' had been purged; a good deal too had been reformed and absorbed into 'official' literary entertainments: the Coventry hocking reappeared, with a rustic *bride-ale*, among Queen Elizabeth's Princely Pleasures at Kenilworth in 1575 (see below, p. 35). Folk play was later encapsulated or transformed by Nashe and by Jonson in his masques and was sent back to the provinces, spruced up by the metropolitan stage as jigs.[9] Copying manuscripts of the Chester plays and shows became a minor industry and, with the 'yeerely celebration of Mr Robert Dover's Olimpick Games upon Cottsold Hills' (commemorated in *Annalia Dubrensia* (1636) by Michael Drayton and others), antiquarianism set a paternalistic hand to the plough for the preservation of the 'folk'.

FOLK DRAMA BEFORE THE REFORMATION

Baskervill hypothesised that English folk plays were formed when the traditional *games* of ploughmen or shearmen were taken as *play* offerings to the obligatory feasts held by their overlords. This theory (for which Baskervill had no textual evidence) has recently received support from the identification of a plough play from about 1500.[10] The song text describes an intricate ballet performed by plough 'hinds' for their 'laird', to whom they offer their service in return for pasturage rights. In the action of the drama a tired 'old ox', impersonated by the leader, is 'broded' to death by the sticks of a circle of dancers. The head is removed and set on a 'new ox' and members of the team, called by rustic or heroic names, are renamed as oxen and 'bound' together before the plough. The company is blessed and the team moves off. The play is an offering, its action affirming social bonds, duties and rights.

Such offerings were not always respectful, and the bulk of the medieval evidence shows authority suspicious of folk dramatic practice. Welsh villagers observed by Giraldus in the twelfth century celebrated a saint's day by dancing in church and churchyard and performing mimetic versions of their workaday tasks: 'the hands of one laid to the plough, another driving oxen as if with a goad'; others 'sheared sheep' and 'spun'.[11] Gerald notes that these occupations have been forbidden on holidays. It seems that the dancers mock authority and they are later made to show their penitence. It is as likely that medieval churchmen condemned popular *ludi* because they felt themselves threatened as to suppose that their concern was simply for the souls of the participants. One motive can perhaps be located in the irrational fear of masks and disguise, often connected with paganism and witchcraft.[12] There was also the fear of civil unruliness. A proclamation by the Mayor and Aldermen of the City of London in 1418 charged that,

no manere persone, of what astate degre or condicion þat euere he be, duryng þis holy tyme of Cristemes, be so hardy in eny wyse to walk by nyght in eny manere mommyng, pleyes, enterludes, or eny oþer disgisynges, with eny feynyd berdis, peyntid visers, disfourmyd or colourid visages in eny wyse, vp(on) peyne of enprisonement of her bodyes.[13]

Offering *to* can easily become offering *at* and it may be a perennial function of folk drama to express the social antagonism of a lower class against 'authority'. (A recent sociological study of Christmas mummings in Newfoundland has described the use of seasonal disguise and nocturnal visitations within a small community as a licensed form of name-calling. The intruder has freedom to mock from behind his mask but must reveal himself before moving on to the next house.[14])

In *Sir Gawain and the Green Knight* (*c.* 1400) the Green Knight's boisterous challenge of Arthur's court to a Christmas 'game' can be seen as the courtly transformation of a folk mumming, coming as it does to interrupt the feast. It is as such an 'enterlude', fitting the Christmas season, that the king tries jestingly to pass off the frightening events. In the course of the finely wrought narrative two recurrent patterns of the folk drama are completed: the hero faces the monster and survives beheading; the 'vileyn' who comes to dispraise the feasting nobles removes his 'mask' and gives friendly blessing. The reverberations of the 'eldritch challenger' in Elizabethan drama have been suggested by Muriel Bradbrook in *English Dramatic Form*.[15] The line runs through Dunbar's May-time prologue, *The manere of the crying of ane playe*, in which the grandson of Gog Magog, slayer of King Arthur and phallic champion in search of a wife, urges the 'noble merchandis everilkane' to take bow and arrow and 'in lusty grene . . . follow furth on Robyn Hude'. This monster of lust and violence is tamed by the offer of a boozing can into dispensing blessings on 'madin, wyf, and man' in the name of the 'Haly Rude'.[16]

The radical ambivalence of these folk play creations towards both Christianity and authority could be illustrated at length in the French medieval drama, where Adam de la Halle's *Jeu de la Feuillée* (*c.* 1276) provides a model repertory of popular themes and conventions. The play has been seen by Mikhail Bakhtin as the carnival expression of proletarian feeling; I prefer to view it as a literary poet's transformation of a traditional revue. Either way, there can be no doubt that this strange drama is subversive of both *ecclesia* and *urbs*.[17] In Adam's play Christian belief and pagan licence, respect for authority and holiday misrule are crammed oddly and explosively together. The play's occasion (apparently the coincidence of a summer festival of the Virgin Mary with a non-Christian 'feast of mothers') supposes a formal hostility of the sexes, such as was practised in the fifteenth-century Coventry hocking plays. Thus the men in the play leave the acting-place in order to light candles at the shrine of the Virgin, while the women, led by an old *dame* who has been shown to be 'miraculously' pregnant, follow the fairy sisters, threatening violence to any man they find to have maligned them. Husbands complain of wives, fathers complain of sons. A fool enacts an obscene cow-and-bull game (known in Irish wake games[18]) with his father, and gets beaten. Voices are raised against all forms of restraint, family, city, church. Popes, magistrates and nobles are named in scorn. Tavern law is set up in opposition to the church, whose representative, the monk, is cheated and beaten; his relics are stolen and mocked, his authority parodied by the taverner. Certain formal features of the *Feuillée* are also characteristic of the English tradition, as it can be glimpsed through fragmentary records and clerical condemnations: the construction of an arbour of greenery; feasting and drinking; the fact that the audience is nocturnally visited by perambulatory actors who bestow 'luck' or curses; the dressing-up and carrying of human effigies; the use of at least one fantastic headdress and wearing of little bells. The play has a loose, improvised appearance in its alternation of formal set-piece and topical reference, and it lacks story.

Adam's play cannot be matched in English for its scale. From the same period we have only the *Interludium de Clerico et Puella* and *Dame Sirith* (both *c.* 1300), two versions (for actors and for solo mime) of the same fabliau wooing. These professional entertainments, *for* the people rather than *by* the people, skilfully manipulate the stereotypes of blasphemous fool-lover, bawdy old hag and 'nice' lady, spicing the whole with anti-religious humour.[19] Evidence from the fifteenth century is fuller and allows one to sketch in a tradition of English folk play in the half-century before the Reformation. 'Comedies' among the 'foolish vulgar' concerning Robin Hood are scorned by a historian of the 1440s and a fragmentary text survives from about 1475. It is all that remains of a play that may have been performed annually by servants in the Paston household.[20] In common with other early Robin Hood plays it is constructed around physical combat and shows the flouting of law and the redress of social differences. The story of the first fragment comes from the ballad of Guy of Gisborne;

the extant text deals only with Robin's resisting arrest and killing of Sir Guy, and with the Sheriff of Nottingham's capture of Robin's men. The dialogue is simple and formulaic, the merest induction to a series of physical contests. In sixteen lines Robin and Guy have met, competed at bow shooting, cast stones, heaved the axletree, wrestled, fought with swords to the death. Robin then disguises himself in Guy's clothes. Why he must cut off Sir Guy's head and bear the head in his hood is never made clear. In the next 'scene', the sheriff overcomes and binds all Robin's outlaws, threatening to hang them. Presumably Robin later rescues them.

In a post-Reformation text, printed by Copland *c.* 1560 ('verye proper to be played in Maye games') Robin and Friar Tuck vaunt and fight with staves. Robin fails to make the friar bear him over the water and is thrust in. Each calls his men to combat, but they are reconciled when Robin gives the friar a 'Lady fre' (presumably a grotesque, played by a man). Friar Tuck rejoices in his sexual prowess, telling the audience:

> Go home ye knaves and lay crabbes in the fyre
> For my lady & I wil daunce in the myre for veri pure joye.   (lines 149–50)

A further episode (or an alternative 'game') repeats the territorial combat with Robin and a potter, whose wares Robin has broken and from whom he demands 'one penny passage to paye'. Here Robin is a 'good yeman' and a 'gentylman' (there is even the suggestion of Roman tribute in the penny) and he is worsted at the potter's hands. Little John undertakes a fresh combat on Robin's behalf as the play ends. Robin here seems to be villain, but the function of the play remains the same: the redress of social inequalities. Binding and beheading, capture and release are recurrent actions in these early English folk plays. Their style is vigorous, an assertion of virility by dancing and combat using sticks.

It will be apparent that even very simple and naive forms of folk play may involve some conscious transformation of traditional forms for a specific social context. The Scots plough ceremony survives as a courtly amusement in a repertory of songs which has been associated with the royal chapel. Copland's lusty friar, though he has a long dramatic ancestry, appears in a post-Reformation printing. Early in the fifteenth century Lydgate transformed the matrimonial 'flyting for maistrye' of 'rude upplandisshe people (compleynyng on hir wyves, with þe boystous aunswere of hir wyves)' into a Christmas mumming at Hertford fit for a king. Contemporary clerical dramatists recognised the entertainment value and thematic potential of the folk drama which offered them ready-made modes of action with which to characterise evil within a larger design. The folk-play antics of the vices in *Mankind* (mock-beheading, showing the big-head devil, collecting from the audience, naming local gentry) have been commented on before, as has the intrusion of a quack-doctor and his boy in the Croxton *Play of the Sacrament* (*c.* 1470).[21] In the earliest printed plays – didactic interludes intended for popular playing by professionals – folk play traditions are assimilated and reformed in a number of new ways, before being returned to the folk as a kind of instruction.

TRANSFORMATIONS OF FOLK PLAY IN THE INTERLUDES

Youth is demonstrably one of the most popular moralities (written *c.* 1515 and printed six times by the 1560s).[22] The dialogue is vigorous, formulaic, allusive, referring to a known tradition of acting, rather than evoking character. That Youth himself is a folk play hero and Morris dancer is suggested by the formulaic detail coupling leaf and ale, body gesture and hazel stick:

> My name is Youth I tell the
> I florysh as the vinetre . . .
> My hearre is royall and bushed thicke
> My body plyaunt as a hasel styck . . .
> My chest bigge as a tunne
> My legges be full lighte for to runne
> To hoppe and daunce and make mery . . .
> I am the heyre of my fathers lande . . .   (AIv)

In the course of Youth's choosing his companions, this folk play energy is shown to run headlong from pride and wrath into gluttony and lechery. Charity sets out to instruct the audience, greeting them by 'Jesu that his armes dyd sprede', but Youth enters with a roistering challenge, 'A backe, felowes and give me roume!' brandishing a dagger, and chases him 'out of this place'. Youth struts about, enjoying his power over the 'place' and over the audience. There can be no action until a new character is 'called on'. Riot is summoned in a sequence reminiscent of the calling of Tityvillus in *Mankind*; he looks for a combat with Youth, but seems to be hindered by a grotesque mask: 'But my lyppes hange in my lyght'. He is welcomed 'in the devels waye' and answers the old riddle correctly:

> *Youth.* Who brought the hither today?
> *Ryot.*   That dyd my legges I tell the.   (A4)

In the cryptic dialogue of this antic crew a whole gamut of topics is hinted at: hanging, beheading, binding in chains, neck-ropes and mayoral collars, salt-fish in Lent, 'holy catifs'. They make sense only as the shorthand evocation of a familiar carnival spirit in which taboo subjects can be named. In the play's structure these elements serve together to oppose Charity's message of social and moral responsibility, but there are elements not so neatly assimilated, where social criticism is not 'placed'. Such is Youth's repeated boast, 'I am heyre of my fathers land'. (The tag is preserved in a nineteenth-century ploughmen's play – a good example of the conservatism of popular drama in its reverence for textual formulas, however inappropriate or cryptic they may seem.) Pride's sing-song mockery captures the spirit of the play's popular appeal:

> Thoughe his clothes be never so thine
> Yet he is come of a noble kinne,
> Though thou give him suche a mocke
> Yet he is come of a noble stocke. (B4)

Henry Medwall's *Fulgens and Lucres* (*c.* 1497) is a much more elegant production than *Youth* and was originally meant for a select audience in the household where Thomas More was a page. But here too the play's social criticism is the cue for inclusion of folk elements. Medwall makes a distinction of decorum between the 'substance of the play' (a humanist dispute about noble birth and plebeian merit) and the more popular 'tryfles and iapys' interspersed:[23]

> Dyvers toyes mengled yn the same
> To styre folke to myrthe and game
> And to do them solace:
> The whiche tryfyllis be impertinent
> To the matter principall. (Part II, lines 22–6)

The trifles – the by-play of the servants A and B with the audience and their bouts of comic quarter-staff wrestling for the favours of a kitchen wench – are not, of course, 'impertinent to the matter principall'. Rather they work to de-fuse the impact Lucrece's preference of the virtuous plebeian might have for an audience of courtiers and foreign nobles in Cardinal Morton's household.

Later in the sixteenth century Sir David Lindsay uses devices from folk drama in his *Satire of the Three Estates*. One such, a complete playlet, used as prologue to the serious matter, concerns the obscene wooing of a 'Bessy', wife of an old man, by a fool with the key to her chastity belt. The folk elements here expand a play originally performed, it is thought, for James V at Linlithgow in 1540 into a public entertainment on Castle Hill at

Cupar in Fife in 1552. Folk play insinuates that the common people are
firmly behind the reforms of church and state ordered in the play by John
of the Commonwealth. In John Heywood's *Play of the Weather* (printed
1533), the Vice, Merry Report takes down the Gentleman, who has claimed
to be 'head of the commonwealth' with rustic beheading antics. The newly
proposed Henrician title of Supreme Head of the Church of England is
playfully held up to scrutiny. Heywood died a staunch Roman.

   In the educational interludes, where humanity's goal is seen as wisdom
rather than salvation, folk play is used to suggest forces hostile to learning.
A giant Tediousness lives under Mount Parnassus in Redford's delightful
Wit and Science (*c.* 1530–40); he 'cumth in with a vyser over hys hed',
swinging a great club, calling for 'room', threatening to beat the foolish
Wit to dust. The Master of the Children of St Paul's has built his allegory
of the progress to wisdom upon a popular sub-text; although Wit 'fallyth
downe and dyeth', and Tediousness strikes the prostrate body, threatening
decapitation, the hero's resurrection, conjured within a circle of dancers is
fully expected. Eventually he will slay the giant and win the Lady, though
he shows few signs of deserving her. The pattern was familiar already to
the audience, and the model of the fool's wooing eases the triumph of the
weak-kneed but irrepressible Wit, just as on the religious stage it had
sustained the tottering, impotent old bridegroom Joseph with his magic
yerde.

   John Rastell's extensive use of folk play in *The Nature of the Four
Elements* (*c.* 1517) seems to have gone unnoticed. The interlude is constructed on the principle of (almost) separable instruction and *game*; as in
Mankind and *Youth*, the serious and comic characters observe different
conventions of acting. The cosmography lesson is interrupted by Sensual
Appetite demanding 'room'. A taverner is 'called on' with much resistance
and, for no reason inherent in the story, threatens the audience: 'Beware,
syrs, how, let me have room'. Sensual Appetite, a self-appointed marshal
of revels, has decided notions on how the entertainment should go; within
a few lines of entering he has outlined the subjects and style he wants:
physical combat, strife of the sexes, the holiday law of the tavern, parody
of the church, a fool blessing and cursing his 'sons':[24]

(*Enter*) *Sensuall Apetyte.* Well hyet, quod hykman, when that he smot
                       Hys wyffe on the buttockys with a bere pott.
                       Aha, now, god evyn, fole, god evyn.
                       It is even the, knave, that I mene.
                       Hast thou done thy babelyng?

Studyous Desyre. Ye, peradventure, what then?

Sensuall Apetyte. Than hold downe thy hede lyke a pretty man
      And take my blessyng.
      Benedicite, I graunt to the this pardon
      And give the absolucion.
      For thy soth saws stande up Jack daw,
      I beshrew thy faders sone.
      Make rome, syrs, and let us be mery . . .   (B2)

Jesting about food and decapitation ensue and a company of dancers is brought in. Ignorance sings a ballad of Robin Hood.

In *Four Elements* the use of 'folk' language is controlled and functional, forming part of Ignorance's assault on learning. Rastell, with his press, his theatre, his reformist principles, had strong ideas about the role of English, proposing in his Prologue:

      Consideryng that our tonge is now suffycyent
      To expoun any hard sentence evydent,
      [Clerks] myght yf they wolde in our englyshe tonge
      Wryte workys of gravyte somtyme amonge . . .
      yf connynge laten bokys were translate
      Into englyshe wel correct and approbate . . .   (A2v)

Both Nature and Experience pride themselves on explaining cosmography with clarity and simplicity. It is against this ideal of discourse that Ignorance invokes Robin Hood. Rastell has adopted the traditional nonsense of folk ballad, which mismatches subject and object in its carnival celebration of 'heroic deeds', to characterise Ignorance's strenuous opposition to any official interpretation of the shape and workings of the world.

      Robyn hode in barnysdale stode
      And lent hym tyl a mapyll thystyll . . .
      He tok a gose nek in his hande
      And over the water he went.
      He start up to a thystell top
      And cut hym downe a holyn clobe
      He stroke the wren betwene the hornys
      That fyre sprange out of the pyggys tayle . . .   (E8)

In the charming interlude of *Thersites* the satire on chivalry that was implicit in folk play is rehearsed to a more 'classical' treatment of the theme and presented at court (October 1537). Much of the fun comes from the spectacle of a diminutive young veteran from Troy who 'cometh in first, having a club upon his neck' and demanding, 'Aback, give me room' in the manner of a folk devil, summoning King Arthur's knights to fight with him, then hiding behind his mother's skirts when his dragon appears in the form of a snail. His sexual prowess is similarly part of his popular heritage; he addresses the audience:[25]

> Fye, blusshe not, woman, I wyll do you no harme,
> Excepte I had you soner to kepe my backe warme.
> Alas, lyttle pums, why are ye so sore afrayd?
> I praye you show how longe it is sence ye were a mayd . . .
> Well, let all go; whye, wyll none come in
> With me to fyghte that I maye pare his skyn?   (B1v–B2)

and not even his mother is exempt. She is an 'old trot' whose spells can charm worms from the son of great Ulysses (he lies on stage 'with his belly upward'). Thersites beats her about the stage with his club ('He will pricke me, he will stycke me!') until she revokes her curse and gives him her blessing. There is delight too in the mere listing of places and people and food: Godfrey Good-ale, Tom Tumbler of Tewksbury, 'the tooth of a titmouse, the turd of a goat'. This Brueghelian colour – the condescending evocation of a quaint, proverbial, low-life world – is not wholly innocent of meaning. Mater's splendid catalogue of relics works an old vein of parody:

> The vertue of the tayle of Isaackes cow
> That before Adam in Paradyse dyd lowe,
> Also the joyste of Moses rod,
> In the mount of calvarye that spake with God
> *Facie ad faciem*, turninge tayle to tayle
> Cause all these wormes quickly to fayle!   (D2)

The humour is at the expense of popular witchcraft and also of the excesses of the Roman Church. A comparison of Mater's bizarre collection with the printed list of relics owned by the church of Luther's youth in Wittenberg (*Wittemberger Heiligthumsbuch*, 1509) is sobering. Once again, the mockery implicit in folk dramatic practice is worked into a humanist and courtly play. The court was celebrating the birth of Prince Edward and all the satire is lighthearted and confident. By 1537 Erasmus had said as much, Tyndale a good deal more.

'LA CELESTINA' REDUCED TO AN INTERLUDE

The folk play episodes discussed so far make no pretence whatever to represent contemporary life realistically. Indeed, England appears to have entered the era of print lacking a dramatic tradition capable of sustained mimesis of a secular story. In the professional mimic or burlesque tradition represented by the *Interludium de Clerico et Puella* and *Dame Sirith* the impersonation of 'real people' is severely curbed by the satirical function of stock figures in a fabliau action. The biblical cycle plays made extensive use of contemporary language and dress to naturalise sacred history and also found room for episodes of a purely secular kind; in some cases these must already have been developed independently as 'plays': the matrimonial flyting of the Wakefield Noahs, the gallows comedy of Cain and Pickharness, the clowning and wrestling of the shepherds, the Chester alewife, the pantomimic coupling of the Cornish smith's wife and a soldier as they forge nails for the crucifixion. But these scenes all verge on folk drama: they are boisterous, self-contained 'games'; they are not the representation of 'story'. In the morality tradition, similarly, direct representation of contemporary life was subservient to abstract models of plot: the journey of life, the ages of man, the conflict of vice and virtue, the ordering of a household, debate. At the end of the fifteenth century *Fulgens* experiments with the framework, but the 'matter principall' of the picture is stylised from a pure line of humanist debates. Granted the loss of some plays on romantic or chivalric subjects, there are few signs of a developed tradition of secular realism. There was no prose in the drama before 1500 and very little for a long time after.[26]

Calisto and Melebea (printed by John Rastell, *c.* 1529) offers the unique case of an early English interlude based on a novel. Its source, *La Celestina*, is usually thought of as the first (it is arguably one of the greatest) of European novels, and tells a story of illicit and fatal love in a precise social setting. The well-born lovers are brought together by the machinations of Celestina, queen of a vivid and seamy underworld. All three die violently. The notorious Spanish book, originally printed as *La comedia de Calisto y Melibea* (Burgos, 1499), was expanded as *La tragicomedia ...* (Seville, 1501 and subsequently). Composed in sixteen, then twenty-one, 'acts', in dialogue without narrative, deriving from a line of Spanish Terentian imitations it seemed to invite adaptation for the stage.[27] However, *La Celestina* was the work of a sceptical Jew and cramful of vicious life – too much so for the censorious Vivés, under whose aegis it is supposed the English playwright worked. It was within the pious discipline of the 'Thomas More circle' that our innocent truncation, *A new comodye in Ynglish in maner of an enterlude*, was made in Chaucerian rhyme royal.[28]

In the right dramatic climate a version of *La Celestina* could have revolutionised English drama overnight; that this did not happen may be explained by three factors: the lack of a secular drama that could absorb so much realism in a living stage play; the dominance of other dramatic traditions; and preoccupation with morality and reformation.

The Spanish novel's dialogue form allows Fernando de Rojas to express the characters' thoughts and feelings with a startling frankness which the stage had not yet (except, perhaps, in the Italy of Machiavelli's *Mandragola*, *c.* 1513–20) dramatic language and gesture for. Physical intimacy requires highly developed stage conventions if it is not to turn into indecent burlesque. There was thus a great deal in the novel which the English poet could not possibly make into an interlude: the old bawd's eager fondling of Areusa as she undresses; Melebea's flashing jealousy when her maid welcomes Calisto with a kiss; the 'background' raillery of thievish servants discussing Celestina's business, or of whores imagining to one another the vile poultices Melebea must use to keep her beauty. These are the 'scenes' of a great novelist, whose psychological skill and social observation are far ahead of the resources of the English stage. The Spanish Calisto, torn between proud vengeance for his slain servant and the paralysing shame of incipient discovery, between anxious lust and metaphysical gloom, will not reach the English stage until the age of Romeo and Giovanni. Not till then will the accent of true tragedy be heard: '¿Por qué me dejaste triste y solo in hac lachrymarum valle?'[29]

The English interlude is not a translation but a free adaptation, using only four acts-worth of the story, enough, that is, for about an hour-and-a-half, 'in maner of an enterlude'. From the turbulence of the novel the English poet selected only what was susceptible to his received notions of dramatic form and subject. The result is a comic-satiric wooing play which has some interesting affinities with the Middle English *Interludium* and *Dame Sirith* and which is also a temptation-and-fall morality. His story ends at the point where Melebea gives her girdle to Celestina to take to Calisto, and his play concludes with a scene (not in the Spanish) of Melebea's contrition for a sin not carnally committed and with her father's forgiveness. The English omits altogether the tragedy and violence: Celestina stabbed in a quarrel with Calisto's servants, Calisto's brains dashed out falling from a ladder, Melebea's eloquent leap from the tower of her father's house. Whether or not the audience is expected to supply the sequel is an intriguing question.

The novel's cast of fourteen is reduced to six (a regular number for interludes) by discarding Melebea's mother and maid, two of Calisto's

servants, two of Celestina's girls, a lecher and a pimp. The dialogue is pruned of speculative ramifications and purged of such gross pleasantries (sodomy among the angels) as might offend English sensibilities. The three main characters are simplified. The Spanish heroine is transformed to an English blue-stocking who warns the audience against the instability of love by reference to Petrarch and Heraclitus. 'These folysh lovers' is the key note; she is tired of the old pretence –[30]

> O, hys lamentacyons and exclamacyons on Fortune
> With similytude maner as one that shuld dy.
> But who shall pyte thys? In fayth not I . . .
> What, a mys* woman? Now, Cristes benedicite!   *naughty
>   (23–34)

Calisto is a Petrarchan fool of Fortune, a spiritless moon calf, who breaks into complaints against Fortune as soon as he is left alone on stage:

> Lo, out of all joy I am fallyn in wo
> Uppon whom advers Fortune hath cast her chauns   (74–5)

who sends for his out-of-tune lute and 'must nedys sit for very feblenes'. Celestina herself is the best creation; though plucked, she still has the gayest feathers and speaks the liveliest dramatic language. But she too has been given a leitmotif – a conspicuous piety, with frequent oaths and blessings. Her first words are to the audience:

> Now the blessyng that our lady gave her sone
> That same blessyng I gyve to you all.
> That I com thus homely I pray you of pardon –
> I am sought and send fore as a woman universall.   (313–16)

Our unease about her piety is to grow in the course of the play. Celestina's greeting indicates also that she is poorly dressed (hence, that the audience is probably a 'gentle' one) and that she expects to be recognised. When she leaves the stage for the last time, well satisfied with her work, she boasts,

> That I am well worthy to bere the name
> For to be callyd a noble arche dame.   (927–8)

There is something very English in the attitude behind these three voices, in the tongue-in-cheek scepticism of romantic love, in the preference for satire, in the moral sense alerted through the use of religious language. The voices had been heard long before on the popular stage. Here they are in the oldest English 'interlude':[31]

> *Puella.* Do way! By Crist and Leonard,
>   No wil Y lufe na clerc fayllard* . . .   *ne'er do well
>   (7–8)

> By Crist of heuen and Sant Ione,
> Clerc of scole ne kep I non,
> For many god wumman haf þai don scam.   (27–9)
>
> *Clericus.* Y lydy my lif wyt mikel dole:
> Me wor leuer to be dedh
> þan led þe lif þat Hyc ledh!   (42–4)
>
> *Mome Elwis.* Son, welcum, by San Dinis . . .
> A, son! vat saystu? Benedicite!
> Lift hup þi hand and blis þe!   (38, 63–4)

and in the solo mime's version of the same story, *Dame Sirith*:[32]

> *(Margeri)* þat wold I don for non þing,
> Bi houre Louerd, heuene king . . .   (88–9)
> þilke time ne shal neuer bitide
> þat mon for wouing ne þoru prude*   **pride/lust*
> Shal do me scham.   (124–6)
>
> *(Wilekin)* Bote if hoe wende hire mod,   **Unless she change her mind I shall*
> For serewe mon Ich wakese wod   *go mad or kill myself*
> Oþer miselue quelle.*   (181–3)
>
> *(Dame Sirith)* Benedicite be herinne!
> Her hauest þou, sone, mikel senne.
> Louerd, for his suete nome,
> Let þe þerfore hauen no shome!   (193–6)

I am not suggesting here that the Tudor playwright is indebted in a literary way to these medieval analogues, but rather that, as he floundered with his rich Spanish prize, he recognised familiar land and struck out for it. In any case, it is probable that many versions of the wooing play were current in popular repertory. That the English poet felt himself at home is suggested by the fact that the epilogue which he invented for his version of the *Celestina* makes use of an important motif from the *Dame Sirith*: the weeping bitch. In the Middle English, Dame Sirith wins over the lady by claiming that her bitch (whose eyes testify to a recent dosing with pepper and mustard administered in full view of the audience) is really her own daughter, transformed magically by a cunning clerk whose love she refused. In *Calisto* the 'foule rough bych' appears in Danio's dream, 'straykyng her body along on the gras', 'leppyng and fawnyng' round about his daughter, luring her from the path to a 'holesome bath' right to the edge of a 'pyt of foule stynkyng water'. Mortified by the premonitory symbolism, Melebea confesses her weakness and interprets:

> The prikeryd curr and the foule bych
> Which made her self so smoth and fayre to see

> Betokenyth an old quene, a baudy wych
> Callyd Celestyne – that wo myght she be!
> Whych with her fayre wordes ay so perswadyd me
> That she had almost brought me here unto
> To fulfyll the foule lust of Calisto. (1009–15)

The weeping bitch is infrequent enough in folk tale to suggest survival through popular dramatic performance by a gleeman and his dog. I have elsewhere pointed to its recurrence in medieval Latin mimic entertainment.[33] The transformation of the motif in Lance's dog is but one aspect of a Shakespearean heritage that is worth a brief digression.

One scene of *Calisto* is notable in the development of English dramatic form. It contains, so far as I am aware, the first attempt at a complete anecdote in monologue form using reported speeches. (There are snatches of this method in the vices' account of their off-stage villainy in *Mankind* and in the story of London's red-light district in Medwall's *Nature*.) The striking thing about this opening monologue of Celestina's is that it reduces to narrative a scene which occurs as dialogue in the original Spanish; in doing this it calls for a special kind of acting. The anecdote is of a simple ruse played at Celestina's house, where the unexpected return of a regular has necessitated his girl's incumbent beau being shoved hastily upstairs. Celestina recounts her own quick-witted stage management, how she turned a difficult situation to sport by identifying the noise upstairs as coming from a wench sent to her by a friar. (A further reference to the friar has been neatly sliced from the page of the only extant copy.) In telling the story Celestina recalls her own words and those of the quarrelling lovers, catching the idiom of natural common speech:

> Cryto in my chamber above that was hyddyn
> I thynk lay not easyly and began to romble.
> Sempronio hard that and askyd who was within
> Above in the chamber that so dyd jomble.
> 'Who?' quod she, 'a lover of myne'. 'May hap ye stomble',
> Quod he, 'on the trewth, as many one doth.'
> 'Go up,' quod she, 'and loke whether it be soth.'
>
> 'Well,' quod he, 'I go'. Nay, thought I, not so,
> I sayd, 'Com Sempronio, let this foole alone . . .' (355–63)

The voices are distinct, the to and fro of friendly badinage skilfully paced by a comfortable and ingratiating Pandarian presence. The narrative scene is complete in itself: Celestina offers it to the audience as a 'pretty game' to fill the time before Sempronio returns to the stage, and she concludes with an apt reflection on the waste of time which returns the audience neatly to the present. A curtain is drawn over a vivid world-within-a-world, on a cast of characters some of whom we shall not see.

In the original Spanish the incident occurs in the expanded (1501) version of Act I and is our first introduction to Celestina's house. The reader must imagine Crito pushed through a door from the scene of dialogue, but otherwise the episode differs no way in method from other scenes of the novel. What is interesting for the present argument is that the English author recognised in the farcical material the possibility for dramatic monologue and for a particular *kind of acting* which he asks only of his Celestina. She (he) is a mimic, playing assumed roles, in an old tradition which links her with Dame Sirith and Mome Elwis. Celestina's tale and another speech, on sensual delight (lines 567–87) are treated as *mimic* set-pieces. Not a little of the delight for the original audience would have been in watching a man playing an old woman imitating a man. Shakespeare knew the value of mimic entertainment and that may be one reason why in his comedies, as C. L. Barber has observed, 'the clown's part is satisfactory from the outset'.[34] In the middle of *Two Gentlemen of Verona* (11.3.1–32), an improvised puppet show by Lance, the go-between and his dog, Crab, using a pair of shoes and a staff, indecently mimics family life in a miniature comedy within a comedy.

Returning to my main argument, I suggest, then, that the poet of the interlude, confronted by the wealth of 'scenes' and the uncertain moral purpose of the Spanish novel, saw the possibility of organising his play as a satirical wooing play in which the lady's consent and the triumph of the bawd marked the conclusion of the action. In place of the lusty pagan celebration which ends *Dame Sirith*, with its ploughing image ('And loke that þou hire tille!') we are given virginal shame, repentance, moral analysis and paternal exhortation.

What, though, does the printer mean by the 'maner of an enterlude'? What is the English poet's idea of stage-craft? The dialogue of *Calisto* gives no indication of scenic properties; the playing area is a neutral space, never supposed to be anything but itself (though at one point Calisto bids farewell to the 'lordys' in the audience and promises to pass a little time walking 'up and down within myne orchard'). This conception is alien to the simultaneous staging of medieval religious drama and to the various house-and-street experiments of early Terentian followers. It is closer to the conventions of popular medieval drama. Despite the Terentian influence endemic in the play's plot materials (especially the servant types),

there seems to be none in the plotting. The development is in three almost
equal acts (not indicated) and an epilogue (lines 1–312, 313–639, 640–928,
929–1099). The divisions fall when no-one is on stage and they may mark
pauses for the original serving of courses at a banquet. Each act has a
similar pattern: X enters solo, addresses the audience, is joined by Y or Z,
one of whom is left at the end to take farewell of the audience.

Even more than usual in interludes the dialogue is audience-oriented.
The actors promise to bring new characters 'unto this place' or to 'come
again anon', make bids for attention ('Have I not hyed me lyghtly?') and
mocking asides ('I will not moke, this foule is a lover'). Some sparks flicker
into a sustained ironic exchange of actors and audience, as when Melebea
is afraid of entering the empty place alone:

> I pray you, came this woman here never syn?
> In fayth to entre here I am half adrad
> And yet, why so? I may boldly com in
> I am sure from you all I shall not be had.
> But Iesus, Iesus, be these men so mad
> On women as they sey? How shuld it be?
> Yt is but fable and lyes, ye may trust me.   [*Intret Celestina*].
>   (640–6)

What is she afraid of? The speech hardly makes sense as it stands, for
Melebea as yet knows nothing of Celestina. Her reference to 'this woman'
after an evident break in the action suggests that Celestina has been improvising during the interval. Later in the scene, Melebea, outraged by the
bawd's immoral purpose, turns to the audience for help: 'Som good bodi
take this old thefe fro me!'

The audience involvement, which is a feature of all early English popular
drama, reinforces the morality structure. The audience is asked to judge
Melebea's progress in a moral conflict from the moment she declares,

> Nay, nay, he shall never that day see
> Hys voluptuous appetyte consentyd by me   (35–6)

and

> I promyse the where thou art present
> Whyle I lyff by my wyll I wyll be absent.   [*Et exeat*.] (72–3)

In her uncompromising declaration the terms of a traditional wooing
comedy are refined. With Melebea's Gawainian standards the mere granting
of a girdle will be a moral catastrophe. The English playwright has discovered a formula for compactness. In fact, he draws attention to his

truncation of the Spanish plot and omission of the fateful acts of lust and
their tragic consequences. Left alone on stage to gloat over the hard-won
girdle, Celestina drops a proverb:

> Now know ye by the half tale what the hole doth meane   (919)

to provide the audience (in a manner approved by Erasmus) with a key for
interpreting the structure.

FROM REFORMATION IRONY TO REFORMATION SATIRE

The conspicuousness of religious language in *Calisto* has already been
touched on. A large number of oaths and blessings occur in Celestina's
lines and are not found in the Spanish. This religiosity works to underline
the theme of Christian chastity tempted, but it has further reverberations.
In the course of the play both virgin lady and bawdy witch are shown to
be equally daughters of Eve, subject to the 'auncyon malyce', as 'it is
resytyd in the fest of Seynt Jhon '(Midsummer Day). This seems unfair to
Melebea whose overt sin is slight. She has her modern champions; Pearl
Hogrefe writes:[35]

In the English play Melebea is the ideal maiden, or nearly so . . . Even her wavering, in
the scene where Celestina makes her shrewd approach, is based on appeals to her compassion for Celestina's age and for Calisto's toothache, and on her religious feeling. Thus
the wavering is not entirely irrational, not motivated by a real response to seduction . . .
Even Vivés might concede that her inner feeling of chastity had been scarcely touched.

But this is to see character in too naturalistic a light. In a play where the
most conspicuous piety and the most 'religious' arguments come from the
lips of the old bawd, is it safe to assume that all Melebea's 'religious feeling'
is good? Certainly Melebea shows little response to the pleasures of illicit
love and only tacit approval of the catalogue of Calisto's heroic virtues. The
real temptation and seduction of Melebea is far subtler and arises precisely
from religious feelings. It begins with the compassion of virtuous youth
for vicious age ('In dede age hath aray thee!') and works through Celestina's
Virgin-worship:

> And Mary, goddes mother, that blessyd vyrgyn,
> Preserve and prosper your womanly personage
> And well to injoy your youth and pusell age . . .   (652-4)
>
> O angelyk ymage! O perle so precyous!
> O how thou spekyst, it rejoysyth me to here!

> Knowist thou not by the devyne mouth gracyous
> That agaynst the infernall feend Lucyfere
> We shuld not only lyf by bred here
> But by our good workys, wher in I take some payn?   (704–9)

In the 1520s these terms are not idly chosen. Melebea, concedes:

> To do a good dede is lykyng to god,
> For good dedys to good men be alowable.   (752–3)

Just when she ought to send the old brothel packing, the heroine succumbs to an appeal to her own saint-like power:

> It is for a prayer, mestres, my demaundyng,
> That is sayd ye have of Seynt Appolyne
> For the toth ake wher of this man is in pyne.
>
> And the gyrdle there thou weryst about the,
> So many holy relykys it hath towchyd
> That thys knyght thynkyth his bote* thou maist be.   *salvation*
>   (841–6)

and gives up her girdle to cure the man's 'toothache'. With Celestina's triumphant, 'For Gabriell to our lady with Ave Maria/Came never gladder than I shall to this knyght', and her promise that she and Calisto will become the maiden's beadsfolk, the double-edged Virgin-worship concludes.

In *Calisto* then, the traditional Catholic emphasis on good works and on the efficacy of relics is questioned; in pious virgin and pious bawd Mariolatry is spoofed. Earlier in the play the doctrine of purgatory had been humorously glanced at.[36] The humour is equivocal rather than reformist, close to that of Erasmus's *Colloquies*. But the reformist intention is plain when it is revealed in the epilogue that Melebea has been saved from deed of sin by regular morning prayer, and more earnest tones are heard insistently urging parents to bring up their children to useful trades and to reform their own social attitudes.

Looking at *Calisto* in the historical perspective of folk drama and noting the English poet's introduction of so much religious language, one can see that he recognised in the Spanish bawd an old anti-type of the Virgin Mary, the dame of a cult purely erotic and anti-ecclesiastical. A figure shaped by the licensed mockery of folk practice is placed in a new critical light and made the apologist for attributes of the contemporary Roman church. Without being sure of the play's author, date or auspices of performance, it is hard to gauge the adventurousness of its attitudes. Certainly the poet 'nothing affirmeth' contrary to orthodoxy.

Within ten years of *Calisto* John Bale had reincarnated the dame on stage as Idolatry. Directions for *A comedy concernynge thre lawes* (c. 1538?, printed 1548) say, 'Let Idolatry be decked lyke an olde wytche'.[37] Sodomy ('a monke of all sectes') tells us,

> She can by sayenge her Ave marye,
> And by other charmes of sorcerye,
> Ease men of toth ake by and bye,
> Yea, and fatche the devyll from hell.   (B3)

The 'vice', Infidelity, recalls her ancestry in dramatic folk festivals:

> At Christmas and at Paske
> Ye maye daunce the devyll a maske,
> Whyls hys great cawdron plawe.*   *boils*
> Yow soch a prati mynyon,
> And yow now in relygyon?   (B3)

Midwife, fortune-teller, quack doctor, charmer of the plough, she works with 'holye oyle and waiter', 'tyrdles' and 'gyrdles' and 'our blessed ladyes psaulter'. Her first words are rustic dialect and 'though she be sumwhat olde', her behaviour with Sodomy is wanton ('What, wylt thu fall to mutton... Afore thys Companye?')

Bale's propaganda works through a censorious identification of folk play. The basic dramatic method of his well-articulated five-act morality is simple: the characters address the audience or dispute with one another. But this blunt didacticism meets headlong with a different version of 'acting' in the person of Infidelity. He bursts into Act II, singing,

> Brom, brom, brom, brom, brom. Bye brom, bye, bye.
> Marry, God geve ye good even
> And the holy man saynt Steven,
>   Sende ye a good newe yeare...
> I wyll my selfe so handle,
> That ye shall have a candle,
>   Whan I come hyther agayne,
> At thys your soden mocyon,
> I was in soch devocyon
> I had nere broke a vayne.   (A6–v)

His vigour and gnomic speech, his properties of broom and candle, identify Infidelity as a Robin Goodfellow.[38] As presenter his job is to sweep the acting place and bring luck at Christmas ('saynt Steven'); he must go and 'come again' with speed, shedding curses and good luck ('it was but a fart ... for noyaunce of the howse, / For easement of your toth'). At his

conjuration Idolatry and Sodomy appear and help maintain possession of
the acting place. In each act he calls on a new protagonist to fight against
God's champions of law. Thus, throughout Bale's *Comedy*, folk play provides ready-made models of action; relationships between characters do
not have to be developed, since they can be assumed. In Act III Ambition
and Avarice are shown as 'praty boyes' who are beaten by their 'folysh'
father Infidelity until they kneel and beg his blessing. A fresh 'playe' is
contrived to deal with the Evangelist in Act IV. When John the Baptist is
finally taken out to be burned as a heretic (a new use for Midsummer
bonfires?), Infidelity's triumph as folk play champion is complete; he calls
for a Bessy and ale:

> Well, thys valeaunt George hath made them all to stoupe
> Cheare now maye I make, and set cocke on the houpe.
> Fyll in all the pottes, and byd me welcome, hostesse,
> And go call me hyther, myne owne swete mynyon Besse.   (F2v)

Bale thus makes popular drama stand for 'poperye'. Threatened with a
sword of fire by Vindicta Dei, Infidelity runs from the place, crying,

> Credo, credo, credo, I say, credo, credo, credo,
> To the devyll of helle, by the Messe I wene I go.   (F5)

As one might have anticipated of a man working on Cromwell's propaganda programme, Bale's transformations of folk play are the most radical.
But he has identified the enemy with rather too much certainty: by the
time he published *Three Laws* (1548) he was safe in castigating Reginald
Pole, and the Edwardian reformation was in full swing. Dramatic irony
has given way to satire and abuse. The most delightful and creative period
of the Tudor interlude lay behind, in the decades of transition. The earlier
dramatists were less self-conscious about folk play; they used it in a more
exploratory way to test out feelings and to entertain criticism without
having to state it, to give shape and focus to attitudes which could not yet
be admitted as 'official'. In the best interludes folk play was sub-text rather
than text.

The Tudor mask and
Elizabethan court drama

MARIE AXTON

A mask performed at the court of Henry VIII was both a pastime and a sanctioned occasion for the release and reharnessing of social tensions. Though its lavish costume and display suggest affinities with the Jacobean *masque*, a Tudor mask fiction was not always an idealisation of the court or monarch. Henrician court entertainments contain conflict, protest and mockery; Elizabethan masks sometimes express criticism of the queen. It may be argued that drama was better suited, by dialogue and direct imitation, to express such tensions. As the century wore on, indeed, plays became the lively vehicles of political protest and experiment. However, there are Elizabethan entertainments strongly influenced by the Henrician mask and disguising – mask-dramas, if you like – which can be more fully enjoyed if the usual association of mask and flattery is set aside. It may be one of the secrets of Tudor statecraft that these masks cannot happily be compassed by the terms Stephen Orgel has used for the Stuart entertainments:

Every masque is a ritual in which the society affirms its wisdom and asserts its control of its world and its destiny. The glories of the transformation scene express the power of princes bringing order to human and elemental nature.[1]

The scenes and machines of Jacobean masques may, as Orgel suggests, bypass conflict with wonderful changes of perspective; in the Tudor revels individuals simply change costume. Transformation emphasises disguise and poses questions of identity.

In his *Arcadia*, Philip Sidney explores the mind of a prince reluctantly disguised as a shepherd and reveals an aspect of Elizabethan courtly role playing which I want to discuss. Dorus laments:

> That I become a vision,
> Which hath in others' head his only being

And lives in fancye's seing.
O wretched state of man in selfe division[2]   (lines 162–6)

That is, delight in role-playing depends on who chooses the role. Henry VIII selected his own contrasting roles, danced, jousted and paid for his fictions, but despite his very real political power, he never appeared as a god, and, further, he interspersed his heroic roles with defiant villains, outlaws and enigmatic recluses. The more parsimonious and decorous Elizabeth did not so often foot bills or measures; during her reign the most publicised and expensive revels were devised and offered to her by her nobles and lawyers of the Inns of Court. The difference is crucial. For the first twenty years of both these reigns – periods long enough to establish conventions and iconography – the man who paid the piper called the tune. Under these conditions of patronage, mask conventions for portraying versions of a divided self were developed and explored.

Henry's roles were not idealisations of the Prince; rather, each figures forth an aspect of the man. The difference is worth emphasis, for the later Jacobean apotheosis of kingship has blurred this important distinction. Henry was fond of donning several disguises in one evening. To a knowledgeable courtier the temporal sequence of Henry's contrasting roles, as well as the almost instantaneous costume change of a joust transformation, might imply *simultaneous* conflict. Even partial recovery of this perspective suggests that each court entertainment is not a separate self-contained fiction. To us, the court revels may seem like Aristotle's huge animal, too large for aesthetic appreciation; the time span revealing form and unities may be the twelve days of Christmas or the whole calendar of the year's festivities. Henry's courtier could relate the separate disguises of a mask fiction to each other as well as to the play which preceded it and to the tournament which followed the next day. He could compare the king's successive personae throughout the length of an ambassador's visit, and note his change of role as the court returned three years in succession to Greenwich for May jousts; he would remember, or ask, what had been done on previous midsummer eves, or when two monarchs last met.

Despite his famous egotism, Henry's preference in role playing is that of the English repertory actor rather than the Hollywood star. In his noblest disguise, Cœur Loyal, jousting and dancing for Queen Katherine, Henry entered in a pageant accompanied by wildmen and foresters. Only days later the king himself donned this forester or outlaw disguise. The forester role was a royal favourite: sometimes suggested by the season of May revels, it could also be adopted by Henry in flagrant disregard of the

festive calendar – when he burst into Queen Katherine's chamber one
January morning dressed as Robin Hood, danced a morris and departed.
Multiple roles, in harmony or discord with the festive season, expressed
Henry's complex power and invited comparison and interpretation from
his court.

Two main problems confront the modern student. First, few mask texts
survive. Second, even in those that do, it is difficult to gauge the element
of impersonation in the original role-playing. For a distinctive feature of
the Henrician mask and tournament was the nobility of many of the performers. Holinshed's *Chronicle* describes 'shews of delight wherein great
persons were actors'. The writer may imply the simplest sixteenth-century
dictionary meaning of the word: actor – the doer of the deed; or more subtly
– in law the plaintiff or demandant; or – a player of interludes.[3] The first
and second meanings seem most apt for the Holinshed list: 'the king
runneth at tilt in his owne person; the king with other nobles disguised like
Robin hoods men for disport; the king and others disguised after the
Turkish fashion; a maske wherin the king was an actor'. Noble maskers
and jousters used neither dialogue nor naturalistic impersonative gesture;
instead they danced, fought on horseback and on foot and occasionally
(when the enemy was female) hurled persuasive weapons such as roses and
comfits. Words crucial to the role were often embroidered on a masker's
costume or a knight's horse bard; these were called 'reasons' or 'poyses'.
When the conceit required, a herald or a trunchman introduced the noble
performers with a narrative relating their disguise to the present festive
occasion. Some of these explanatory devices survive as songs, or in heralds'
manuscripts or as miscellaneous pieces amidst a poet's collected works.
Disjunction between verbal meaning and traditional gesture left the spectator to make crucial connections when the disguised king saluted in the
tiltyard, when he chose a dancing partner, or removed his mask. Clearly
some interpreting was necessary when Henry burst into the hall dressed as
a turbaned Turk flourishing a scimitar and later the same evening, costumed
in a short tunic, danced with black Egyptian ladies. Sometimes the contrast
was self-explanatory as on the night he appeared first as a German then
some hours later as an English nobleman who danced conjugally with a
lady of Spain. Queen Katherine remained in the audience for most of these
shows but she was often symbolically represented in the 'reasons' or (as on
the occasion just mentioned) by another masker.

Conflicts implied by changes of costume or of role can be most easily
seen in the tournament fictions. The elaborate disguises of afternoon

challengers were often simply carried over into the evening's costumed dancing; mask and tournament were interdependent. The mutable disguises of Henry's friend and jousting companion, Charles Brandon, provide the earliest and clearest examples of significant role-changing. Brandon honoured the Princess Mary in jousts and revels many years before he won and married her. In 1507, when Henry VII promised his daughter to Charles of Castile, Brandon initiated the jousts of May and June.[4] The betrothal generated in the Princess's English champion a conflict of loyalties which he visualised in colour and gesture as a contest between the months. Dressed in green and wearing a green cockle-shell, Brandon maintained the superiority of Dame May over all the wintry months; in blue the following month he protested his fidelity to Henry VII, although the king had given Brandon's May Lady to a prince beyond the sea. Three years later Brandon celebrated the birth of Henry VIII's first son in a joust in which he enacted for the assembled audience the psychological liberation consequent on the birth of a prince. Brandon entered the tiltyard imprisoned in a tower 'lyke a recluse or a religious person . . . without dromme or noyse of mynstralsye'. Halting the pageant before Queen Katherine a gaoler opened the prison with a large key and delivered Brandon's pilgrim staff and beads to Katherine, together with a letter asking permission to joust in her presence – 'if not then he woulde departe as he came'.[5] At the queen's assent the suppliant 'cast from hym hastely his clothyng, berd [beard] and hat and shewed hym self in brygth harneys, and forthwyth smote his horse wyth the sporys and rode a lusty pace unto the tyyltys end.'[6] The first persona is *visually* effaced by the Queen's intervention, but the pilgrim–prisoner makes a vivid impact on the viewer as a latent possibility, a state of mind, which the combatant strives to overcome permanently by participation in the court triumph. Unhappily, the young prince died a month later and Henry had no legitimate male heir until 1537.

This personal loss did not stem the imaginative flow of early court festivities in which Henry and Brandon played. Their most frequently repeated disguise was the one in which Brandon had made his debut: the forester champion of May. So dressed they danced or jousted as occasion demanded. A break with tradition was remarked when in May 1514 they failed to appear in Kentish kendal, but rode into the tiltyard as hermits. Their motto 'who can hold that wyl away' related their disguise to the imminent departure of the king's sister, Mary, to join her betrothed husband, Charles of Castile.[7] The king entered as a white hermit; Brandon as a black hermit. When they finally threw off their religious garb they reversed colour; Brandon was the white knight, Henry the black. Whether black indicated mourning or villainy, the reversal neatly divided the burden of meaning between the two friends and admitted to the court both Henry's commiseration and the friends' accord in this necessary act of state. Diplomacy took unexpected turns that year and pageantry immediately reflected it. Mary was for a few hectic months the unfortunate pawn in an international power game. When the Prince of Castile, humiliatingly, failed to claim her, she was swiftly betrothed to his enemy, the ancient and recently widowed King Louis of France. Marriage jousts were held in November in Paris where each day the French nobility appeared in new costumes; Brandon (with Henry's consent) jousted each day dressed as St George. Louis opportunely died on 1 January after scarcely three months of marriage, and Brandon again crossed the Channel to negotiate Mary's return. As insurance against further unhappy experiments in the international market, Mary secretly married him and informed King Henry of the fact. Whereupon the king's council, excepting only Wolsey, agreed to have Brandon put to death or imprisoned. A final letter of appeal directly to Henry on 22 April preceded the return of Mary and her husband. Suddenly Henry pardoned Brandon, scrapped his previously planned entertainments and celebrated his friend's triumph in the most elaborate maying of the reign. Matching green velvet and gold costumes were prepared for the king and his brother-in-law who, in company with Robin Hood and his outlaws, feasted Queen Katherine and Queen Mary in the forest. This resumption of their mutual revels' disguise in 1515 re-associated Henry with the law-breaker who had defied him. As propaganda, it may be evaluated in the light of a Parisian despatch which reported shortly before the couple's return 'the Duke of Suffolk did not dare leave the King of England's house, as he would have been killed by the people for marrying Queen Mary'.[8]

Two songs in Henry VIII's manuscript preserve the conceit of the forester–hermit transformation and may well have been sung at these revels. The song of renunciation is appropriate to the hermit disguise of May 1514 and is the lament of a forester (or foster) who has been spurned by Beauty and has become a beadsman. Its persistent refrain, 'Yet have I bene a foster', is turned to triumph in the second song, which suits the resumption of the virile foster persona in May 1515:

> Wherefore shuld I hang up myne arrow
> Opon the grenwode lynde?
> I have strengh to mak it fle

And kyll bothe hart and hynd:
I am a joly foster.

Wherfore shuld I hang up my horne
Upon the grenwod tre?
I can blow the deth of a dere
As well as any that ever I see:
I am a joly foster.

Wherefore shuld I tye up my hownd
Unto the grenwod spray?
I can luge and make a sute
As well as any in May
I am a joly foster.[9]

In mask, tournament and disguising the inner circle at court celebrated
its personal and public triumphs or defeats in iconographic fictions understood fully by a select few and more imperfectly by a widening audience.
As John Stevens has said, 'The "game" is private but it is played in public'
(p. 187). A London citizen chronicler who watched the Cœur Loyal joust
in 1511 completely missed the point. Delighted by King Henry's several
costume changes, he spotted his monarch each time by the gold letters on
his coat which he singlemindedly translated: 'h for henry and k for kyng'.[10]
The more knowledgeable chronicler, Edward Hall, a lawyer familiar with
court iconography, usually amplified the 'reasons' correctly as he recorded
Henry's revels and the varying forms of the king's tribute to Queen
Katherine, tribute he offered as late as 1527 in both tournament and mask.
But an observant courtier closer to the king would notice more: remembering the king's light-hearted mask of Youth in 1518, he would, in 1524, see
omens of stress when Henry entered as a feeble old knight with long white
beard to joust for the Castle of Loyalty. In 1518 a mask of old men with
silver beards had preceded the king and six youthful companions, and as
foil amused the ladies with their stiff, antiquated dancing. In 1524 the
disguised king asked permission, despite his infirmity, to joust for the queen.
When Katherine consented, Henry removed his beard and withered visor
and galloped into combat. Conflict latent in the two roles was overtly
expressed in the subsequent ritual combat – the attack and defence of the
Castle of Loyalty. In the revels of 1524 Henry's mask of age was lightly
removed but it was nevertheless a formal acknowledgement to the court of
the king's ever-increasing anxiety. The following year he elevated his
bastard son to the Dukedom of Richmond.

The conflict between Henry's public loyalty to Katherine and his irrepressible wish for a legitimate male heir was embodied in the first mask danced by Anne Boleyn at court in 1522. In this siege of the Chateau Vert, Henry and seven other allegorically named knights wooed Lady Beauty and her ladies to descend from the castle and dance. Sydney Anglo believes that Henry dressed as Ardent Desire in flame-coloured taffeta. Though that character expressed his wishes, I think Henry was more circumspect. Hall's punctuation is ambiguous:

Then enterd eyght Lordes in clothe of golde cappes and all, and great mantell clokes of blewe Sattin, these lordes were named Amorous, Noblenes, Youth, Attendaunce, Loyaltie, Pleasure, Gentlenes, and Libertie, the kyng was chyefe of thys compaignie, thys compaygnye was led by one all in Crymosyn Sattin wyth burninge flames of golde, called Ardent Desire, whyche so moued the ladies to geue ouer the Castle, but Scorne and Disdain sayed that they woulde holde the place, then Desire sayd the ladies shoulde be wonne, and came and encoraged the knyghtes, then the lordes ranne to the castle.

(q2)

I think it likely that William Cornish, as Master of the Chapel, took the speaking role; Desire addressed the besieged court ladies but was answered by the boys of the Chapel, who, dressed as ladies of Inde, with 'Scorn' and other shrewish names embroidered on their gowns, defended Beauty and her women. Henry as one of the identically dressed blue and gold lords expressed a silent affinity in colours which matched those of the equally silent castle ladies, who finally consented to dance. The king's personal dilemma was solved by simultaneous visual representation of conflicting states of mind: Desire, Loyalty, Nobleness and so on. The king had danced both Youth and Loyalty in previous masks; there was no certainty that he did so that night. The courtiers had to find the visored king among his allegorical companions – a game Wolsey also had to play. After a mask in 1527 he humbly offered the chair of state to Sir Edward Neville whom he mistook for the king.

It may be helpful to look more closely at this word *mask*. I have used it loosely in the discussion so far and talked more about tournament than dance because both as word and form *mask* can only be extracted with difficulty from the essentially fluid Henrician revels. Sydney Anglo rightly insists upon the mutability of forms in the early Tudor festivities. Despite a growing preference for the word *mask* which gradually replaced *disguising* in contemporary descriptions of court revels, a fixed form for the mask cannot be isolated until the seventeenth century. Anglo's cogent assessment of early Tudor revels might be extended to the Elizabethan scene.[11]

The young Elizabethan lawyers who, in planning their Inns of Court festivities, pored over Hall's *Chronicle* in the evenings would not find *mask* in the index prepared by the printer Grafton in 1550, though they would find *pageant*, *shew* and *maying*. Perhaps Grafton ignored the term, which occurs frequently in the chronicle, because of its imprecision. Anglo has found the earliest use of the word in an ambassadorial despatch of 1527.[12] Hall was writing in the 1540s, many years after the entertainments he had witnessed, so that when he initially uses *mask* in his book to describe an Italian innovation Henry introduced in 1512, he is not using a word current in that year. On that occasion Henry crossed the customary boundary between performers and audience by choosing a partner from the uncostumed onlookers. This seems to be an innovation in form, but a few pages later Hall uses the new word to describe perfectly usual disguisings with pageant cars and dancing that does not include the audience. He often uses *pageant* or *shew* as synonym for *disguising* or *mask*. By mid-century Grafton saw no reason to index *mask* as a key to such miscellaneous material.

Throughout the sixteenth century the meaning of *mask* as visor or disguise predominates over all other meanings and it is from the choice of visor that the Tudor danced-mask took whatever form it had. Poets and patrons seem to have been concerned that all parts of the entertainment should relate coherently to the chosen disguise but they showed little interest in the decorum of abstract form; a mask might begin or end in any way the patron chose. Since excellent studies by Enid Welsford and Stephen Orgel have traced the development and emergence of the well-defined Jacobean masque from this welter of experiment, aspects which remain stubbornly Elizabethan – in particular the conventions and iconography of the divided self – may repay a little study. Conflict and drama are part of the sixteenth century mask tradition and if these qualities did not enrich the Jacobean masque, the cause may well be James's imperviousness to the difference between suggestion and flattery.

Sixteenth-century denunciations of the mask canvas some evidence for its origins and social purpose: among these, however, political objections have received less modern attention than the vociferous and rather indiscriminate Puritan attacks on dancing and Italianate customs. Yet the impetus for mask fictions cannot lie solely in the joyous nocturnal dancing and Italianate immorality castigated in this typical extract, an English translator's gloss on *bacchanalia*:

wherein men use to company dissulutely wyth women in the night, in such wise that it is shame for christen menne to speake of, muche lyke our shewes or daunces called maskes in England, and bonefires as they be used in some partes of the realme.[13]

The early Elizabethan mask was a political weapon and as such it was feared. The court disguisings in Kyd's *Spanish Tragedy* (I.v) and the menacing dance of Diana in *Woodstock* re-create some of the associations the term *mask* raised in the minds of Elizabeth's subjects. The royal viewers in the *Spanish Tragedy* are puzzled by the 'mystery' which they try to interpret and Woodstock, in the play of that name, is swept to his death in an apparently complimentary mask he has failed to understand. Holinshed's *Chronicle* contains an apt entry in its full and useful index (1587 edition): 'a mask with intended mischeefe'. The reader is directed, quite anachronistically, to the year 1400 and a plot by the Earls of Salisbury and Huntington to carry King Henry IV to his death in a 'mask'. Here, 'mask' is an Elizabethan translation of Thomas of Walsingham's 'sub simulatione ludorum natalitiorum' – literally 'under the pretence of nativity [or Christmas] games'.

'Mask with intended mischeefe' would be an appropriate heading for a series of entertainments provided for Queen Elizabeth by Robert Dudley, Earl of Leicester. They were familiar to the compiler of the Holinshed index, Abraham Fleming. They caused hostility and suspicion in rival factions at court and with good reason.

The first of these masks might equally be called, according to Walsingham's freer terminology, a Christmas game. It originated at the Inner Temple and aimed, not at Elizabeth's life, but at control of the throne. In alliance with the Inner Temple and Gray's Inn, Dudley in 1561/2 made the first of several bids to draw the queen into marriage.

Traditionally at Christmas the lawyers of each Inn chose a monarch who danced, jousted, commissioned plays and presided over a revels council which was an educational parody of the actual government at Whitehall. By these Christmas king-games the Inns of Court men prepared themselves for government service. Their revels kingdom differed in one crucial aspect from its model; while England was ruled successively by a boy and two women, the lawyers always chose a king. When they took their plays and masks to Greenwich or Whitehall to entertain Elizabeth, their Christmas Prince rode in triumph through London with all the pomp appropriate to a monarch. The lawyers' hierarchy affirmed a 'god-given', male-dominated, power structure broken by the death of Henry VIII. The model, too, for their dancing, jousting monarchs seems to have been Henry VIII, rather than Henry VII who had sat firmly aloof on his hard-won throne while his court revelled. Elizabeth, like her grandfather, preferred to be a spectator, though undisguised, she would sometimes consent to dance.

In 1561 the Templars chose Robert Dudley as their Christmas Prince, at a time when the queen made no secret of her preference for him. There were high hopes in legal circles that England would have a king before the end of Elizabeth's fourth regnal year. However, Elizabeth had frankly spoken of her personal wish to lead a single life. No one, of course, believed her. It was her duty as a woman and a monarch to marry and provide an heir for the kingdom.

The tournament, mask and play which Dudley took to court in January 1562 displayed variations on the theme: marry or declare a successor to the throne. Sackville and Norton's *Gorboduc* chronicled the destruction of Britain by rival claimants to the throne; this first Elizabethan history play was followed by a lavish mask whose theme and iconography were described in a book published later in the same year.[14] Publication of Dudley's princely revels in a book of heraldry, Gerard Legh's *Accidens of Armory*, marks a new departure in the dissemination of court entertainment. Hitherto tournaments, royal entries and revels had been recorded chiefly in chronicles or ambassadorial despatches. For the period between 1507 and 1558 a few slim printed pamphlets survive, unpretentious news-sheets describing royal triumphs for ordinary subjects. Gerard Legh's elegantly produced *Accidens* describes the mask and revels of a Tudor subject whose princely persona was entirely fictitious.

Dudley chose as his first offering to the queen a version of Henry VIII's mask of Desire and Beauty. Elizabeth is given two fictional personae, following in this the legal decorum of the coronation pageants which had honoured her as 'royal queen' and 'most beautiful lady'. Desire woos Lady Beauty and the goddess Pallas gives consent for the marriage. Dudley himself is also given multiple roles; this was more audacious. When Desire receives the consent of Pallas to wed Beauty he is transformed to Perseus; later the knighting ceremony represents him as an Olympian. The ostensible logic of the successive transformations lies in an allegory of the Olympians as moral virtues. But the presumption is patent; if Pallas represents the queen's majesty then Dudley's Olympian role elevates him to the rank requisite for a potential consort. Pallas, within the fiction transforms Desire to Perseus by her consent to the marriage; only then does the conceit open out to include the queen herself. The maskers celebrate the marriage by choosing partners from 'Beauty's dames' in the

audience; dancing signifies matrimony. This invitation to Eliza to affirm
the fiction and dance at her own wedding was mischievous but in the rest
of the mask the queen's two capacities are kept respectfully distinct.
Desire woos the lady but it is the goddess who gives consent. However
subsequent political events show no such happy accord and later masks
reveal more strain. Muriel Bradbrook has suggested that the power of
Elizabeth's legend lay in the fact that it was not a static but a dynamic
affair.[15] It grew gradually and sometimes painfully from conflicting ideas of
a female monarch's duties. Pallas and Juno symbolized martial and marital
ideas for which Elizabeth had little sympathy. Yet despite her lack of
enthusiasm for these poetic versions of her majesty she took no steps to
publicise alternative visions; the content of her own modest court masks is
unremarkable and no texts of performed masks survive.[16] Apart from
masks of Acteon and Diana in 1558, the iconography of chastity is nowhere
in evidence. Fishwives and fishermen, swart rutters and Italian women fill
the columns of the early revels accounts.[17] The cult of Cynthia or Diana
was not imposed; it was a hard-won personal triumph, not firmly established until the 1580s.

A struggle for maistry between the queen and her male subjects in
Parliament and the Privy Council is reflected in several of the entertainments offered to Elizabeth in the first decade of her reign. Gray's Inn
staged an entertainment in 1565; before the dancing began Juno triumphed
over Diana in debate. The queen turned to the Spanish Ambassador and
remarked 'This is all against me'.[18] Elizabeth was guest at a marriage in
1566; in the mask penned by a gentleman of Lincoln's Inn, Diana was
described as a hearty red-faced athlete, and the golden apple of Beauty was
bestowed, not on the queen, but on the bride, who had fulfilled her proper
destiny of marriage.[19] This harsh critical version of the judgement of Paris
stands in stark contrast both to the pageant offered to the queen's mother,
Anne, on the day of her coronation in 1533 and to Peele's later graceful
tribute to the aging Elizabeth in the *Araygnement of Paris*.

Accounts of several of Dudley's entertainments were published (probably
with propagandist intention) during the queen's lifetime: the well-known
Princely Pleasures at Kenelworth (1575) the *Lady of May* (1578) and the
Fortress of Beauty or *Four Foster Children of Desire* (1581). Dudley employed first-rate poets including George Gascoigne and his own nephew
Philip Sidney to write new instalments of the twenty-year saga of Desire
and Beauty. Dudley's entertainments link directly with the masks of Henry

VIII through their re-use of the king's mask iconography and through Dudley's adoption of multiple personae and therefore the same perplexing question about who impersonated Desire must be asked. In 1561 it is clear that Desire represented Dudley's wishes, Perseus and Jove his royal hopes; how far he impersonated these figures when, as prince, he danced in the mask, Legh's narrative does not reveal. At Kenilworth Dudley himself was not disguised; the offerings of 1575 are perhaps best called mask-drama; the different disguises were animated by learned protégés and poets but they revealed aspects of the patron. An important point of decorum may be suggested by a final comparison with Henry's revels. In these, the king appeared as rival to himself alone; his successive roles signalled self-conflict, even when this meant sometimes appearing as the villain. Dudley's king-games, too, admitted no other competitor; a spectator was not, I think, invited to find the face of Dudley's court rivals or even direct reflections of the patron or his queen. Instead, the fictions embody the facets of divided selves caught in an interminable wooing game.

The entertainments during the nineteen days at Kenilworth are only sometimes overtly allegorical but almost all require some form of interpretation. The episodic nature of the pageants has been emphasised by David Bergeron, who sees recurrent praise of the queen as liberator.[20] But this is only half the picture; who is responsible for the tyranny and enchantment that precede liberation? George Gascoigne, in charge of the *Princely Pleasures*, had been trained at Gray's Inn and was adept in the lawyers' coercive criticism. The entertainments relate to each other thematically; a conflict of maistry runs through the historical Hock Tuesday combat of the English women and Danes, the burlesque country bride-ale and the courtly wooing games. The queen as sovereign is petitioned to redress wrongs for which, as 'most beautiful lady', she is partly responsible. She is asked to liberate characters from different forms of enchantment; the idea of actor as plaintiff is apt and one of the patron's themes emerges – that of *Responsibilities*:

> Pardon that for a barren passion's sake
> Although I have come close on forty-nine
> I have no child.

If Elizabeth was unmarried in 1575 it was largely her fault. But Dudley's shows acknowledge that many people (rightly or wrongly) blamed him for preventing more suitable royal matches. Some of the entertainments still propose marriage, but two suggest disengagement as an alternative. The familiar Olympian-sovereignty fiction recurs throughout the visit, carrying the positive marriage bid while parallel Arthurian and allegorical pageants suggest the emotional struggle and press for release.

As the queen crossed the bridge to Kenilworth castle on 9 July, she received presents 'from the gods'. Among the gifts Mars's protection for the nineteen-day visit was singled out for particular attention by Dudley's own heraldic device – the bear and ragged staff. Jupiter's fireworks were allegorised as the visible emblems of Desire. The Lady of the Lake welcomed Elizabeth and introduced the Arthurian fiction, recounting fears which had kept her confined to the lake during successive invasions of England by Saxons, Danes and Normans; she admitted her fear even of the present owner of Kenilworth. Later, on 19 July, her present fears were dramatised in the device of her imprisonment by Dudley's darkest persona, the lustful Sir Bruse sans Pité. Neptune told the queen that the besieged Lady on her floating island could only be released by 'sovereign maiden's might', reminding the audience of the difference between the 'most beautiful lady' who needs the protection offered by Mars and the queen who does not. Neptune nevertheless warned the queen that 'the cheefest Gods' supported Sir Bruse's matrimonial siege. Undeterred the queen freed the Lady, rejecting Sir Bruse and his Henrician siege tactics with the same firmness shown by the country women who routed the invading Danes in their 'storial show' for Elizabeth's amusement on the next day, 20 July. Juno was to have the last word in a marriage debate planned by Gascoigne for performance in the forest on 21 July. The show, in which Mercury and Iris were to descend from clouds, was not given but its conceit was salvaged for the queen's departure on 27 July in a narrative delivered by Gascoigne dressed as the wood god, Sylvanus. What he lost in performance, Gascoigne gained in print; in his book of 1576 both the show of Zabeta and the gods, and the narrative of Zabeta and Deepdesire are described for a wider public. In the Zabeta devices Gascoigne draws a contrast between Elizabeth's private and public capacities. Diana searches the forest for her lost nymph and learns that Juno's gift of sovereignty has transformed nymph to goddess. Diana finally recognises Queen Elizabeth as Zabeta and exits cheered by her militant virginity. Iris takes the lawn with harsh recollections of Zabeta's imprisonment during the previous reign and reminds her royal spectator that Diana had been powerless to aid her. Freedom was the gift of Juno, goddess of sovereignty and marriage:[21]

> Then geve consent, O Queene to Juno's just desire,
> Who for your wealth would have you wed   (p. 514)

Juno's just desire is the keynote of the Kenilworth farewell. Gascoigne, dressed as Sylvanus confronts the departing queen with the emasculating effects of her women's liberation policies. The wood god pleads to the queen against the enchantress, Zabeta, who transforms her suitors to trees:

Well notwithstanding these examples of justice I will now rehearse unto your Majesty such a strange and cruel metamorphosis as I think must needes move your noble minde unto compassion. (p. 520)

Despite Gascoigne's eloquence and the gods' lament sung by Desire, the queen left Desire to spend his life with Sylvanus and the foresters, a prey to the restless pricks of his privy thoughts. The poet's outspoken criticism of Zabeta's inadequate response to Desire is the most remarkable feature of the entertainment:

All which she hath so rigorously repulsed, or rather (to speake plaine English) so obstinately and cruelly rejected. (p. 518)

At Kenilworth, then, Dudley proposes but the queen disposes dramatic illusion. If he had hoped in the early 1560s to draw Elizabeth into a public expression of her love for him by dancing in his mask fictions, he had abandoned that hope in 1575. What he did create by his patronage is a mask-drama, dependent upon the iconography of Henry's entertainments, vigorous enough to challenge the queen to a public demonstration of her own unpopular preference for virgin life or for *metaphoric* marriages. Dudley's patience wore thin and he finally challenged the queen to face the political consequences of her maistry.

The Lady of May was presented to the queen as she walked in Robert Dudley's Wanstead garden in May 1578. In this dispute of shepherd and forester for the hand of the May Lady Elizabeth chose the contemplative shepherd with 'smale desertes and no faults' rejecting the rival forester, a man 'with manie desertes and manie faultes'. The date of the entertainment is a happy certainty since the recovery of the original epilogue.[22] Bitterly humorous, this recently discovered epilogue (suppressed in Sidney's *Works* of 1598) asks Elizabeth to see the consequence of her choice; it is spoken by the pompous Latinate schoolmaster, Rombus, who reveals that Master Robert of Wanstead has become a 'huge Catholicam'. The transformed Robert has been found at his beads daily, murmuring 'Pater noster', then 'Semper Elizabeth'. Solemnly Rombus presents the confiscated agate rosary to the queen; comic Latin doesn't conceal Dudley's decisive abdication from the king-game. Contemplative pastoral life favoured by the queen is equated with the hermit's life; her beadsman

disables himself by renouncing all jurisdiction in the country and she is
urged to love him better:

he hath deparded all his Iuriousdiction and yt is forfayted tibi dominorum domina
accipe therfore for he will never be so audacious to reclamat yt againe beinge Iure
Gentiorum this manumissor   (p. 119)

Although the epilogue itself is undated its conceits are echoed in Dudley's
letter to Christopher Hatton on 8 July 1578. That summer Dudley was at
Buxton taking a cure.[23] Elizabeth caught him unaware by suddenly deciding to visit Wanstead – as it turns out for the second time that year – in her
summer progress. The master of the house could not be there to receive
her. His half-alarmed letter not only fixes the date of Sidney's entertainment as May 1578 but also confirms that the contention between shepherd
and forester was the struggle between anti-selves. In discussing his troubled
relations with the queen Dudley refers to his own 'too, too many faults'
and to 'Master Robert at his beads.'

One thinge hath troubled me not a litell to heare that her ma[jes]tie should come to
Wansteed, and her ⁓ ⁓* nott there to receave her. I feare, that litell likyng to it she
had before will thorowe to, to many more faultes, breede her lesse love hereafter . . . Butt
god grante, I maye heare, that her ma[jes]tie doth both well rest and fynde all thinges
ells there to her good contentment; and that the goodman Robert, she last hard of there
were founde at his beades, with all his Aves in his sollytarye walke.[24]

* Elizabeth's cipher for Dudley was her 'eyes'.

Sidney's *Lady of May* is usually included in discussions of Tudor masks,
although it took place one afternoon and did not end with dancing; it was
probably performed by professional actors, animated by realistic gesture,
dialogue and a singing contest. It is fully dramatic in ways that the Henrician mask and tournament were not. However, it is mask-like in Sidney's
expectation that disguise exists to be penetrated and conflict to be resolved
by the queen in the audience. Like Mary Tudor in Brandon's joust of May,
the queen is in the audience and in the fiction; she is both sovereign and
May Lady. Elizabeth chooses the May Lady's husband, declares her own
preference in love and thus determines the identity of Sidney's indecisive
Lady. A May queen took her character from the coarse or courtly devo-
tions offered to her, as can be seen in *Richard Edwards his May*, a poem
which runs a punning gambit from courtesan to the blessed May, mother
of Christ. At Wanstead, then, the queen's choice of Espilus, the shepherd
with no faults, content to contemplate his lady from a distance, neatly

side-steps the country matters of marriage and childbearing. Therion, the forester, demanded the lady herself.

Sidney's show begins as a cry 'justice, justice' is heard from the woods; a countrywoman accosts Queen Elizabeth and asks her to decide the May Lady's future. Her petition immediately acknowledges two aspects of Elizabeth: her beauty which enchants and hurts the bravest, and her political authority by which justice is done. The shepherd and forester burst from the woods, haling and pulling the May Lady from side to side. The difference between the suitors is not immediately apparent in their behaviour, nor in the schoolmaster's description of them. The May Lady is 'hunted as you wolde say pursued, by tooe, a brace, a cupple, a caste of younge men'. When the Lady presents her suitors to the queen, she says Espilus is one 'who hath neuer donne me anie wronge, but feedinge his sheepe sittinge vnder some sweete bushe, some tymes they saie he recordes my name in dolefull verses'. Therion steals venison for her from the forests and 'many other prettie and prettier services' (pp. 110–12).

The suitors engage in a singing match in which Espilus is distinguished as a poet, a man of metaphor; Therion is blunt and direct. Espilus vows himself the slave of his lady; he lives in thoughts more high than stars; a shepherd later equates these thoughts with Espilus's sheep. Therion remarks that Espilus, by his own conceit, is the servant of his sheep. They have different linguistic approaches to courtship.[25] Espilus hopes to possess 'thie grace'; Therion uses no elegant circumlocutions, addresses the Lady as 'you' and wants to hold her in his arms:

> Two Thowsande Deere in wildest woodes I haue
> Them can I take but you I cannot howlde
> he is not poore whoe can his freedome save
> Bounde but to you no welth but you I woulde   (p. 113)

To proceed any further without the text of the first of Henry VIII's foster songs would be to miss some of the delightful resonances Sidney gives to Dudley's suit. Espilus, the contemplative (though he has obvious European pastoral antecedents), and Therion spring from the hermit-foster transformations of Henry's mayings. A foster spurned by Beauty becomes a beadsman. Deer killing in Henry's bawdy *double entendre* is an assertion of virility:

> I have bene a foster
> Long and many a day;
> Foster wyl I be no more

No lenger shote I may;
Yet have I bene a foster ...

Lady Venus hath commaundyd me
Owt of her courte to go;
Ryght playnly she shewith me
That beawtye ys my foo
Yet have I bene a foster ...

Now will I take to me my bedes
For and my santes booke,
And pray I wyll for them that may,
For I may nowght but loke;
Yet have I bene a foster.[26]

Why is Sidney's forester called Therion? And what exactly are his many faults? Sidney's tact is admirable, for both the name and the offence are presumptuous. A forester is merely a keeper; deer belong to the monarch and may only be hunted with a royal warrant. As Manwood's *Treatise of Forrest Lawes* put it, 'The forest . . . is a place of recreation and pastime meete for the royal dignitie of a Prince'.[27] Deer-killing is a crown privilege. Thus at Wanstead in 1578, on the edge of Epping Forest, only the queen can absolve Therion of the presumption his act and name imply. Therion means beast or lower animal. Sidney probably derived it from a proverb of Aristotle: 'η θηριον 'η θεος; it had some currency in English as 'solitary man is either a god or a beast'. It seems likely that Sidney had the context of the *Politics* in mind when he lightly but firmly blamed Elizabeth for the isolation of both shepherd and forester and asked her, as queen, to end it. Both suitors are solitary figures, both might be seen as less or more than a man depending on how a spectator valued the contemplative or active life. Therion himself hurls the word 'beast' at his rival, implying that a shepherd content with thoughts is less than a man.

The context of the *Politics* and Sidney's reminder that the queen's suitor is an Inner Templar emphasise the serious political strand in the conceits of these king-games. Both Aristotle and Sidney explore, in their own ways, the nature of the political bond which links state and subject. Sidney sees the state personified in his queen, yet his concern for political identity is close to this passage of Aristotle:

A man who is incapable of entering into partnership, or who is so self-sufficient that he has no need to do so, is no part of a state, so that he must be either a lower animal or a god.

For Sidney, the queen justly or unjustly decides the terms of Aristotle's bond:

For as man is the best of animals when perfected, so he is the worst of all when sundered from law and justice . . . justice . . . is an element of the state; for judicial procedure which means the decision of what is just, is the regulation of the political partnership.[28]

Therion argues for active participation in that political partnership; Espilus will settle for a passive role. Therion is resisting a transformation which is fully described in a dispute between a *young* forester and an *old* shepherd. Old Dorcas praises a life of retired contemplation as suitable for 'Templars' driven to despair by the queen's remote beauty:

yf contemplacion as clarckes saie be most excellente, which is so fitte a life for a Templer as ours is? which is nether subiecte to violente oppression nor servile flattery how many courtiers (thincke you) I haue hard vnder our somer bushes make theire wofull com-playntes some of the greatnes of theire mistris estate, which dazeled theire eyes and yet burned theire hartes some of the extremytie of her beautie cupled wyth extreme creweltie some of to much witte which mad all these theire Lovinge Labors folly O how often haue I hard one name sounde in many mouthes makinge our valleyes wytnesses of theire dolefull Agonies so that with longe loste Labor fyndinge theyre thoughte bere no other wolle but Dispaire, of you(ng) courtiers they grewe owlde shepheardes.   (p. 116)

Elizabeth's choice of the shepherd confirms this transformation before an audience of courtiers and statesmen at Wanstead. Espilus wins the Lady, but on such terms that he must be content with 'her grace' and not her person. The rubrics in both manuscript and printed text give Espilus a final song. In his excellent edition, William Ringler unnecessarily, I think, divides this song between Therion and Espilus. The rivals are alternative selves; when the queen chooses the shepherd, the forester has no further independent existence. Espilus quite properly sings for him, voicing in one person both triumph and defeat.

Dudley publicly accepted the queen's choice; he refers to himself as beadsman in the letter to Hatton, but he continues to reflect on the 'too, too many faults' of the presumptuous Therion. He never again sought the queen's hand in princely pleasures. The shepherd had won the field and Queen Elizabeth found more congenial iconography in subsequent offer-ings; just four months after the Wanstead maying Dudley married the queen's more tractable cousin, the Countess of Essex.

Elizabeth's final courtship by the Duc d'Alençon occupied the years from 1578 to 1581. There were many plays at court but only the trace of one mask; it concerned knights and Amazons. Earlier in the reign, at the

marriage of the Earl of Warwick in 1564 when Dudley had ordered Amazons
to celebrate his brother's wedding, Hippolyta's countrywomen had ridden
docilely beside the tilting knights as spear-carrying squires. The Amazons
paid for by the queen in 1578 fought against their knights at barriers and
only after combat consented to dance.[29]

The most elaborate entertainment during the French courtship took
place at Whitsun in 1581: the *Fortress of Perfect Beauty*, or the *Four Foster
Children of Desire*. Sir Philip Sidney tilted on successive days as one of the
Foster Children and he probably helped to devise the entertainment. A
pamphlet version of the two-day triumph was printed that year and was
incorporated in the second edition of Holinshed's *Chronicle* in 1587.[30] For
the French commissioners, twenty years of revels struggle between Desire
and Beauty were drawn together and assessed in song and combat. The
queen in her gallery at Whitehall sat in the fortress of perfect beauty. The
mutations of Henry's earlier Chateau Vert mask are interesting. Anne
Boleyn in her pageant castle in 1522 had been defended by Chapel boys;
against such adversaries Henry and Desire had brought her down with a
rosebud. Sidney is only an adoptive (or outlaw – depending on the con-
notations of *foster*) child of Desire. He claims Beauty for himself. In 1581,
however, she is defended at tilt, tourney and barriers by all the knights of
the court who maintain that this Beauty belongs to no man in particular
but to all by contemplation. The Duc d'Alençon's agents would have done
well to pay attention to the pageant ending. Sidney and the Foster Children
admit defeat at the end of the second day. From this moment, chronicled
in Holinshed, the cult of Cynthia or Diana becomes Elizabethan orthodoxy.

The court flattery and Platonic idealism of this cult have often been
recognised. There is, however, a legacy of resistance and criticism of the
virgin ideal which finds expression in the court plays of John Lyly. In this
respect he is the direct heir of Gascoigne; techniques for multiple personae
developed by the Inns of Court mask writers give subtle flexibility to his
drama and call for the informed participation of a court audience. Lyly's
mask-drama runs in the Dudleian–Sidneian vein, not the Jonsonian. I do
not think he could have written *Woman in the Moon* or *Endimion* without
the backing of a powerful patron and a spirited court audience.

The pastoral *Woman in the Moon*, though it may be later than *Endimion*,
provides a helpful approach to the masterpiece. Lyly sends up the conventions of court flattery by proposing a woman – not at first situated in
the moon – endowed with the qualities of all the gods. This Pandora is

given to the shepherds of Utopia to bear a child but, as each god in turn descends to exercise his influence on the heroine, she is by turns loving, wrathful, imperious, lustful and lunatic; so wildly inconsistent and indecisive is she that her suitors are alienated and procreation quite impossible. She is finally placed in the moon where, at a distance, her perfections may be appreciated. The moon, we are reminded, has at least three aspects, Diana, Cynthia and Hecate.

In *Endimion* Lyly revolved more seriously the plight of the shepherd who loves the chaste but changeable goddess. He chose the myth which would most fully express the struggle between physical desire and contemplative devotion; one in which the moon, herself, was seductress. Pausanias had written of children born to Cynthia and her shepherd. Lyly manages the erotic myth in the manner of Gascoigne; he gives the moon several disguises. Endimion is enchanted by the mortal aspect of Cynthia; her destructive and beneficent powers are expressed as different phases of the moon: the dark phase, when the goddess deserts heaven and walks on earth, is represented by Tellus, a lady of Cynthia's court. In the play Tellus loves Endimion, enchants him to sleep and tries to have him moved into an obscure cave. In the received classical myth these actions are Cynthia's and they suggest that *she* descended to earthly love rather than that her shepherd ascended Platonic heights. This is the version known to Spenser's E. K.:

Endimion whom the Poets fayne to haue bene so beloved of the Moone that he was by her kept a sleep in a cave by the space of 30 years for to enjoy his company.[31]

While earlier poets had demurred, Lyly accepts the identification of the queen's majesty as the chaste Cynthia but he reserves the right to criticise the destructive effects of her evident femininity, as Spenser did in his Belphoebe stories. Lyly uses the struggle between Cynthia and Tellus much as Sidney had used Espilus and Therion to externalise inner conflict. Lyly's mixture of exasperation and reverence finds its counterpart in the letters, written in the 1570s and early 1580s by Hatton, Sidney and Dudley. From her courtiers Elizabeth habitually asked a devotion on terms of friendship which some found difficult to maintain. The idiom of Elizabeth's actual suitors furnished many of the dramatic metaphors of later entertainments. Hatton said, 'the Queen did fish for men's souls, and had so sweet a bait that no one could escape her net work'.[32] In one of her letters Elizabeth recognised that her correspondent desired her as a woman; demanded that he master his desire and then blandly, on those special terms, promised to be his.[33] But some of her suitors had loved her as a woman and courtly revels found conceits to express the impasse: Zabeta the malicious enchantress of Kenilworth, the indecisive May Lady at Wanstead. Edward Dyer in 1572 advised Hatton, infuriated by the queen's capricious favour, to remember the two persons of the queen, 'though she descend very much in her sex as a woman, yet we may not forget her place as our sovereign'.[34] Hatton wrote to Elizabeth on another occasion in 1584 that if he were over-presumptuous of her favour, nevertheless he had had royal encouragement.[35] The argument is respectful but the queen is the temptress.

In Lyly's play, we find Cynthia's court full of discontented, bickering lovers: a society and, allegorically, a psyche in a state of conflict. Order, both external and internal, is restored when Cynthia finally demonstrates her ability to control Tellus in Act V. In Tellus Lyly concentrates forces of procreation and the fecundity of the earth so that in scenes with Endimion, who is struggling to offer a chaste love to Cynthia, Tellus functions quite simply as the Vice. She employs a witch to enchant Endimion. As Tellus moves among the court, she provokes and reciprocates physical desire. In the course of Acts I and II, Endimion falls victim to earthly enchantments and laments the waning of Cynthia's favour. Tellus explains to the audience how she will bring him to desire the *woman* in the moon.

In Act II she tempts Endimion, as Eve does Adam, to forget the distinction between gods and men and to bring Cynthia down from her heavenly place. Here myth and allegory resonate with unusual power, for the dark phase of the moon, visually embodied in Tellus, is also the darkening of Endimion's mind by desire. At first he refuses to admit mortal thoughts which might debase Cynthia but when Tellus whispers, 'She is but a woman and a virgin' he begins to indulge his fantasy in a series of comparisons; while apparently complimenting her he finally denies her immortality:

> *Tellus.* Why, she is but a woman.
> *End.*   No more was Venus.
> *Tellus.* Shee is but a virgin.
> *End.*   No more was Vesta.
> *Tellus.* She shall haue an ende.
> *End.*   So shall the world . . .
> *Tellus.* Wilt thou make her immortall?
> *End.*   No, but incomparable.[36]   (II.1.79–89)

At this point, the shepherd overcome by the enchantments of Tellus falls upon a bank of lunary, his heart bruised by amorous desires.

Cynthia's first response to the malicious Tellus is inadequate. Tellus is banished from court under guard of a martial captain called Corsites (place of the heart). The human heart is too weak a prison for Tellus who soon persuades Corsites to move Endimion to an obscure cave.

Mercifully all this passionate intensity is relieved from time to time by a comic subplot which explodes some of the Platonic absurdities; Sir Thopas's hilarious apostrophe to his ancient mistress allows the audience to return refreshed to matters immortal with the thought that Cynthia herself must by now be very aged. The physical incongruities which are bound to occur when a sexual union is re-defined as a political one are brilliantly manipulated in the love stories of Cynthia's courtiers. During Acts III and IV Endimion is immobilised by his sensual dream but like the recumbent Adam of the icons his salvation is worked out in the stories enacted around him. In these cameos Cynthia demonstrates her ability to master Tellus or the earthly imperfections of their love. The triumph of friendship over passion in the story of Eumenides, hopelessly in love with the malicious Semele, assures Endimion's return to favour; this story precedes and thus defines the kiss with which Cynthia awakens Endimion. In similar allegorical fashion the compromising story of the cave on Latmus hill is enacted so that the audience sees this as part of Endimion's dream of lust, part of the enchantment Tellus throws upon him. Corsites is commanded by Tellus to move Endimion to the dubious cave, whereupon fairies enter to punish the heart singing:

> Pinch him pinch him black and blue
> Sawcie mortals must not view
> What the Queen of Stars is doing
> Nor pry into our Fairy wooing (IV.iii.29–31)

The fairies kiss Endimion and depart; but the shepherd is not alone. Corsites lies emblem-fashion, black and blue, beside his sleeping counterpart demonstrating Endimion's earlier admission that his heart has been bruised with amorous desires. At this point Cynthia appears and heals the bruised heart thus ensuring Endimion's recovery. As Cynthia intervenes to protect Endimion from the destructive aspect of her own beauty, Tellus's power is broken. Cynthia's concession to his mortality is her kiss which awakens him. It is a kiss of friendship. Endimion wakes as an old man with a white beard and expounds his dream in terms which also describe Cynthia's inner conflict 'After long debate with herself mercie overcame anger and a look of divine *Majestie* on the face of my mistress ravished

me with delight'. In the end their love, like that of Espilus and the May
Lady, is consummated in a metaphor of state. The court and psyche are
allegorically re-ordered in the courtiers' marriages which Cynthia arranges.
Affirming her immortal constancy amidst the illusion of change she resolves
their conflicting desires by union and obliquely expresses and interprets
her own love. These marriages belong to the tradition of the *Faerie Queene*,
where Truth tempers Holiness and Chastity tames Justice. The moon's
darker phases – Tellus, the enchantress Dipsas, the scornful Semele – lose
their independent power when Lyly shows that Cynthia's 'words are deeds,
and her deeds virtues'. Cynthia accepts the *word* love and Endimion is
released from his long beard and white hair, the last emblem of Tellus's
enchantment. In this final metamorphosis, though he does not spring up
a jolly foster, Endimion is restored to youth. He, like his mistress, will now
be impervious to mutability. The word is taken for the deed, union is
complete. This shepherd, like Espilus, has learned to live in metaphor.

Because critics have insisted upon equating Cynthia's courtiers with
historical people, the play's pattern has been obscured. Lyly, like the Inns
of Court men, dramatised his love story with multiple mirrors and left his
audience to decide whether the earthly or heavenly lady offered the truest
reflection.

EPILOGUE

The Gray's Inn mask of Proteus, presented to the queen in the winter of
1595, is a complete and indisputable Elizabethan mask text; it is therefore
too often seen as typical of the entire reign. After its single performance
this text lay unpublished until 1688, whereas reports of the earlier Inns of
Court and Dudley entertainments were printed and circulated widely
within the queen's lifetime.

The Proteus mask is flattering and celebratory. If I read it rightly it
reassures an aging Cynthia of the unshakeable loyalty of her lawyers who
are not tempted by the wonders of Proteus's Adamantine Rock which
'always draws the needle to the north'. At a time when the Earl of Essex
and other courtiers were securing the future by secret, ingratiating letters
to James of Scotland, the Gray's Inn Christmas Prince, Henry Helmes,
brings the boasting sea god to the queen's throne. The action hinges on
the premise that Proteus misunderstands his own iconography. The opening hymn in praise of Neptune's empire is a direct challenge to Cynthia's
supremacy which the lawyers counter as they insist that Cynthia's power
over the ocean comes not from Adamantine Rocks which ensure perfect

navigation, but from the hearts of men; through this powerful political bond she rules the sea. Cynthia's presence breaks open the Adamantine Rock and dancing lawyers issue forth. Here, truly, is the form of masks to come.

Another name might be invented for the earlier entertainments of the reign. They certainly began as masks; they drew upon Henry's masks for story elements and allegorical devices; but they took their shapes and impetus from the wishes and personality of their patron. Chronicled for succeeding generations these king-games ultimately exerted more influence on Spenser's *Faerie Queene* and the drama than on subsequent court masks. They did not always please the queen but they had unquestionably more impact on Elizabethan culture than the revels the queen herself ordered and financed.

Comic form in Ben Jonson:
Volpone and the philosopher's stone

LEO SALINGAR

> Oh, 'tis imposture all:
> And as no chymique yet th' Elixir got,
> But glorifies his pregnant pot,
> If by the way to him befall
> Some odoriferous thing, or medicinall,
> So lovers dreame a rich and long delight,
> But get a winter-seeming summers night.
>
> Donne, *Love's alchymie*

Ben Jonson regularly presented an image of himself, in and beyond his comedies, as a figure of monolithic assurance, consistency and integrity; he could never publicly have agreed with Yeats that a poet makes rhetoric (merely rhetoric) out of his quarrels with others, but poetry out of his quarrels with himself. Behind this image of himself that Jonson projected there were the impulsions of an ideal – an ideal both of the Stoic sage, like his own Crites in *Cynthia's Revels* ('humble in his height' but 'fixed' and self-sufficient as 'a circle bounded in it selfe'), and of the humanistic orator–poet as moral instructor, 'the interpreter, and arbiter of nature, . . . a master in manners'. Jonson could reply with some justice to his detractors that it was 'the offices, and function of a Poet' he was proclaiming, not simply his personal and private merits. But it has always been difficult to distinguish cleanly between learning and pedantry in these proclamations of his, between self-assertion and arrogance. Other motives, such as competitiveness, ambition and vanity, seem to be mixed with his affirmation of a noble ideal. Self-advertisement was a professional deformation he shared with other humanists – and charlatans as well – in the world of the Renaissance. And deeper needs to commend himself seem to have been at work. In his anger with the 'loathsome' ignorance and 'impudence' of his public, there may have been the spark of a suspicion that his own humanism was out-of-date. Worse still, it may have been prompted by the suppressed recognition that his own comedies were not, after all, consistently the best he felt himself capable of. So much, at least, was tactfully hinted by Thomas Carew, the most penetrating of Jonson's 'sons', after the older poet's explosion of 'immodest rage' over the fiasco of *The New Inn*.[1] Had Jonson's self-approval been as firm and stoical as he professed, he would not have betrayed such an 'itch of prayse'. He would have acknowledged, without flinching, that

> 'tis true
> Thy comique Muse from the exalted line
> Toucht by thy Alchymist, doth since decline
> From that her Zenith;

and he would have carried his laurels with indifference towards 'the extorted prayse / Of vulgar breath'. In the end, 'the quarrell lyes', not with the public, but 'Within thyne owne virge'.

Drummond of Hawthornden had already drawn, in harsher terms, a similar conclusion about Jonson:

He is a great lover and praiser of himself, a contemner and Scorner of others, . . . jealous of every word and action of those about him (especiallie after drink, which is one of the Elements in which he liveth), . . . a bragger of some good that he wanteth . . . He is passionately kynde and angry, carelesse either to gaine or keep . . .: oppressed with fantasie, which hath ever mastered his reason, a generall disease in many poets.

And, if one can attribute something here to the resentment of the provincial host who had been browbeaten by his London guest in his cups, Jonson had evidently provoked the apparently surprising remark about his own oppressive fantasy by such things as his stories of tricking a lady by dressing up as an astrologer, and 'consum[ing] a whole night' in contemplation of imaginary battles circling round his great toe. Similarly, fantasy, or poetic 'madness', is the theme of the tribute published by James Howell, addressing himself to Jonson as one of his 'sons':[2]

you were madd when you writt your *Fox*, and madder when you writt your *Alchymist*, . . . but when you writt your *Epigrammes*, and the *Magnetic Lady* you were not so madd; Insomuch that I perceave ther be degrees of madnes in you; Excuse me that I am so free with you. The madnes I meane is that divine furie, . . . which *Ovid* speaks of.

Howell and Drummond both agree with each other and with Carew in this, that they see strong impulses in Jonson that are at odds with his public image of himself.

Although Jonson's impatience with 'the loathed stage' of his own day never subsidised very far below the surface, his confidence in an ideal art of comedy never wavered. Nevertheless, there are differences of emphasis in some of his statements of the ideal, which partly correspond to the differences between his own view of his genius and that of his friends. In his earlier, more propagandist, statements[3] he dwells, as if in assured anticipation, on the effects of comedy, 'a thing throughout pleasant, and ridiculous, and accommodated to the correction of manners'; the poet writing comedy 'is said to be able to informe yong-men to all good disciplines, inflame growne-men to all great virtues' and even 'recover [old-men] to their first strength' – apparently by the sheer force and 'justice' of his 'doctrine'. However, to 'sport with humane follies' sounds less peremptory. And in the private notes he put together for *Discoveries*, late in his career, he shifts his attention, though still within the framework of the theory he had always held, from the remote or alleged effects of comedy to the means towards those effects, to what is directly perceived. Of all types of Poet, it is the Comic, he says there, who 'comes nearest' that established model of humanist culture, the Ciceronian Orator:

Because, in moving the minds of men, and stirring of affections (in which Oratory shewes, and especially approves her eminence) hee chiefly excells. What figure of a Body was *Lysippus* ever able to forme with his Graver, or *Apelles* to paint with his Pencill, as the Comedy to life expresseth so many, and various affections of the minde? There shall the Spectator see some, insulting with Joy; others, fretting with Melancholy; raging with Anger; mad with Love; boiling with Avarice; undone with Riot; tortur'd with expectation; consum'd with feare: no perturbation in common life, but the Orator findes an example of it in the Scene.   (lines 2532–43)

The variety and liveliness of the stage, and the 'perturbation' of characters 'oppressed with fantasie' – these are the features of comedy that stand out in Jonson's mind here, rather than the 'doctrine' or 'justice' of the satirist behind the scenes. And these, of course, are the features of his own successful comedies, as distinct from his 'dotages' and comparative failures. No doubt his finest achievements depend at every step on Jonson's rational control, his unrelaxing pursuit of measure, decorum and justice. But they depend no less on the release of energy from those sources in the poet that Drummond called fantasy and Howell, madness.

Granting the general bias of Jonson's mind, it seems likely that they depend even more, as Howell said, on the latter sources. Jonson never forgets his obligations as a rhetorician, moralist and contriver of intrigues in his comedies. But in half of them, his machinery is too ponderous for his material; he takes himself too seriously; there is no proportion between the intellectual power exerted and the triviality or the merely schematic significance of the characters. *Every Man in his Humour* is an exception, but there Jonson is altogether unusually light-hearted. We only see him at his full stretch in his comedies of sustained 'perturbation', in *Volpone*, *The Silent Woman*, *The Alchemist* and *Bartholomew Fair*. And even among those, there is surely a distinction between the two prose works and his two generally acknowledged masterpieces. *The Silent Woman* and *Bartholomew Fair* have a crowded vigour that no other English dramatist, I believe, can match, but even so, they remain top-heavy because the comic butts are too cramped, too limited to repay the full benefit of Jonson's laughter at their expense; he presents them as eccentrics rather than types. What distinguishes *Volpone* and *The Alchemist* is not simply the resonance and mock-heroic grandeur of Jonson's verse, but the generality of their comic themes. Their people can still be described as caricatures, but they are caricatures of deep-rooted human impulses, which seem universal even in the distorted form that Jonson imposes on them. Indeed, the distortion is necessary to the impression of universality, since it develops in each play from a common imaginative centre, with the result that the characters reinforce one another, with all their variations and extensions of gullibility and greed.

I want to suggest that there is essentially one theme at the centre of both plays, namely the idea of alchemy, or what Jonson found in it; to borrow the term Mr Ray Heffner has applied to *The Silent Woman* and *Bartholomew Fair*,[4] alchemy is the 'unifying symbol' in *Volpone*, where it is latent, as well as in the companion masterpiece, where it is declared. Whatever psychological causes may have favoured the choice, this theme gave Jonson the release he apparently needed for both sides of his personality at once, the rational and the fantastic, more than any other theme in his comic repertory. For one thing, the hope of converting base metals to gold epitomised the acquisitiveness that Jonson saw as both a permanent human failing and the special driving force in his own world, in an age of mercantilism, inflation, and social pushing.[5] Secondly, the hope of finding in the philosopher's stone an elixir of life, a panacea for all diseases and a sort of hormone-substitute to confer prolonged vitality, represented a clinging to life even more primitive and deep-seated than the desire for easy money; it is the force of this motif that makes one of the principal differences between *Volpone* and *The Alchemist* on one side, and on the other, *The Devil is an Ass* and *The Staple of News*, where Jonson's allegory is more barely economic. And alchemy, which was particularly flourishing in the century after Paracelsus, offered not merely a fertile ground for quackery and delusion, as Chaucer and Erasmus had shown, but a satirically attractive pseudo-religion, with its overtones of occult theosophy and its carapace of jargon.[6] Because of its pretensions as a philosophy of nature and an esoteric tradition, it provided Jonson with the most general symbol he could probably have found for the self-willed shams he wanted to attack in the learning, religion and social behaviour around him – more general, certainly, in its intellectual applications, than puritanism or the ballyhoo of the market-place or the humours of gentility. It was a supremely typical example of fantasy in thought and action. Treated as a 'unifying symbol', alchemy fitted in with Jonson's admiration for the classical satirists and for the humanism of More and Erasmus; at the same time, it enabled him to carry further his ambition to adapt some of the basic forms of Old Comedy to the Elizabethan stage. He made of it the image of a latter-day world-upside-down, a counter-Utopia.

Like other Elizabethans, Jonson learned much of his art in comedy from Plautus and Terence and their Italian followers. And he paid much more attention than his rivals to Renaissance theory, including the principle of concentration of interest implied in the unities of time and place, and the principle of calculated progress towards a climax implied in the parallel between plays and orations. His 'art', as he says, 'appears most full of lustre' when his humourists are 'laid flat' just as they have reached their 'flame and height'; he puts his comic intrigues together like the parts of a 'clock', so that all the pieces interact, but the 'catastrophe' is delayed or 'perplexed', 'till some unexpected and new encounter breake out to rectifie all, and make good the *Conclusion*'.[7] At the same time, Jonson develops his own distinctive method of construction, whereby he sets going a number of interests or intrigues that are separate at first, but are drawn together and inter-involved, like the currents in a whirlpool, at significant centres of action (such as Paul's Walk and then Saviolina's apartment at court in *Every Man out of his Humour*, or the pig-woman's booth and then the puppet-show in *Bartholomew Fair*). This is one of the main resources behind his crescendo effects.

Insofar as Jonson drew his separate characters together by the allurements of a common folly or vice, he was plainly following the example of the Tudor moralities. But the principal stimulus behind his methods of construction must have been the example of Aristophanes (in whom the art of comedy 'appeared absolute, and fully perfected', in spite of his 'scurrility').[8] Aristophanes provided Jonson not only with precedents for topical satire including instruction and horse-play and 'a mingling of fantasy and realism', but suggestive examples of 'a comic structure centered . . . on the exploration of an extravagant conceit'.[9] The typical ground-plan of an Aristophanic comedy could be described as the execution of a pre-posterous scheme which brings characters of all sorts flocking round its originator. So, in *Plutus*, for example, the neighbours flock to Chremylus's house as soon as it is known that he is lodging the Wealth-god there after hitting on the idea of curing the god of his blindness – and not only the neighbours, but a host of strangers, a Just Man, an Informer, an Old Woman who has lost her kept lover, the Youth in question, Hermes (the jack-of-all-trades among the gods), the Priest of Zeus, and even Zeus the Preserver himself. So, similarly, people flock to a common attraction in *Volpone* and *The Alchemist*, and Volpone can boast that his reputation

> drawes new clients, daily, to my house,
> Women, and men, of every sexe, and age.   (1.i.76)

And they flock for comparable reasons: Aristophanes' account of Plutus (who is not only blind at first, but does not know his own powers)[10] is the prime literary source for the god that Volpone and his 'clients' worship,

> Riches, the dumbe god, that giv'st all men tongues:
> That canst doe nought, and yet mak'st men doe all things.   (1.i.22)

Both dramatists build on similar premises. It is true that Aristophanes has been given a variety of interpretations. And his comedies expound Utopian schemes, patently fabulous, though allegedly beneficial; whereas the schemes Jonson invents for his tricksters are plausible, but fraudulent. The 'extravagant conceit' that Aristophanes develops in *Plutus* and his earlier plays involves the poetic fiction of restoring Athens to a golden age, whereas the talk of a golden age in *Volpone* and *The Alchemist* is an impudent cheat. Nevertheless, Jonson's debt to the Greek poet is vital, in that he constructs his plays around a fantastic project that overturns the values publicly honoured by society, a project that is alluring precisely because it is outrageous and defies the limits of nature. The sexual licence and the dream of rejuvenation or perpetual vigour that Jonson associates with the golden metal in *Volpone* and *The Alchemist* also belong to the scheme of things in Aristophanes.

Though *Plutus* has lost rank with modern students of Aristophanes, it was the favourite among his comedies with Jonson's age.[11] And, for Jonson, the critique of money it contains was reinforced by later classical satirists, particularly Lucian, whose 'mery conceytes and jestes' had already 'delyted' the wise Utopians.[12] Lucian's *Dialogues of the Dead*, some of which Erasmus had translated, are prominent among the sources commonly cited for the plot of legacy-hunting in *Volpone*.[13] Even more important in this connection, I think, was Lucian's *Timon*, which Erasmus had also translated. In this semi-dramatic dialogue, which darts across Lucian's characteristic satiric themes of mythology, superstition and philosophical imposture, the principal topic, following Aristophanes' *Plutus*, is the inequality and instability of wealth, and its moral consequences. Timon clamours to Zeus because in his poverty he is ignored by the very men he had flooded with gifts when rich; Zeus at last deigns to listen, and sends Plutus with Hermes down to him with a gift of treasure; whereupon Timon hugs his lucky gold to himself – and beats off the train of sycophants who have immediately hurried to renew his friendship. A cluster of details from the dialogue reappear in *Volpone*. For instance, Hermes points out to Zeus the advantages of shouting loudly (like Voltore) when pleading in court (*Timon*, 11); Zeus refers to the type of a miser, defrauded by 'a cursed valet or a shackle-burnishing steward', like Mosca ('*aut sceleratissimus famulus, aut dispensator*');[14] Plutus compares some of the misusers of wealth to a man who (like Corvino) 'should take a young and beautiful woman for his lawful wife' and should then 'himself induce her to commit adultery' (16). In the manner of the *Dialogues of the Dead*, Plutus also sketches the case of legacy-hunters who find that all their 'bait', their expectant gifts, have been wasted when the will is published, while the estate may pass to some 'toady or lewd slave' (like Mosca, again) who promptly gives himself airs, changes his name, and 'insults gentlemen', before squandering his gains on flatterers in his turn (22–3). Those who 'gape' after money are not necessarily blind, Plutus explains, but have their vision darkened by 'Ignorance and Deceit, who now hold sway everywhere' (27). They are repeatedly compared to birds and beasts; for instance, Hermes calls Timon's hangers-on during his first prosperity so many 'ravens and wolves' and 'birds of prey' (*corvi, lupi, vultures*).[15] Here Jonson could have found the principal suggestion for his animal fable and the names of his Venetians.

Moreover, Timon's reaction when he strikes treasure with his pick foreshadows the ethic that Volpone is to live by:

O Hermes, god of gain! Where did all this gold come from? Is this a dream? I am afraid I may wake up and find nothing but ashes. No, . . . it is coined gold . . .

'O gold, thou fairest gift that comes to man!'
In very truth you stand out like blazing fire, not only by night but by day . . . Now I
am convinced that Zeus once turned into gold, for what maid would not open her bosom
and receive so beautiful a lover . . . ?   (41)

He resolves to build a tower for himself alone over the treasure, where he
intends to be buried; and he promulgates for himself a law of egoism:

'Be it resolved and enacted into law, . . . that I shall associate with no one, recognise no
one and scorn everyone. Friends, guests, comrades and Altars of Mercy shall be matters
for boundless mockery. To pity one who weeps, to help one who is in need shall be a
misdemeanour and an infringement of the constitution [*morum subversio*]. My life shall
be solitary, like that of wolves; Timon shall be my only friend, and all others shall be
enemies and conspirators. . . .Tribe, clan, deme and native land itself shall be inane and
useless names, and objects of the zeal of fools. Timon shall keep his wealth to himself,
scorn everyone and live in luxury all by himself, remote from flattery and tiresome
praise . . . Be it once for all resolved that he shall give himself the farewell handclasp
when he comes to die, and shall set the funeral wreath on his own brow . . .'   (42–4)

Volpone's tactics, of course, are to be directly opposite; he is to be a fox,
not a wolf. But his egoism is a variant of Timon's misanthropy. When he
opens his 'shrine' in the first scene, he too hails his gold 'like a flame, by
night; or like the day / Strooke out of *chaos*'; he too adorns it with poetic
fables, as 'the best of things: and far transcending / All stile' – 'inane and
useless names' – 'of joy in children, parents, friends'. For him, as for
Timon, the very idea of commiseration for others becomes a subject for
scorn, as in the flattery he laps up from Mosca –

> You lothe, the widdowes, or the orphans teares
> Should wash your pavements; or their pittious cryes
> Ring in your roofes.

His basic motive for alluring clients instead of beating them off is the same
as Timon's:

> What should I doe,
> But cocker up my *genius*, and live free
> To all delights, my fortune calls me to?
> I have no wife, no parent, child, allie,
> To give my substance to; but whom I make
> Must be my heire: and this makes men observe me.

And even his final and fatal trick of tormenting his dupes by spreading
in person the rumour of his own death keeps in line with Timon's earnest
wish to be chief if not sole mourner at his own funeral. In short, it appears

as if Jonson, while inverting the circumstances, has taken over the moral scheme of Lucian's satire. Conceivably – to go a step further – it was Jonson who aroused Shakespeare's interest in *Timon*.[16]

His debt to Lucian did not end with the legacy-hunting plot. The grotesque interlude Mosca has devised for Volpone's private delectation is taken (with reinforcements out of *The Praise of Folly*) from Lucian's dialogue of *The Dream, or The Cock*, which again combines economic and philosophical satire, this time emphasising the Pythagorean doctrine of the transmigration of souls. And, as Harry Levin has claimed, the notion of metempsychosis goes 'to the core' of *Volpone* and of much in Jonson's later writing.[17] It stands for much more than a philosophical fantasy. On one side, Jonson makes it analogous to the transformation of substances in alchemy. On the other side, he relates the notion of shifting and transformed identities to the theatrical business of disguise or deception, to the principle of acting a part.

When Marlowe makes Barabas boast of his enormous profits, 'Infinite riches in a little roome', his language is arrogant and highly coloured, but there is nothing bizarre or mysterious about it; the merchant is simply a sharp operator exploiting favourable conditions. Volpone's attitude towards his gold is decidedly more complex. He too is clearly intended to dominate the world of the play in and by fulfilling that 'desire of gold'[18] whose compulsion most of those around him are too hypocritical to acknowledge. But it is also clear from the outset that neither Volpone nor his creator is to be satisfied with that dramatic function alone. From Volpone's first lines to his hoard, 'my *saint*', 'the worlds soule, and mine', it becomes clear that he is not content merely with beating the rest of the world at their own game, but sees himself as the discoverer of a truly human destiny, which other men in their vanity have been simply blind to; he is full of scorn at their expense, but he does not adopt the pose of a disillusioned cynic. On the contrary, he sounds more like a man with a revelation, an enthusiast. According to C. H. Herford, his opening speech is a 'hymn' which 'transfigures avarice with the glamour of religion and idealism'.[19] To this comment, L. C. Knights has objected that it omits the essential, Jonson's irony; the speech 'brings the popular and religious tradition into play, but that is a different matter; religion and the riches of the teeming earth are there for the purpose of ironic contrast'.[20] But this, in turn, understates Jonson's scope and resourcefulness in his rhetoric.

No doubt Volpone brands himself with egregious folly when he speaks

of his gold 'darkening' the sun and 'far transcending' love or companion-
ship; with perversity, when he exclaims,

> Well did wise Poets, by thy glorious name,
> Title that age, which they would have the best;

and with grovelling superstition, when he repeats the word, 'saint', and
offers to

> kisse
> With adoration, thee, and every relique
> Of sacred treasure, in this blessed roome.

Nevertheless, 'popular and religious tradition' would hardly dispose of
him automatically for a Jacobean (not to speak of a modern) audience.
When, for instance, in line 3 he hails gold as the world's 'soule', is he a
sophist – or perhaps a mystic? There is awe, as well as impish belittlement,
in his image of 'the teeming earth' beholding 'the long'd-for sunne / Peepe
through the hornes of the celestiall *ram*'; and his awe takes on a biblical
splendour when (in the image probably suggested by Lucian's Timon) he
compares his gold not only to 'a flame, by night' but to

> the day
> Strooke out of *chaos*, when all darkenesse fled
> Unto the center.

For his next epithet, 'O, thou son of SOL', Volpone borrows the language
of alchemy; and even though Jonson diverts the effect at once towards
anti-climax – with '(But brighter then thy father)' – some hint remains of a
mystical faith or system at work behind the speaker's rhapsody. While an
audience can be sure that Volpone's mythology is false, they are not likely
to be supplied with a prompt retort from tradition; surely 'wise Poets',
purveyors of secrets as they were, must have had some arcane reason for
giving the 'glorious name' of golden to the 'best' of ages? There is a similar
hint of clairvoyance within his impudence when Volpone makes gold 'far
transcend' human love – the vain 'stile' of it, – 'Or any other waking dreame
on earth'. As he works towards a climax, our confident suspicion that
nevertheless he has merely been juggling with paradox is brought crashing
against the gross facts of common experience (or common opinion) about
the power of money –

> That canst doe nought, and yet mak'st men doe all things;
> The price of soules; even hell, with thee to boot,
> Is made worth heaven! Thou art vertue, fame,
> Honour, and all things else!

And even though Mosca is allowed to deflate his patron by means of an equivocal assent –

> Riches are in fortune
> A greater good, then wisedome is in nature, –

Volpone has still a higher card in his hand:

> Yet, I glory
> More in the cunning purchase of my wealth,
> Then in the glad possession; since I gaine
> No common way . . .

He is not, like Barabas, simply first among equals, but belongs to a different order of being; beside his cult of gain, the usual avenues to profit are destructive as well as trivial, so that 'nature' appears to be on his side, in addition to 'fortune':

> I use no trade, no venter;
> I wound no earth with plow-shares; fat no beasts
> To feede the shambles; have no mills for yron,
> Oyle, corne, or men, to grinde 'hem into poulder;
> I blow no subtill glasse; expose no ships
> To threatnings of the furrow-faced sea;
> I turne no moneys, in the publike banke;
> Nor usure private –

On returning from Utopia, Raphael Hythlodaye had perceived in the so-called 'commen wealth' at home nothing better than 'a certein conspiracy of riche men', stained with 'fraud, theft, ravine' and yet undermined with 'feare, griefe, care, laboures and watchinges';[21] Volpone has blandly appropriated some of this stern radicalism, combining it with a solicitous concern for Nature. And though we may feel positive already that he is practising some confidence trick, we have not been told yet what his 'cunning purchase' is. Our first general impression of him includes an uneasy perception that he is something more esoteric than a superlative swindler. Mystification is part of his character.

Volpone speaks like a virtuoso or an artist, in the special Renaissance sense of one initiated into Nature's secrets. He does not practise alchemy (he need not take the trouble), but he both nourishes and feeds upon the same extravagant hopes. According, for example, to Cornelius Agrippa – writing for the time being as an authoritative critic, with inside knowledge, – it is doubtful whether alchemy should really 'be termed an Arte, or a counterfaite colouring, or a pursuite of nature', but in any case it is certainly 'a notable and a suffered deceipte'[22] –

the vanity whereof is easily perceyved in this, that it promiseth the thinges whiche nature in no wise can abide, nor attaine, whereas no Arte can surmounte nature, but doth imitate, and folowe it aloofe of[f], and the force of nature is farre stronger than of Arte. . . . Whilst that they go about to alter the kinds of thinges, and suppose to forge (as they say) a certaine blissed stone of Philosophers, with the which like *Midas*, all bodies touched become golde and silver: moreover they endeavoure to make a certaine *Quint essence* to come down from the high and inaccessible heaven, by the means whereof they promise us not onely more riches than *Croesus* had, but also expelling olde age, do promise us youth and continuall health, and almost immortalitie togither with great substance. . . .

Such fallacies are smiled at in Volpone's Venice, as when Mosca greets Corbaccio, carrying his 'bag of bright *cecchines*' (I.iv.69):

> This is true physick, this your sacred medicine,
> No talke of *opiates*, to this great *elixir*.

But Corbaccio is goaded by precisely the delusions that alchemy fosters, as Volpone proclaims the moment his doddering visitant has left:

> So many cares, so many maladies,
> So many feares attending on old age,
> Yea, death so often call'd on, as no wish
> Can be more frequent with 'hem, their limbs faint,
> Their senses dull, their seeing, hearing, going,
> All dead before them; yea, their very teeth,
> Their instruments of eating, fayling them:
> Yet this is reckon'd life! Nay, here was one,
> Is now gone home, that wishes to live longer!
> Feeles not his gout, nor palsie, faines himselfe
> Yonger, by scores of yeeres, flatters his age,
> With confident belying it, hopes he may
> With charmes, like A E S O N, have his youth restor'd:
> And with these thoughts so battens, as if fate
> Would be as easily cheated on, as he,
> And all turnes aire! (I.iv.144)

Volpone mocks Corbaccio as if the old man believed literally in the myths of rejuvenation from Aristophanes, and he draws a conclusion exactly parallel to the fate in store for Subtle and his companions: 'Selling of flyes, flat bawdry, with the *stone*: | Till it, and they, and all in *fume* are gone'. Volpone speaks with a crushing sense of physical reality, with the weight of a long-tested moral tradition behind his words.

But the very tautness of Volpone's irony here demonstrates the pull of the opposing illusion. And Volpone himself is a kind of quintessence extracted from the vices of his clients, greed, double-dealing, loquacity and perversion. When he diagnoses Corbaccio's folly, he has already been heard responding to a piece of flattery from Mosca that could have been taken from the *Dialogues of the Dead*:[23]

> when I am lost in blended dust,
> And hundred such, as I am, in succession –
> – Nay, that were too much, MOSCA. – You shall live,
> Still, to delude these *harpyies*. – Loving MOSCA...   (1.ii.119)

And the whole of his 'cunning purchase' depends, of course, on shamming the condition of men like Corbaccio, with

> my fain'd cough, my phthisick, and my gout,
> My apoplexie, palsie, and catarrhes.   (1.ii.124)

So that when he jumps from his pretended sick-bed to ridicule Corbaccio, Volpone is tacitly acting for his own benefit the illusion he professes to pierce in others.

The sense that Volpone pursues an elixir, or believes he already possesses an equally magical secret, is all the more potent in the play because his obsession is not directly named. Not to say what he is after is part of his mystification; and, if anything, he thinks of himself as a Machiavellian, rather than a vulgar adept; (part of the effect of Sir Pol's role in the comedy is to throw light on this kind of self-deception among the Venetians). But Volpone is an adept in spite of himself. As soon as his imagination has been inflamed by the mere description of Celia, the course he takes to see her is to disguise himself as a mountebank, with a 'precious liquor' for sale:

O, health! health! the blessing of the rich! the riches of the poore! who can buy thee at too deare a rate, since there is no enjoying this world, without thee? Be not then so sparing of your purses, honorable gentlemen, as to abridge the naturall course of life . . . For, when a humide fluxe, or catarrhe, by the mutability of aire, falls from your head, into an arme, or shoulder, or any other part; take you a duckat, or your *cecchine* of gold, and apply to the place affected: see, what good effect it can worke. No, no, 'tis this blessed *unguento*, this rare extraction, that hath only power to disperse all malignant humours...   (II.ii.84)

And, once he has caught Celia's attention from her window, he tries to hold it with praise of an even rarer secret, his powder –

of which, if I should speake to the worth, nine thousand volumes were but as one page, that page as a line, that line as a word: so short is this pilgrimage of man (which some call life) to the expressing of it. . . . It is the poulder, that made VENUS a goddesse (given her by APOLLO) that kept her perpetually yong, clear'd her wrincles, firm'd her gummes, fill'd her skin, colour'd her hair; . . . where ever it but touches, in youth it perpetually preserves, in age restores the complexion; seat's your teeth, did they dance like virginall jacks, firme as a wall . . .   (II.ii.228)

Volpone here is acting, but acting with conviction; he is not trying simply to deceive the ignorant crowd, but to make an impression on the woman he intends to seduce. His rhapsody of perpetual 'life' is an ironic sequel to his diagnosis of Corbaccio.

Similarly, when he tries to seduce Celia, it is the dream of sexual vigour perpetually renewed that animates him, as he throws off his disguise of decrepit age:

> I am, now, as fresh,
> As hot, as high, and in as joviall plight,
> As when (in that so celebrated *scene*,
> At recitation of our *comœdie*,
> For entertainement of the great VALOYS)
> I acted yong ANTINOUS.   (III.vii.157)

A Jacobean spectator, struck by that precise reference, could have reflected that the role had been hardly flattering to the actor's virility, and that the famous 'entertainement' was some thirty years back. In any case, the present Volpone must be old enough for the rumour of his physical decay to be believed. Yet what riles him, when Celia holds him off, is the horror reflected in his own lucrative pretence:

> Thinke me cold,
> Frosen, and impotent, and so report me?
> That I had NESTOR's *hernia*, thou wouldst thinke.   (III.vii.260)

It is significant that the turning-point of the play should come here, in a scene of attempted rape, and not in an episode of fraud. References to health, medicine, disease, images connected with the life-force, are even more insistent than thoughts and images connected with money. And with an exact sense of the appropriate, Jonson has Volpone sentenced at the end, not for obtaining money under false pretences but for simulating disease:

> our judgement on thee
> Is, that thy substance all be straight confiscate
> To the hospitall, of the *Incurabili*:
> And, since the most was gotten by imposture,
> By faining lame, gout, palsey, and such diseases,
> Thou art to lie in prison, crampt with irons,
> Till thou bee'st sicke, and lame indeed.   (V.xii.118)

Volpone has been 'by bloud, and ranke a gentleman', stooping to a beggar's cony-catching tricks. But his essential crime has been an offence against Nature.

When Shakespeare discusses drama, in *Hamlet*, for instance, his mind is chiefly on the actor; when Jonson discusses it, in his many prologues and inter-scenes, he is concerned with the poet. In Shakespeare's comedies, disguise, or play-acting within the play, usually creates a beneficial illusion; in Jonson, it usually expresses imposture, and the removal of a disguise is the exposure of a sham. He is altogether more aloof towards the players than his rival. Nevertheless, he must have observed the technique of acting very closely, and the thought of acting stood for something influential in his general view of life. 'I have considered', he was to write in *Discoveries* (1093–99),

our whole life is like a *Play*: wherein every man, forgetfull of himselfe, is in travaile with expression of another. Nay, wee so insist in imitating others, as wee cannot (when it is necessary) returne to our selves: like Children, that imitate the vices of *Stammerers* so long, till at last they become such; and make the habit to another nature, as it is never forgotten.

The comparison of life to a play was of course a Renaissance commonplace, but Jonson's particular application of it here was unusual, if not unique. It contrasts sharply with his public image of himself. It suggests that there were motives arising from self-inspection and self-protection behind his repeated attacks on 'humours', charlatanism and social apery.

Volpone expresses this side of Jonson's vision of life more completely than any other of his characters. Materially speaking, the magnifico does not need to go in for fraud. He does it for his private 'glory', to 'cocker up [his] *genius*'; he feels a compulsion towards play-acting, preferably with a strain of the abnormal or the exotic. He needs spectators, but secret spectators whom he governs, including 'the curious' and 'the envious', whom he imagines spying on his love-making with Celia (III.vii.236–9). Above all, he needs to act a part, to the accompaniment of his own applause. A man of mature age, he feigns senility. As a would-be love-adventurer, he mimics a charlatan. Having recalled, to impress Celia, an image of himself as a youthful actor, he tries to dazzle her, beyond the pitch of '*vertigo*', with the prospect of making love 'in changed shapes', copied from Ovid's *Metamorphoses* and then furnished from a collector's wardrobe of exotic 'moderne formes' (III.vii.219, 221–55). Finally, escaping, thanks to Mosca, from the fear of exposure, his immediate recoil is to look for 'Any device, now, of rare, ingenious knavery, / That would possesse me with a violent laughter' (v.i.14), so that he brings retribution down on himself by way of his superfluous disguise as an officer of the law. Jonson has calculated Volpone's assumed roles so as to reflect back on his real personality; or rather, to reflect back on a being with a compulsive ego but no firm identity, a man perpetually 'forgetfull of himselfe' and 'in travaile with expression of another'.

In this respect, Volpone is by no means alone in the play. Except for Celia and Bonario, who are necessary symbols rather than characters, all the people of the play, English as well as Venetian, are engaged in pretences, stratagems real or imaginary, or sudden and opportunist changes of front. Even the court of law, at the end, is not exempt. Indeed, the theme of systematic insincerity is first put clearly into words with regard to the lawyer, Voltore, when Mosca flatters his hopes of inheriting Volpone's fortune:

> He ever lik'd your course, sir, that first tooke him.
> I, oft, have heard him say, how he admir'd
> Men of your large profession, that could speake
> To every cause, and that mere contraries,
> Till they were hoarse againe, yet all be law ...   (1.iii.51)

The ironies of the word 'profession' are carried over from *The Jew of Malta*, but Mosca develops them with a zest of his own –

> That, with most quick agilitie, could turne,
> And re-turne; make knots, and undoe them;
> Give forked counsell; take provoking gold
> On either hand, and put it up: these men,
> He knew, would thrive, with their humilitie.

And it is fitting that this cinematograph of the hypocrite in motion should come from Mosca, the Fly, the mobile demon of equivocation. When (developing a theme possibly suggested by one of the dialogues under Lucian's name) Mosca dilates on the praise of his own life-style, it is the physical, existential qualities of the affair that receive his fondest attention:

> I feare, I shall begin to grow in love
> With my deare selfe, and my most prosp'rous parts,
> They doe so spring, and burgeon; I can feele
> A whimsey i' my bloud: (I know not how)
> Successe hath made me wanton.   (III.i.1)

He feels a biological transformation –

> I could skip
> Out of my skin, now, like a subtill snake,
> I am so limber. . . .

And, for Mosca, it is precisely versatility, changefulness, that distinguishes 'your Parasite' in the scale of creation:

> All the wise world is little else, in nature,
> But Parasites, or Sub-parasites.

The parasite's 'mystery' is 'a most precious thing, dropt from above'; by rights, a liberal 'science':

> And, yet,
> I meane not those, that have your bare towne-arte,
> To know, who's fit to feede 'hem;

nor does he mean those with a merely animal flexibility –

> With their court-dog-tricks, that can fawne, and fleere,
> Make their revenue out of legs, and faces,
> Eccho my-Lord, and lick away a moath.

No, Mosca's true-born parasite is a 'sparke' so volatile that he has no position in space or discernible identity at all:

> your fine, elegant rascall, that can rise,
> And stoope (almost together) like an arrow;
> Shoot through the aire, as nimbly as a starre;
> Turne short, as doth a swallow; and be here,
> And there, and here, and yonder, all at once;
> Present to any humour, all occasion;
> And change a visor, swifter, then a thought!

Puck or Ariel could not do better. Poetically, Mosca deserves to out-manoeuvre his patron; he does not act metamorphoses, metamorphoses are the element he lives in.

Jonson restates the principles Mosca stands for in *The Alchemist*, with fresh embellishments of burlesque: for instance, in the scene (II.v) where Subtle calls on the well-schooled Face to recite 'the vexations, and the martyrizations / Of metalls, in the worke', and to 'answere' Ananias, 'i'the language':

> S: – Your *magisterium*, now?
> What's that? F: – Shifting, sir, your elements,
> Drie into cold, cold into moist, moist in –
> to hot, hot into drie. S: – This's *heathen Greeke* to you, still?
> Your *lapis philosophicus*? F: – 'Tis a stone, and not

A *stone*; a *spirit*, a *soule*, and a *body*:
Which, if you doe *dissolve*, it is *dissolv'd*,
If you *coagulate*, it is *coagulated*,
If you make it to *flye*, it *flyeth*.   (36–44)

In this brilliant parody, which reproduces the technicalities of the Hermetic art with a minimum of distortion,[24] Jonson incidentally defines the speaker's role as well. Face is like the claims for the philosopher's stone because he can be almost anything or everything at once – which means that (until he declines again to Jeremy, the butler) he is really nothing at all, or an actor's mask. He embodies Mosca's philosophy of metempsychosis, of the being that is a non-being because it is incessantly something else; and for this dramatic purpose, his connection with alchemy supplies no more than a habitation and a name. But the dramatist had already seized on the connection in *Volpone*, and had sketched it in with reference to Mosca himself. When Mosca and Volpone are gloating over their successful imposture at the first trial, and are planning already to 'vexe' the dupes further with Volpone's new – and reckless – 'device', Mosca introduces the metaphor of alchemy, with his customary ironic reservations, and Volpone, self-blinded, carries the metaphor on:

M: – ... My Lady too, that came into the court,
To beare false witnesse, for your worship – *V*: – Yes,
And kist mee 'fore the fathers; when my face
Flow'd all with oyles. *M*: – And sweate, sir. Why, your gold
Is such another med'cine, it dries up
All those offensive savors! It transformes
The most deformed, and restores 'hem lovely,
As 'twere the strange poeticall girdle. JOVE
Could not invent, t'himselfe, a shroud more subtile,
To passe ACRISIUS guardes. It is the thing
Makes all the world her grace, her youth, her beauty....
V:...   – I'le to my place,
Thou, to thy posture. *M*: – I am set. *V*: – But, MOSCA,
Play the artificer now, torture 'hem, rarely.   (v.ii.95–111)

Already, by metaphor, Jonson has given Mosca the tasks of 'vexing' and 'torturing' metals that he was later to assign to Face. And the qualities Jonson finds in Mosca's metaphor are the essential poetic characteristics of the play as a whole – animal, mineral and vegetable properties 'transformed' into one another, emotional and moral values rendered 'false' in the utterance, poetic hyperbole gilding deceit.

In a world where hardly anyone follows fixed principles, nearly anything can happen, as the rogues in *Volpone* find to their cost: Corvino rushes his wife into the trap 'too soone' for Mosca's plans (III.vii.1), Mosca snatches too eagerly at Volpone's last deception. Jonson constructs his play by making the compulsive fantasies in his characters collide with one another in a 'vertigo', in a dizzying spiral. He repeats this method, with even greater virtuosity, in the action of *The Alchemist*. The rogues there manipulate their dupes as before, Sir Epicure's dream of endless vigour in an age of gold is much the same as Volpone's, the intrigue shifts, as before, from money to sex. The dupes in *The Alchemist* are more numerous and varied. And, with 'the language' to support him, Jonson deploys his rhetoric in a bacchic extravaganza of impostures of speech – technical jargon, varieties of London slang, Spanish, fairy vocables, Puritan cant, theosophical claptrap – until meaning itself (in Dol's assumed frenzy) threatens to disintegrate, like the materials submitted to Subtle's furnace, into

> *the antient us'd communion*
> *Of vowells, and consonants – . . .*
> *A wisedome, which* PYTHAGORAS *held most high. . . .*   (IV.v.19)

But although *The Alchemist* gives a further range to Jonson's command of rhetoric, he had already prepared for it in *Volpone*. He had already discovered there the poetic value for him of the idea of alchemy, as a latent symbol unifying mystification and power-fantasies with images of 'Pythagorean' transformations and comic myths adapted from Aristophanes and Lucian. In several of his masques he returns to the same complex of themes – the revival of Nature, 'that impostor Plutus' impersonating Cupid, and alchemy as the rival of genuine art and learning.[25]

Though alchemy was a controversial subject when Jonson was writing, the theory enjoyed exceptional prestige, even (or especially) among scientists. Jonson must have owed the spirit, though not the details, of his own critique largely to Bacon, whom he praises, in *Discoveries*, more unreservedly than any other contemporary. And it also seems possible that he owed the crystallising touch in *Volpone* to *The Advancement of Learning*, which he could have read in 1605, just before the rapid composition of the play. Years later, in *Discoveries*, Jonson summarised a section of the *Advancement*,[26] following Bacon's words closely, in the course of a discussion (lines 2031–124) of a question vital to the poet, speech as an image of the mind:

It was well noted by the late L. St. *Alban*, that the study of words is the first distemper of Learning: Vaine matter the second: And a third distemper is deceit, or the likenesse of truth; Imposture held up by credulity.   (lines 2090–3)

In Bacon's words, deceit is the 'foulest' disease of learning,

as that which doth destroy the essential form of knowledge, which is nothing but a representation of truth: for the truth of being and the truth of knowing are one, differing no more than the direct beam and the beam reflected.

This conjunction of knowledge and reality, and hence of learning and life, evidently impressed the dramatist deeply; and Bacon continues by defining, in effect, the psychological laws of Volpone's world – even providing a theoretical justification for the introduction of the prattling Sir Pol and Lady Would-be, to mimic the Venetians:

This vice therefore brancheth itself into two sorts; delight in deceiving, and aptness to be deceived; imposture and credulity; which, although they appear to be of a diverse nature, the one seeming to proceed of cunning, and the other of simplicity, yet certainly they do for the most part concur: for as . . . an inquisitive man is a prattler, so upon the like reason a credulous man is a deceiver. . . .

And finally, Bacon lists alchemy among the 'arts' or 'sciences' most productive of deceit 'for the facility of credit which is yielded' to them:

The sciences themselves which have had better intelligence and confederacy with the imagination of man than with his reason, are three in number; Astrology, Natural Magic, and Alchemy; of which sciences nevertheless the ends or pretences are noble. For . . . alchemy pretendeth to make separation of all the unlike parts of bodies which in mixtures of nature are incorporate. But the derivations and prosecutions to these ends, both in the theories and in the practices, are full of error and vanity; which the great professors themselves have sought to veil over and conceal by enigmatical writings, and referring themselves to auricular traditions, and such other devices to save the credit of impostures.

In this section, which Jonson summarised as a whole, Bacon was not dealing with any picturesque illustration for argument's sake, or any freakish sideline, but with a major entanglement of contemporary thought. For Bacon, the section contained the germs of his subsequent aphorisms on the Idols of the Mind. For Jonson, it seems hardly too much to say, it contained the germs of both *Volpone* and *The Alchemist*.

Bacon has reservations, particularly in favour of alchemy. He does not reject the claims for it outright, and there was no sufficient reason in the science of the period why he should. Nor does Jonson show that he rejects them completely. On the contrary, he makes Subtle draw more varied customers, and arouse more varied feelings, than the cheats and visionaries satirised by Chaucer or Erasmus; and he could hardly have thrown so much force of mind into the play if he had assumed that Subtle's art stood for no more than a transparent fraud or a hopelessly discredited fallacy. Bacon had said that 'confederacy with the imagination' was the source of deceit in alchemy, not ignorance or blatant falsehood; and Jonson's attitude towards the theory of the subject seems like an unwilling suspension of disbelief. He could not have brought so much life into the organisation of *The Alchemist*, or of *Volpone*, if his attitude towards the idea at the centre of both plays had been remote, and single-minded.

He that plays the king:
Ford's *Perkin Warbeck* and
the Stuart history play

ANNE BARTON

In the Prologue to *The Chronicle History of Perkin Warbeck: A Strange Truth* (1633), John Ford claimed that he was reviving a mode now conspicuously 'unfollowed' and 'out of fashion'.[1] Historians of the theatre have agreed. Apart from a few belated survivals, among which *Perkin Warbeck* itself and Shakespeare's *Henry VIII* stand out, the chronicle history seems to have died with Elizabeth. Various explanations have been advanced for the disappearance of plays focused upon the reigns of more or less historical English kings: a decline in 'national spirit', the accession of a Scottish king, the rarefied tastes of the private theatre audience, a tendency to transform history into romance, or merely the inevitable exhaustion of what was perhaps a limited dramatic form. The massive achievement of Shakespeare's nine Elizabethan histories, plays dealing with the reigns of seven English kings from John to Richard III, may well have contributed to a contemporary feeling that the chronicle history had fulfilled its potentialities and should now be put aside. Certainly Shakespeare's decision, at the beginning of the seventeenth century, to turn from English to Roman history seems (quite apart from its own internal artistic logic) to herald the general abandonment of the genre. Plays concerned with the lives of English kings had been written during the last decades of the sixteenth century not only by Shakespeare, but by Marlowe, Peele, Greene, Heywood, Munday, Wilson and by all those anonymous authors responsible for such works as *The Troublesome Raigne of King John* (1588), *Edward III* (1590), *Jack Straw* (1591), *The True Tragedy of Richard III* (1591), and *Woodstock* (1592). Many other plays of this type have been lost. The decline, after only one year of James's reign, in the popularity of a dramatic genre which flourished so richly under Elizabeth raises questions about the genre itself. It may also lead one to ask whether theatrical interest in the nature and development of the English monarchy really did fail abruptly in the early seventeenth century, or whether it simply went underground, manifesting itself in new and characteristically Stuart forms.

Any list of the English histories written between 1603 and the closing of the theatres in 1642 must always be subjective, conjectural and incomplete. Some plays have vanished. Others survive only as disembodied titles suggestive of a type. Even the extant histories reliably assigned to the period can be difficult to disentangle from lost, Elizabethan plays on the same subject. Most perplexing of all is the problem of classification. The English history play had been, from the beginning, an amorphous and ill-defined genre, always inclined to blur or submerge its identity in that of the neighbouring, and more established, forms of comedy and tragedy. Elizabethans were notoriously careless about nomenclature, blithely describing the same play as a 'comedy', a 'tragedy', or a 'history' as the humour took them. Such contradictory baptisms are understandable. Modern critics, confronted with plays like Shakespeare's *Richard III* (1592) and *Richard II* (1595), with Greene's *James IV* (1590), the anonymous *Look About You* (1599) or the second part of Heywood's *Edward IV* (1599), tend to shift their terms in a not dissimilar way. Any decision as to whether *Richard II*, for instance, is properly to be classed as a history or a tragedy is likely to depend less upon objective criteria than upon a particular, critical interpretation of the play. In the Stuart period, as the history play adopts new and subtle disguises, the difficulties increase. *Macbeth* (1606) is surely as much a history play as *Richard II*. The fact that it is almost invariably discussed as a tragedy would seem to reflect not so much its First Folio grouping (*Cymbeline*, after all, appears among the tragedies too), as it does critical preconceptions about the protagonist, plus an underlying and guiding conviction that tragedy is the dominant Jacobean form.

Ironically, in view of its subsequent eclipse, the traditional history play received an invigorating gift of new subject matter as the immediate effect of the accession of James I. During the reign of Elizabeth no one, for obvious reasons, had dared to represent either the great queen herself, or her father Henry VIII, on the public stage. Even Henry VII, the founder of the Tudor dynasty, was sparingly handled. Shakespeare distanced him as a kind of icon of majesty at the end of *Richard III*, an emblem of righteousness and peace more than a fallible, human being. He never wrote a play about Henry VII, attractive though much of the historical material must have seemed to him. Robert Wilson did. Henslowe records a payment to him for the second part of *Henry Richmond* on 8 November 1599. Both this play and its presumed first part are lost, as is an *Owen Tudor* of 1600 on which Wilson collaborated with Drayton, Hathway and Anthony Munday. Judging from the extant *1 Sir John Oldcastle* (1599) produced by the same dramatists, and from the titles of several other lost histories in which Wilson had a hand, his two plays about the Tudors probably tempered fact with a strong and, under the circumstances, prudent admixture of fantasy. The very fact that he called his play *Henry Richmond*, not *Henry VII*, suggests a shying away from the actual reign of Elizabeth's grandfather in favour of passages from his early life: a strategy altogether understandable in 1599. As for Henry VIII, it is significant that the king does not appear as a character in either *Sir Thomas More* (1595) or *The True Chronicle History of Thomas Lord Cromwell* (1600), despite his overwhelming importance to the lives (and deaths) of these two servants of the Crown. Almost certainly, the same was true of the two lost plays concerned with the life of Cardinal Wolsey recorded in 1601.

The beginning of James I's reign, by contrast, is marked by no fewer than five extant histories in which Tudor monarchs are assigned prominent speaking parts: *Sir Thomas Wyatt* (1604), *When You See Me You Know Me* (1604), *1* and *2 If You Know Not Me, You Know Nobody* (1604), and *The Whore of Babylon* (1606). It is just possible that the Dekker and Webster collaboration *Sir Thomas Wyatt* is based upon the lost *1* and *2 Lady Jane* of 1602, but even if it was, that stage coronation of Queen Mary to which the 1607 title-page so proudly draws attention, together with the portrayal of Elizabeth's half-sister herself, must be Jacobean additions. Rowley's *When You See Me You Know Me*, clearly a play with which Shakespeare was familiar, follows Henry VIII affectionately through three marriages and the disgrace of Wolsey, while recording the struggles of emergent English Protestantism, a faith championed most effectively by Will Sommers, the king's canny fool. In Heywood's two-part *If You Know Not Me, You Know Nobody*, Elizabeth strives gallantly to retain her life and liberty despite the persecutions of Queen Mary, to be rewarded at last for her acumen and courage by the great Protestant victory of 1588. *The Whore of Babylon*, an hysterical anti-Catholic blast by Dekker, presents Elizabeth thinly disguised as Titania the Fairie Queene (by courtesy of Spenser, who would not, one feels, have been much gratified) and again moves to its climax with the defeat of the Armada.

In his address to the readers of *The Whore of Babylon*, Dekker claimed that his intention was 'to set forth (in Tropicall and shadowed collours) the Greatnes, Magnanimity, Constancy, Clemency, and other the incomparable Heroical vertues of our late Queene'. These he compares to a pyramid lost in the clouds, beyond the achievement of any pen, or to a stream so profound as to be unfathomable. Time, the presenter of the play, will fetch back 'all those golden yeares / He stole', and 'lay the Dragon at a Doues soft feete'.[2] This is not the language of court flattery – Elizabeth, after all, was dead, and no son of hers succeeded – but of myth. The same kind of glorification of Elizabeth's early reign informs Heywood's diptych *If You Know Not Me, You Know Nobody*, where the very title isolates Elizabeth as the wonder of the western world. Rowley's portrait of Henry VIII is more intimate and personal, never attempting to slur over the king's well known inequalities of temper. Henry emerges, however, with all his idiosyncrasies, as a mythological figure of another, and more traditional, kind. The death of Elizabeth and the consequent replacement of the Tudor by a Stuart monarchy has allowed Rowley to celebrate Henry, most implausibly, as a ballad king-in-disguise: walking incognito among his subjects, talking with them familiarly, proving his physical supremacy by defeating Black William in a hand to hand fight, uncovering and redressing hidden wrongs. The play continues the old, romantic line of *George A Greene* (1590), *Fair Em* (1590), *King Leir* (1590), *Edward I* (1591), *1 Edward IV* (1599), and *1 Sir John Oldcastle* (1599), all of them histories in which a great king pretends for a time to be a private man and, in this disguise, vindicates his inherited right to rule others by demonstrating his personal strength, intelligence, imagination, judgement and compassion.[3] *When You See Me You Know Me* is distinctively Jacobean only in that, before 1603, it would not have been possible to add Henry VIII to this theatrical line of historical kings who acquire the status of folk hero.

The little flurry of plays mythologising the reigns of Henry VIII and his daughter Elizabeth was soon over, Shakespeare's *Henry VIII*, with its ecstatic prophecy of the glories of Eliza's time, standing as a curiously belated example of the phenomenon. After 1604, only a few plays were written which seem to extend the old-style Elizabethan history. Rowley's *The Birth of Merlin* (1608 or possibly 1620) is a conjuror play tenuously linked to the life of an English king, in the manner of *Friar Bacon and Friar Bungay* (1589), *John a Kent and John a Cumber* (1589), or *Look About You*. The anonymous *Welsh Ambassador* (1623) is reminiscent of *Locrine* (1591) or *Edward III* in its delineation of a monarch tempted to be unkingly because of lust. Celebration of the safely distant heroics of ancient Britons, adumbrated in the titles of such lost Elizabethan plays as *1* and *2 The Conquest of Brute* (1598), *Uther Pendragon* (1597), *King Lud* (1599), or *Arthur King of England* (1599), finds its Stuart echo in *Cymbeline* (1609), Fletcher's *Bonduca* (1613), the unintentionally hilarious *The True Trojans* of 1625, and *The Valiant Welshman* (1612). More interesting, however, in terms of the distinctively seventeenth-century development of the English history, are those plays in which a vanished, and usually heroic, ideal of royalty, related to the ideal glorified in the nostalgic Tudor histories written around 1604, is explored without direct reference to the Tudors, and in forms which depart consciously from those of the Elizabethan period.

Nostalgia can assume many shapes. Massinger, in *The Emperor of the East* (1631), surely invokes the memory of Elizabeth in the character of Pulcheria, the wise and good regent of Constantinople, who has in time to surrender her throne to a younger brother who is foolish, uxorious, swayed by his favourites, and weak.[4]

> she indeed is
> A perfect Phoenix, and disdaynes a rivall.
> Her infant yeares, as you know, promis'd much,
> But growne to ripenesse shee transcendes, and makes
> Credulitie her debtor . . .
> Her soule is so immense,
> And her strong faculties so apprehensiue,
> To search into the depth of deepe designes,
> And of all natures, that the burthen which
> To many men were insupportable,
> To her is but a gentle exercise.   (I.i.18–22, 52–7)

This royal paragon, sought after in marriage by many foreign kings, 'scornes to weare / On her free necke the seruile yoke of marriage'.

> And for one loose desire, enuie it selfe
> Dares not presume to taint her. *Venus* sonne
> Is blinde indeed, when he but gazes on her;
> Her chastity being a rocke of Diamonds,
> With which encountred his shafts flie in splinters,
> His flaming torches in the liuing spring
> Of her perfections, quench'd: and to crowne all,
> Shee's so impartiall when she sits upon
> The high tribunall, neither swayd with pittye,
> Nor awd by feare beyond her equall scale,

That 'tis not superstition to beleeue
Astrea once more liues upon the earth,
Pulcheriaes brest her temple.   (1.i.64–78)

The young emperor Theodosius shows signs of repenting of his wicked
ways at the end of the tragi-comedy, but clearly, he will never attain the
kind of magical and epic royalty associated with this elder sister who fades
away so mysteriously at the end of Act V. Massinger's hyperbole, far
exceeding Shakespeare's description of the 'fair vestal throned by the
west', makes one understand how the author (probably Ford) of *The
Queen: or The Excellency of her Sex* (1628) could rely upon his audience to
react instantly against Alphonso, a character who seeks 'to free wrack'd
Aragon from ruin, / Which a fond womans government must bring'. The
Queen, as it turns out, is no Elizabeth. Still, she is not a bad ruler, and
Alphonso's blind prejudice against a 'female Mistriss of the Crown'[5] tells
against him because of the memories of the great queen that are inevitably
aroused.

Nostalgia of a different, and less specific, kind seems to inform Shakespeare's treatment of Duncan and of Edward the Confessor in *Macbeth*.
There are no real analogues to these remote and saintly kings in his
Elizabethan work. Edward's success in touching his subjects for the evil
may indeed represent a compliment to James I; the fact remains that
Edward himself, as he is described by Malcolm and the English doctor, is
a living legend of a kind that even the most assiduous and obsequious of
the Jacobean masque writers could not create around the person of James.
It has sometimes been suggested that there are scenes missing from the
fourth act of *Macbeth*, that it is strange that so much emphasis should be
placed upon the healing and prophetic gifts of a monarch we are never
allowed to see. Edward the Confessor as an absent presence, on the other
hand, obviously contributes to the pattern of a play concerned throughout
to contrast an older, sacramental kind of kingship with something more
brisk and modern. Duncan too is 'a most sainted king' (IV.iii.109) who
becomes, in death, a sort of royal icon: 'his silver skin lac'd with his golden
blood'.[6] (II.iii.112) Both he and Edward represent images of monarchy
associated with the past and, as such, contrasted not only with Macbeth
the savage usurper but also with the young king who inherits the throne
of Scotland at the end. That strange scene in which Malcolm investigates
Macduff's willingness to accept a rightful king who is, by his own con-
fession, a lecher, a miser, and a promise-breaker, devoid of all 'the king-
becoming graces' (IV.iii.91), has always seemed disturbing. One is surely

intended to take Malcolm at his word, to believe that he blackens his character falsely as a way of testing Macduff. And yet, whatever one thinks of Macduff for countenancing as much as he does of this impressive catalogue of royal vice, Malcolm himself emerges from the scene obscurely tainted. Even if he is none of the dreadful things he has artfully pretended to be, it seems clear that he will prove a politic and ordinary king, neither saint nor hero. It is hard to imagine Duncan or Edward the Confessor, however uncertain the times, playing Malcolm's trick upon Macduff. Had Duncan practised such wiles, he might have lived longer, but he would have been a different kind of king.

Interestingly enough, in at least two Stuart histories, men who share some of the mythic quality of Shakespeare's Duncan and Edward are presented as reluctant kings, elevated unwillingly to thrones they have no wish to possess. Shakespeare's Richard II and Henry VI had each had moments of wishing for the status of a private man. These, however, were momentary aberrations, products of despair, or a particularly sinister political situation. Elidure in *Nobody and Somebody* (1604) and Constantius in Middleton's *The Mayor of Queenborough* (1618), by contrast, both regard monarchy as an unwelcome assault upon the integrity of their private lives. Bookish and religious men, they find, as Constantius says, that their 'true kingdom' is within, and wonder that 'men so much should couet care'.[7] Like Duncan, the saintly Constantius is murdered, but not before he has persuaded the future queen of England, Vortiger's consort-to-be, that worldly power is despicable and corrupting. Elidure, after suffering the agony of being crowned three times, as a result of factional strife, is left at the end of his play as an established king who has no choice but to reign. One can only speculate as to the nature of that intriguingly titled lost play, *Two Kings in a Cottage* (1623), but Dekker and Webster's Lady Jane Grey certainly makes it clear that the only kingdom she desires is that of her husband's love, enjoying which, 'What care I though a Sheep-cote be my Pallace?' Were the pains of sovereignty 'rightly scand', she asserts, 'wee scarce should finde a King in any Land'.[8]

Despite some suggestions in *1* and *2 Henry IV* and *Henry V*, this idea of kingship as something which violates and destroys a private life which rivals it in value, would seem to be a peculiarly Stuart phenomenon. It was strengthened by the consciousness of a new kind of rift which had opened, in the seventeenth century, between the private and the public man. Elizabethan histories had often traced the calamities of a reign to a war between man and office, a conflict between the needs of the king's body natural and his body politic. Almost invariably, however, they assumed that the 'king-becoming graces' listed by Malcolm,

> As justice, verity, temp'rance, stableness,
> Bounty, perseverance, mercy, lowliness,
> Devotion, patience, courage, fortitude, (IV.iii.92–4)

were also those to which a private man and good Christian ought to aspire. A great king was by definition a good and complete man, an idea which helps to explain the persistence on the stage of that ballad tradition in which royalty in disguise continues to command the respect and admiration of the unsuspecting subject. Kings like Richard II, or Locrine, or Edward II and III, imperil their thrones when they are tempted to behave in ways that would also be wrong – if less cataclysmic in their consequences – in a private individual.

On the plains of Scythia, or before Damascus, the brilliant ferocities of Tamburlaine might be acceptable. They were not to be admired, even covertly, in an English king. This fact surely helped to shape Marlowe's sudden change of style and attitude when he turned to English history in *Edward II* (1592). The subtle trains and amoral behaviour of Machiavelli's Prince were expected as a matter of course from usurpers like Shakespeare's John, or from characters like Marlowe's Mortimer who were in chase of a crown. Elizabethan dramatists exercised the greatest caution in attributing such qualities, patently at odds with the traditional virtues, to legitimate English rulers. It is extremely interesting to watch Shakespeare, arguably the greatest political realist among the Elizabethan writers of history plays, carefully white-washing the surface of *2 Henry IV*, *Henry V* and (later) *Henry VIII*, while leaving the reality behind the official facade delicately open to question. To what extent did Henry IV (and Prince Hal) approve Prince John's distasteful stratagem at Gaultree? Is the expedition to France really the holy war Henry V and the Chorus claim, or something more Machiavellian? What is the real motive governing Henry VIII's divorce? It is impossible to be sure. Only Shakespeare, perhaps, could have raised such issues, even obliquely, before 1603 in connection with a 'good' English king.

After the death of Elizabeth, it seems to have become increasingly difficult, not only to mythologise the English monarchy, but even to believe that an effective king was necessarily a good man. The changed temper of James's reign was surely responsible, in large part, for this shift of attitude. A great many of Elizabeth's subjects had been perfectly aware of just how hard-headed and devious she was as a ruler. Nevertheless, particularly in her last years, this knowledge co-existed quite happily with an acceptance of her as a phoenix, a secular Virgin Mary, a bejewelled and magical icon of state. She had a way of turning even her miscalculations into triumphs. The so-called 'Golden Speech' of November, 1601 in which she used her defeat in the matter of monopolies as an occasion to express her love for her people, not only strengthened the ties of loyalty to the Crown at the time but, as C. V. Wedgwood has demonstrated, lived on into the Commonwealth period as an emotional weapon to be employed against the Stuart kings.[9] James I's honeymoon with the English people was quickly over. After an initial period of relief that the succession had been resolved so smoothly, dissatisfaction gradually mounted with a king whose foreign policy seemed positively pusillanimous and a betrayal of the Protestant cause at home and abroad, whose ambiguous sexual tastes gave increasing power to his favourites, who could think of nothing better to do with a man like Ralegh than to lock him up, who was personally anything but charismatic, let alone heroic, and whose financial dodges, though cunning, seemed unworthy of a great king. Even Ben Jonson must often have found it trying to be obliged to celebrate a monarch who was inclined to fall asleep during the serious portion of a court masque and, upon awaking, to demand crossly that somebody should dance. The doctrine of the divine right of kings so dear to James's heart was all very well in the abstract: there was little about James personally or his court to encourage dramatists to embody it in a new wave of history plays. The reign of Charles I, although different in quality, proved no more propitious in this respect.

Stuart dramatists who wished to treat English history seriously, without retreating into the mists of pagan Britain, found that they had very little room for manoeuvre. A real king, as the Stuart monarchy reminded them constantly, now appeared to be a practical, cautious, unheroic individual, greatly occupied with questions of cold cash. Elizabeth must have looked fairly grotesque in her last years, but she was a magnificent monster, a mythic beast, which is more than could be said of 'the wisest fool in Christendom', in Sir Anthony Weldon's famous description, with his thin beard and circular walk, his tongue too large for his mouth, weak hams, and shapeless clothes artificially padded out as a protection against possible assassins.[10] As the hero of a play, even if the image was reflected at a distance, such a figure was not artistically attractive. It was always more rewarding to write about Macbeth, or even Duncan, than about Malcolm.

The English history play was created during the reign of Elizabeth: a problematic figure, but nobody's Malcolm. The form withered away after 1603, partly because dramatists seem to have found it difficult to invest historical English kings with majesty and significance once James I confronted them as the visible representative of monarchy. There seem to have been only two lines of genuinely fresh development, neither of them responsible for many plays. Both lines meet in Ford's *Perkin Warbeck*, an achievement magnificent in itself which also represents the brilliant, if temporary, solution of an artistic dilemma.

In the Elizabethan history, love had almost always been something a prince had to overcome, a temptation to him to stray from the path of kingly duty. This is its role in *Locrine*, *James IV*, *Fair Em*, *Friar Bacon and Friar Bungay*, *1* and *3 Henry VI*, *Edward III* and (with a difference) *Edward II*. Davenport's *King John and Matilda* (1631) is the first English history to give the king's name in the title equal weight with that of the lady he loves. The play itself suggests that John's failure to subjugate the beautiful Matilda is quite as important as his defeat by the barons on the field of Runnymede. An impulse largely diffused before 1642 in tragi-comedies (especially those of Fletcher), with only the most tangential relationship to the English history play, the conflict between love and the claims of monarchy became during the Restoration a guiding principle of the English histories written by Crowne, Orrery and Banks. It formed a special sub-section of the general love and honour debate. In his adaptation of Shakespeare's Henry VI plays (1680, 1681), Crowne reinforced virtually every political motive with one derived purely from the heart, even going so far as to make Warwick defect from Edward IV not so much because of the dishonoured French marriage treaty as because Warwick was in love with Lady Grey himself. Orrery managed to suggest, in 1664, that the battle of Agincourt was almost trivial compared with the struggle between Henry V and Owen Tudor for the favour of Katherine of France, while John Banks, in *The Unhappy Favourite* (1681), reduced Elizabeth, that Amazonian queen, to a love-sick maiden who is literally 'no more but e'en a woman' when the machinations of a jealous rival deprive her of Essex, her true love.

Although its Restoration and eighteenth-century progeny were more numerous, the Stuart love history is ultimately less interesting than a little group of plays in which an amoral and unglamorous monarch, a warrior for the working day, is used to set off a king figure of another and more nostalgic kind. In this latter character, traditional 'king-becoming graces' like those enumerated by Malcolm and celebrated in Elizabethan history plays and ballads are resurrected. Shakespeare, earlier, had created a contrast of this kind in *Richard II* and in *King John*. It was plain, however, that the charismatic figures there, Richard and the young Arthur, were the true kings of England, even if they were forced to yield both their thrones and their lives to a politic usurper. The Stuart plays are different. In them, the individual who looks and speaks like a monarch is, in some sense, a pretender: a claimant whose actual title to the throne, whatever the emotions aroused by his personality, is fictional, or impossible to prove. They seem to turn the ancient story of 'the waking man's dream' upside down, with results that are characteristically Stuart.

The sleeping beggar who awakes in splendour, to be assured by everyone that he is a prince whose memories of rags and poverty are all an unfortunate delusion, then finds himself back in his old life when the 'dream' breaks, was traditionally a comic figure. The ineptitude of his attempts to behave like a nobleman amused Haroun al Raschid in *The Arabian Nights*, Shakespeare's nameless Lord in the induction to *The Taming of the Shrew* (1594) and, presumably, the historical Philip the Good of Burgundy and the Emperor Charles V, both of whom are said to have practised the trick. The ineptitude was, indeed, the point of the joke, Christopher Sly, elevated to the aristocracy, remains unable to suppress his plebeian appetite for beef and small ale, or to address his 'wife' and servants as a great man should. Bottom encounters similar difficulties as the consort of the fairy queen. The dream of monarchy in which Ancient Pistol is more or less permanently lost appears to be entirely self-induced, but again the effect is comic for everyone but Pistol himself. In *2 Henry VI*, even the followers of Jack Cade find his lunges at kingly rhetoric ('We John Cade, so term'd of our suppos'd father' iv.ii.33) and his claim to be the son of Mortimer and a Plantagenet mother, hilarious. Falstaff fares no better when he tries to impersonate Henry IV in the Boar's Head, only to be met by Prince Hal's amused contempt: 'Dost thou speak like a king?' (*1 Henry IV*. ii.iv.433) These Shakespearean examples, various though they are in terms of the characters and situations involved, are typical in their view of the pretender figure as funny. Not until the seventeenth century does the man who plays the king begin to appear more genuinely royal than the legitimate monarch.

Almost certainly, there was a Stuart play about Perkin Warbeck before Ford's. Gainsford mentions one in 1619, and implies that it took a strongly denigratory view of Perkin. Given Gainsford's own hostile attitude towards the pretender in his *True and Wonderfull History of Perkin Warbeck* (1618), one of the prose sources for Ford's play, this is scarcely surprising, and may not be an accurate reflection of the lost work. The dedicatory verses to the quarto edition of 1634 suggest that even in the case of Ford, contemporary opinion was oddly divided with respect to the right way of responding to Perkin. Of the five poems printed, two, after making it prudently clear that they do not support the pretender's claim to be Richard, Duke of York, nonetheless celebrate him as 'Glorious Perkin', whose 'lofty spirit soars yet', Another reduces him to a trickster who 'ran his wily ways', while the remaining two decide to ignore the issue entirely. Subsequent criticism has perpetuated this uncertainty of attitude. Within recent years, however, the number of Perkin's admirers has tended to increase, while Henry VII, a character scrupulously passed over in all five of the 1634 poems, now seems a more dubious figure than nineteenth- and early twentieth-century critics were prepared to admit.

In an important article published in 1970, '*Perkin Warbeck* as antihistory', Jonas Barish first queried the conventional reading of Ford's play as a lesson in kingship in which Henry emerges as an admirable or even, in some interpretations, an ideal monarch while Perkin himself, for all his personal grace, becomes an interesting study in aberrant psychology. Barish stressed Ford's strange and persistent refusal to commit himself as to the truth of Perkin's claim. The historical Perkin confessed, before he died, that he was an impostor. The dramatic character does not. 'As in *Richard II*', Barish concludes, 'we find a contrast between the storybook monarch, the one who plays the king beautifully, and the manipulator who rules adroitly without commanding love. . . . Perkin Warbeck reminds us of how, in our dreams, we would like kings to appear, and how in reality, it is nearly impossible that they should'.[11]

Even more recently, Philip Edwards has linked *Perkin Warbeck* as a pretender play with Massinger's *Believe As You List* (1631). It is known that Massinger originally wrote his play about Don Sebastian of Portugal. He transferred it to the safe distance of the classical world only because his version of a recent European *cause célèbre* ran foul of the censors. Both dramatists then, as Edwards points out, have taken a pretender who, historically, was discredited and invested him with dignity. Both resurrect the myth of the hero who returns from the dead to save his oppressed people, and they do so in ways which suggest, delicately, that their real subject is England under the rule of Charles I. These nostalgic and conservative plays use Henry VII and Flaminius, Massinger's representative

He that plays the king

of Rome, to personify what seemed at the time to be the dangerous innovation and autocracy of Charles's rule. Standing against these politicians, and doomed to lose, is a king figure of another and more traditional kind: a man who not only 'has a kind of beauty of being', but who 'is the guardian of the idealized, authentic, undivided life, when truth and government were not separated'. Massinger's Antiochus really is a king. Perkin's position is far more ambiguous, but Ford hints, in Daubeney's first speech and in the exchange between Huntly and Dalyell on the subject of Katherine's royal blood, at the uncertainty of all these titles to a throne: 'At best, Henry the usurper faces Richard the son of the usurper'.[12]

Edwards's essay on *Perkin Warbeck* and *Believe As You List* is extremely illuminating, not only in itself, but for what it suggests about the changed form and function of the Stuart history under Charles. Certainly the two plays make a revealing pair, whatever their precise relationship to each other in terms of date of composition and intentionally parallel subjects. Massinger may let his audience know the truth about the pretender, as Ford does not: his title *Believe As You List* stresses the dilemma confronting all the stage characters who meet Antiochus, a dilemma which Ford has simply extended so that it affects the theatre audience as well. We too believe as we like and as we are emotionally and politically predisposed. The total inability of Antiochus, the true king of the Asians, to prove his identity politically, as opposed to personally, suggests that the ironic words of Ford's James IV lie at the heart of both plays:

> Kings are counterfeits
> In your repute, grave oracle, not presently
> Set on their thrones with sceptres in their fists.   (II.iii.37–9)

By implication, the converse is also true: any man actually sitting on a throne, grasping the appropriate regalia, is now by definition a king, whoever he is, and however he got there in the first place. It does not do much for the theory of divine right.

Ford was always a dramatist who liked to invoke and build upon his audience's memory of earlier plays, in particular those of Shakespeare. Often, he seems to use Shakespeare in something of the way Euripides used Aeschylus: to set off and define his own, strikingly different treatment of subject matter superficially similar. *Perkin Warbeck* is filled with deliberate echoes of this kind. Perkin himself, as has often been pointed out, greets the soil of England when he steps ashore at Cornwall in Act IV in words that recall Richard II's salutation of his kingdom's earth when he returns

from Ireland. Again like King Richard, Perkin in chains parts forever from
his wife in a London street, surrounded by ungentle men who make a
mockery of the marriage oath. Most brilliantly of all, perhaps, Richard's
defiance of Henry IV in the deposition scene – 'You may my glories and
my state depose, / But not my griefs; still am I king of those' (IV.i.192–3) –
becomes Perkin's affirmation at the end that he is king at least over death,
and also of one woman's heart.

> Spite of tyranny
> We reign in our affections, blessed woman!
> Read in my destiny the wrack of honour;
> Point out, in my contempt of death, to memory
> Some miserable happiness: since herein,
> Even when I fell, I stood enthroned a monarch
> Of one chaste wife's troth pure and uncorrupted.   (v.iii.120–7)

In Shakespeare's play, Richard's rhetoric is almost always ambiguous,
arousing in his auditors both on and off stage a mixture of admiration and
impatience. Ford calculatedly rendered the already complicated situation in
Shakespeare's play still more mysterious, when he gave this noble, but
oddly anachronistic, language not to an anointed king but to a pretender.

Perkin, however, is not the only rhetorician in the play, nor is *Richard II*
the only play by Shakespeare that Ford invokes. The first two acts of
Perkin Warbeck imitate the structure of *Antony and Cleopatra* (1607) in
the way they alternate, scene by scene, between England and Scotland.
There was, as it seemed, only one woman in the Rome of Octavius, and
she was a political pawn. There are none at all in the court of Henry VII,
or at least none who are granted a stage life. Daubeney reminds us in the
first scene that 'Edward's daughter is king Henry's queen' (I.i.38) but this
queen, the possession of whom constitutes a large part of Henry's title to
the throne, never appears in the play. Ford was probably remembering
what Bacon said about Henry VII's resentment of a queen whose title was
considered by many to be far stronger than his, and his insistence upon
keeping her in eclipse. He was also, as Shakespeare was in *Antony and
Cleopatra*, drawing a contrast between a limited world and one which, for
all its faults, is complete. Of the three other women with whom Henry VII
is concerned, two are, like the queen, important but invisible marriage
tokens. His own daughter, Margaret, is used to buy off James IV. King
Ferdinand's daughter Catherine is, in the course of the play, contracted to
Henry's son Arthur, at the price of the life of the imprisoned Earl of
Warwick – a Yorkist pretender even more alarming than Perkin in that his

identity is beyond question. The third woman, Perkin's Scots wife Katherine Gordon, discovers when she is brought before Henry in Act V that he will not admit the fact of her marriage. It is politically inconvenient, and therefore does not exist. As she tries desperately to speak of her husband, Henry pointedly offers her the compliments appropriate to a young, unmarried beauty, and presses her to accept an annuity of a thousand pounds.

It has often been remarked that the opening scene of *Perkin Warbeck* recalls the beginning of Shakespeare's *1 Henry IV*. Here once again is a king formally 'supported to his throne' by his nobles. Even his opening speech seems, at first sight, to echo that of the earlier Henry:

> Still to be haunted, still to be pursued,
> Still to be frighted with false apparitions
> Of pageant majesty and new-coined greatness,
> As if we were a mockery-king in state,
> Only ordained to lavish sweat and blood
> In scorn and laughter to the ghosts of York,
> Is all below our merits; yet, my lords,
> My friends and counsellors, yet we sit fast
> In our own royal birthright. (I.i.1–9)

There is a querulous tone here absent from Henry IV's declaration, 'So shaken as we are, so wan with care . . .' It seems odd that Ford's king should begin by advertising his own 'merits', and even stranger that he should talk about a 'royal birthright' which, in his case, palpably does not exist. The whole speech, with its nervously repeated 'yet', sounds like a cunning appeal for reassurance, for an affirmation of allegiance. The Bishop of Durham, for the first of many times in the play, provides it, marshalling the other lords behind him in a chorus which seems, in its unqualified abuse of Perkin and celebration of Henry, too unanimous and strident.

In the intricate structure of Ford's play, Durham is a character parallel to Perkin's chief follower Frion. Durham has material of better quality than Frion's with which to work – the peers of England, as opposed to a motley collection of tailors, scriveners, merchants and small town mayors – but he moulds and directs these inferior intelligences in the same way. Consistently, in the early part of the play, Durham is the man who speaks first on all important issues and trains the rest obediently after him. He and Henry operate as a team almost in the manner of Richard III and Buckingham. Consummate actors, they make sure between them, not only that Stanley should die, but that it will be the nobles and not the 'merciful' king who insist upon his execution. There is no evidence that Stanley's guilt in the play extends any further than it did in Bacon's *Life*: a mere unguarded assertion, made to Clifford, who later turns informer, that he would not take up arms against a true Yorkist claimant to the throne. As with the execution of Warwick, announced later in the play, Ford obviously had to be careful how he handled the question of Stanley's 'treason'. There can be no doubt, however, as to the dignity with which Stanley faces death, or to where our sympathies lie in that strange scene in which he marks the informer's cheek with the sign of the Cross. Stanley dies praying for the king (II.ii.67–9, 97–8), but it is not clear which king he has in mind. His last message to his brother, 'that I shall stand no blemish to his house / In chronicles writ in another age' (II.ii.101–2), reinforces the ambiguity inherent in his final couplet:

> I take my leave, to travel to my dust;
> Subjects deserve their deaths whose kings are just.   (II.ii.108–9)

With Stanley out of the way, Durham hastens up north. There, characteristically, he will brush aside the 'gay flourishes' (IV.i.60) of the single combat proposed between King James and Surrey, in favour of a hard-headed and successful appeal to James's self-interest. By now, Durham has the English nobles sufficiently well-trained that they can bark in chorus without a conductor:

> *Hen.* Lords, we may reign your king yet; Daubeney, Oxford,
>   Urswick, must Perkin wear the crown?
> *Dau.*   A slave!
> *Oxf.* A vagabond!
> *Urs.*   A glow-worm!   (IV.iv.31–3)

For services such as these, Henry determines that, should the present archbishop of Canterbury obligingly 'move / To a translation higher yet', his good Fox of Durham 'deserves that see. / He's nimble in his industry, and mounting'. (IV.iv.71–4)

Quite apart from the dubious joke about 'translation', one may wonder if nimbleness and a mounting mind ought really to be the chief prerequisites for an archbishop of Canterbury. Henry's piety, although frequently on public view, is like so much of his behaviour a facade. He may assure his followers that, 'When counsels fail, and there's in man no trust, / Even then an arm from heaven fights for the just' (I.iii.137–9), or claim that

> A guard of angels and the holy prayers
> Of loyal subjects are a sure defence
> Against all force and counsel of intrusion.   (I.i.73–5)

The aphorism by which he actually lives would seem to be: 'Money gives soul to action' (III.i.29). It is like Henry that after the defeat of the Cornish rebels in Act III – men who have rebelled because of his financial exactions, not because of the Yorkist claim – the king should direct that cash should be distributed among his troops, 'which shall hearten / And cherish up their loyalties' (III.i.112–13). 'O happy kings,' he muses after giving this order, 'whose thrones are raiséd in their subjects' hearts!' (117–18). Hearts, in this instance, would appear to be a euphemism for pockets.

Ford's Henry VII is not a villain, like Shakespeare's Richard III or King John. He is simply a king with the soul of an unscrupulous merchant banker. His cash, as he says proudly, 'flows through all Europe', and he likes to think of himself as 'steward' of 'such voluntary favours as our people / In duty aid us with' (IV.iv.46–54). The 'voluntary' nature of these contributions is certainly open to question, but not the skill with which Henry bribes and rewards informers, churchmen, soldiers, foreign ambassadors and other kings. He is a monarch in a new and wholly unromantic style: an administrator rather than 'God's substitute, his deputy anointed in His sight'. Such a concept of kingship is modern, and not very appealing, which is why Henry spends so much of the play pretending to emotions and scruples he does not feel. Whatever Perkin may be doing, Henry VII certainly plays the part of king, in the sense that he tries to conceal the thing he is behind a mask of traditional 'king-becoming graces'. He even essays the personal. Henry's staged grief in the scene in which Clifford publicly impeaches Stanley suggests that he has taken hints from a combination of the deposition scene from Shakespeare's *Richard II* (the mirror) and Henry V's reaction, at Southampton, to the treachery of Scroop. As an actor, Henry VII is not very accomplished. Later, in the speech in which he agrees to Stanley's execution, the truth constantly slips out from behind the pose:

> What a coil is here
> To keep my gratitude sincere and perfect!
> Stanley was once my friend and came in time
> To save my life; *yet to say truth, my lords,*
> *The man stayed long enough t'endanger it.*
> But I could see no more into his heart
> Than what his outward actions did present;
> And for 'em have rewarded him so fully,
> As that there wanted nothing in our gift
> To gratify his merit, as I thought,
> Unless I should divide my crown with him

And give him half; *though now I well perceive*
'Twould scarce have served his turn without the whole.
But I am charitable, lords; let justice
Proceed in execution, whiles I mourn
The loss of one whom I esteemed a friend.   (II.ii.26–41. my italics)

Even without the peevish, and altogether characteristic, emphasis upon reward unprofitably bestowed, it is clear that genuine sorrow would be incapable of Henry's jests. Oxford and Surrey may conclude that the king is 'composed of gentleness'. Durham's comment – 'every man is nearest to himself, / And that the king observes: 'tis fit 'a should' – seems, as usual, more perceptive. (II.ii.50–2)

By preference, Henry avoids personal encounters, even as he avoids participation in a battle (II.ii.143–5). He makes his tender heart the excuse for refusing to see Stanley, although it does not prevent him from eaves-dropping on the whole scene. In Act III, he again declines to see the rebel leaders he has just condemned to death. Significantly, Perkin when captured is thrust into Henry's presence before he has time to prevent it, and with embarrassing results. Peter Ure once pointed out that Perkin accomplishes the seemingly impossible when he manages to take Henry's condescending first speech away from him, turn it in the opposite direc-tion, ennoble it, and set it free.[13] Not even Shakespeare's Richard II had done anything quite like this to Bolingbroke. Language and personal appearance may be all that Perkin has to rely upon; with them he dominates the scene. Even the owlish Mayor of Cork, apparently the silliest of Perkin's tattered followers, begins to sound like a disconcertingly wise fool:

For I confess, respectively, in taking great parts, the one side prevailing, the other side must go down ... For my own part, I believe it is true, if I be not deceived, that kings must be kings and subjects subjects. But which is which – you shall pardon me for that.

(v.ii.105–6, 113–16)

One sees why Henry terminates the interview with speed and refuses, thereafter, to see Perkin again.

Ford never asserts either that Perkin is the rightful king of England or that, if he possessed a throne, he would be a better ruler than King Henry. If anything, the suggestion is that this is a man born out of his time, an anachronism in a world where power now resides in the royal exchequer and the 'king-becoming graces' are an irrelevance. The same is true of Massinger's Antiochus, another man whose royalty must be measured in terms of his language and his personal relationships, and who also goes down in defeat, betrayed (like Perkin) by his own followers. Both pretenders grow in stature in the course of their play. Antiochus learns to put in practice the stoic philosophy he studied in his Athenian exile. He may lose the world, but he gains quiet possession of his own soul. Consigned to the galleys, he knows that 'every place shall bee / A temple in my paenitence to me'.[14] Although, like Perkin, he refuses under torture to deny that he is a king, he carefully prevents the old friends who recognise him at the end from proclaiming his identity and so bringing on themselves the anger of Rome. Perkin's new self-possession declares itself when James IV casts him off. He is entirely aware of the sordid traffic between the English, Scottish and Spanish courts. In a desperate situation he chooses, however, to remember only James's past kindness, not his present treachery nor the breaking of his kingly oath. He asks simply that the wife James gave should remain his: 'Such another treasure / The earth is bankrupt of' (IV.iii.103–4). The speech is characteristic of Perkin in the way it translates wealth into personal value, inverting Henry's normal metaphoric practice. It is like Perkin too that when Dalyell asks to accompany the woman he still loves, in her exile, he grants the suit freely, without jealousy or suspicion.

Through Katherine Gordon, Ford manipulates our feelings about Perkin with particular subtlety. Henry VII, as the play points out more than once, acquired a kingdom through his politic union with Edward IV's daughter. Perkin asks courteously for a kingdom of another kind when Katherine becomes his wife:

> An union this way
> Settles possession in a monarchy
> Established rightly as is my inheritance.
> Acknowledge me but sovereign of this kingdom,
> Your heart, fair princess, and the hand of providence
> Shall crown you queen of me and my best fortunes. (II.iii.78–83)

Half in love with Dalyell at the beginning of the play, Katherine was moved to tears by the pretender's initial speech at the court of King James without placing firm trust in his story, and certainly without desiring him as a husband. Neither a sentimentalist nor a fool, she listens doubtfully to his early promises to crown her 'empress of the West', conceding only that her bridegroom has 'a noble language' (III.ii. 162–3). Yet what began inauspiciously as a marriage high-handedly arranged, against the will of Huntly, and half against that of Katherine herself, ends as Perkin's one, incontrovertible triumph. The English lords are scandalised when Katherine insists upon joining the pretender, a man dishonoured, dirty, racked and tortured, in the stocks. They are sure her father will disown her. Instead, Huntly not only approves her action but, for the first time, accepts Perkin as her husband and a gentleman. In the moments before he goes to his death, Perkin is supported by people who, like himself, cannot be bought for cash. And in Katherine, whose language has come now to express something far more passionate than mere duty ('O my loved lord . . . my life's dearest'), he finds, as Lear did briefly with Cordelia, a personal kingdom that can mock at the pretensions of those packs and sects of great ones, that ebb and flow by th' moon.

Although *Perkin Warbeck* and *Believe As You List* were the most impressive pretender plays written in England during the reign of Charles I, they do not stand alone in their period. Two other dramas survive to indicate that Ford and Massinger were not the only playwrights for whom the old story of 'the waking man's dream' had acquired a new significance. A third play pushes the debate between the new style king and the ghost from the past back into the reign of Edward I. Aston Cockain's *Trappolin Supposed A Prince* (1633) is based upon a favourite theme of the *commedia dell' arte*, one for which a number of scenari survive. Probably, Cockain saw a performance by the Affezionati troupe in Venice in 1632, from which he remembered enough to write a play of his own in which virtually every incident can be traced back to an Italian source.[15] *Trappolin Supposed A Prince* is the closest of the Stuart plays to the traditional, comic treatment of the pretender. Trappolin himself is a simple, sensuous, pacific soul, fond of food and drink and not above a bit of pimping, whose theatrical ancestry stretches back to the comic heroes of Aristophanes. His principal ambition is to get his girl Flametta out of the clutches of the lecherous courtier Barbarino, and marry her himself. Unjustly banished from Florence by Barbarino in the absence of the Duke, Trappolin encounters a kindly magician in a forest who not only transforms him into the exact likeness of the Duke, but gives him the power to change the real Duke, when he returns, into Trappolin. The complications which result are, in large measure, farcical. And yet the mock-Duke is not just a figure of fun in the manner of Christopher Sly. That the Florentine courtiers should believe their prince has gone mad is a comment upon their society and upon the degeneration of a royal ideal quite as much as it is upon Trappolin's inability to assume the airs and graces of the genuine Duke.

'Whatever I do, though never so bad', Duke Trappolin muses at one point, 'passeth with approbation. Poor Trappolin turned Duke! 'tis very strange, but very true'.[16] Ford gave *Perkin Warbeck* the sub-title *A Strange Truth*. It seems impossible to determine in what order the two plays were written, but they are not so dissimilar in their concerns as might appear. Like the traditional king of ballads and folk stories, Trappolin is just, shrewd and personal as the real Duke of Florence is not. 'Tho I am the Duke' he says, 'yet I love to do no hurt, as other men in authority would' (p. 173), and the action of the play bears him out. Like Dekker's Henry V in *The Shoemaker's Holiday* (1599), Trappolin recognises that social snobbery should not keep true lovers apart. The real Duke of Florence has forbidden his sister Prudentia to marry Brunetto because he is only the younger son of the Duke of Savoy. Trappolin, who knows an honest man when he sees one, perplexes Brunetto by treating him as a friend and equal, and unites him with Prudentia. He also presides over a mad court of justice which, examined more closely, is not so lunatic after all. Trappolin's decisions are unorthodox and little beholding to legal conventions, but they are emotionally and personally just – as when he rules that there is something grotesque about a plaintiff who demands money in compensation for a child's death. As a law giver, Trappolin is very like Sancho Panza, who also ends up governing his island more wisely than the real Duke and Duchess had anticipated. It was not just in England that the motif of 'the waking man's dream' underwent important changes in the seventeenth century. Calderón's *La vida es sueño*, in which the dreamer behaves atrociously during his brief reign, is returned to bondage, and then miraculously is allowed to play the king's part a second time and get it right, was written in 1635.

Cokain's Trappolin returns happily to the status of private man at the end of the comedy. The suggestions of social and political heresy dissolve, tactfully, in laughter. Stuart dramatists, after all, were obliged to tread with caution. This was especially true when they found themselves facing a monarch who was both sensitive on the subject of kingship, and an inveterate reader of plays. Charles I objected personally to the title of Massinger's lost *The King and the Subject* (1638) and to a passage describing royal methods of raising money, even though the play seems to have been set in Spain. That unknown J. W. (Gent.) responsible in the previous year for *The Valiant Scot* clearly had to exercise great care in writing a chronicle history about the Scottish rebellion of 1297, given the fact that the king of England was emphatically not his hero. Something very strange has happened to Edward I in this play. Peele's warrior king, and the hero of other, lost Elizabethan history plays as well as of ballads, has shrunk into

a reticent, calculating man who exists chiefly, as it would seem, as a foil for
Wallace and (ultimately) for Bruce. As it is in *Perkin Warbeck*, Scotland is
here portrayed as a romantic, turbulent country where old ideals of chivalry
and personal valour linger on as they do not in England. Wallace himself is
not, as he was in the ballad by Blind Harry which underlies the play, an
uncriticised folk hero. His revenges against the English are excessive, and
destroy the innocent as well as the guilty. He can also be as stubbornly
individualistic and vain as Dryden's Almanzor. The dramatist never suggests that this man should rule Scotland. On the other hand, Edward I, for
very different reasons, is equally incompetent to do so.

Among the English, Clifford behaves in a fashion for which there was
no authority in J.W.'s ballad source. He sets himself passionately to oppose
all the schemes proposed by his party to 'snare' or 'intrap' Wallace, as
opposed to killing him nobly in the field. The hunting imagery here is
exactly that favoured by Ford's Henry VII in describing the campaign
against Perkin. Not only does Clifford repudiate the view held by Edward
and his other nobles, that 'All strategems are lawfull 'gainst a fo'[17]: he goes
so far as to persuade the Scottish Bruce to forswear his allegiance to
Edward and join with Wallace. In this play, a shadow king of Scotland
travels a road exactly opposite to that of Ford's King James. Bruce discovers that he cannot exist with honour in the politic world of Edward I,
and exchanges it for something rougher but more heroic. Bruce's change
of sides comes too late to prevent Wallace from being trapped at last and
sent to execution by Edward, but his first act after being crowned – Edward
having abruptly decided to be magnanimous to the Scots he finds he cannot rule, and give them their own king – is to slay with his own hand the
Scots informer responsible for Wallace's death. What Wallace chiefly
lacked, as Clifford remarks, was the tempering quality of noble blood.
Edward's deficiencies go unspecified, but they are clearly those of a man
content to rule at a distance, through officers of doubtful probity, and
undistinguished in himself for human sympathy or understanding. At the
end, having assimilated the complementary lessons of both Wallace and
Edward, Bruce is left standing on the brink of a mythic career as saviour
of Scotland which the dramatist, understandably, was content to leave
implicit.

Cartwright's *The Royal Slave* (1636), in many ways the most interesting
play of the three, was admired so greatly by Charles I and Henrietta Maria
when they saw it at Christ-church on 30th August that they requested a
repeat performance at Hampton Court by professional actors. Music by

Henry Lawes and unusually elaborate and costly sets and costumes by Inigo Jones have usually been given credit for the quite remarkable success of this play. The answer is unlikely to be so simple. *The Royal Slave* is set in Sardis, in the aftermath of a great battle in which the Persians have defeated an army of Ephesians and taken many of them captive. Persian custom dictates that, after such a conquest, one prisoner should be crowned king and, after taking an oath of fealty to Persia, allowed to reign unchecked for three days, after which he is to be sacrificed to the gods. Arsamnes, the Persian king, examining the possible victims in his prison, finds them all disappointing until the gaoler produces Cratander, a man initially passed over because 'wondrous heavy and bookish, and therefore I thought him unfit for any honour'.[18] Cratander, who appears to have been educated in the same Stoic school as Massinger's Antiochus, unwittingly convinces Arsamnes that he is indeed a worthy candidate for the starring role in *The Golden Bough*. What happens thereafter is surprising. Informed of the dubious honour which has fallen upon him, Cratander fails to emulate all his predecessors and call for the wine and the dancing girls. He contents himself with questioning whether the gods can really feel honoured by a custom so barbaric, after which he gets down to the serious business of ruling Persia: 'Our Reigne is short, and businesse much, be speedy. / Our Counsels and our deeds must have one birth' (B4).

After one day of Cratander's reign, the Persian court is in chaos. Half of Arsamnes's councillors find the pretender so impressive that their desire to extend the duration of his monarchy verges on treason. The other half, although it finds him equally formidable, is passionate to get rid of him. Atossa, Arsamnes' queen, has fallen in love with him, and Arsamnes himself is suffering agonies of jealousy and trepidation. Astonishingly, everything works out happily. Cratander not only spurns (like Antiochus) all the sensual baits laid in his path to trap him, but refuses to betray Persia to Ephesus. The queen manages to convince her husband that what draws her to Cratander is 'a faire likenesse / Of something that I love in you' (B4). He is, in fact, a neo-Platonic essence of kingship, from which Arsamnes can learn to correct what is unkingly in himself: his jealousy, his levity, his endurance of false courtiers and, finally, his deplorable sanction of human sacrifice. Cratander faces death calmly at the end of his three days, when the priests insist. The gods, however, intervene. At the end of the play, Cratander returns to Greece to be a king in earnest, not in jest.

That he should do so is all the more remarkable because of Cartwright's hint that this man was a slave not simply because of his misfortune in war,

but also in his native land. The Ephesians who creep into Sardis in disguise
from the shattered remnants of the army outside the walls tempt Cratander
to 'Come then a king home, that went'st out a slave'. The implication
here is one that Cratander seems to accept in his reply:

> I am so still; no sooner did I come
> Within the Persian Walles, but I was theirs.
> And since, good *Hippias*, this pow'r hath only
> Added one linke more to the Chayne. I am
> Become *Arsamnes* Instrument: I've sworne
> Faith to his Scepter   (B4)

At least one of Cratander's actions in the play, his scornful treatment of a
hard-drinking courtier and of the achievement of remaining upright 'after
the hundreth Flagon', seems to refer directly to an episode in the life of
Charles I as recounted, later, by Clarendon.[19] The implied association of
Cratander, as paragon of kingship, with Charles himself becomes all the
more remarkable in view of Cartwright's refusal ever to make the orthodox
discovery that, really, this man possesses noble blood. Shakespeare's
Perdita seems to everyone who sees her like a queen, but then she truly is
the daughter of a king. The same is true of the nobility of the hero in
Massinger's *The Bondman* (1623). Only Jonson, perhaps, dared to go as far
as Cartwright when he allowed 'Sovereign Pru', Lady Frampull's chamber-
maid in *The New Inn* (1629), to display an innate aristocracy so convincing
during her one day as pretender queen that a real lord, Latimer, recognises
it for what it is and takes her to wife. Cartwright was, of course, a university
man. Like Marlowe's Baldock in *Edward II*, but in very different terms,
Cratander's gentry is really something he fetches 'from Oxford, not from
heraldry'. Cartwright may also have been thinking of Epictetus when he
fashioned his philosopher king out of a common slave. The play seems to
suggest, for all its fanciful and remote setting, and its ornate musical and
visual trappings, the logical end of the Stuart history: as visible kings are
reduced to petty and undistinguished private men, private men of a
certain kind may come to seem like kings as kings once were.

History, however, had the last word. There is something very poignant
about all those Royalist pamphlets which describe the last days of Charles I
as a stage play, laboriously analysing the machinations of Parliament, the
Army, and Cromwell as a drama replacing the suppressed activities of the
public stage. One remembers, too, the haunting little vignette of those stage
players who were surprised in a clandestine performance at Salisbury
Court on the first of January 1649, how 'with many Linckes and lighted

Torches they were carried to White-hall with their Players cloathes upon their backs. In the way they [the soldiers] oftentimes tooke the Crowne from his head who acted the King, and in sport would oftentimes put it on again'.[20] It would be interesting to know the name of the interrupted play. When Marvell immortalised Charles I in his death, in the 'Horation Ode', as a 'royall Actor', a man snared and hunted by his adversary, he was using ideas from the Stuart histories which had attached themselves now to the real king. Charles, moreover, found his own dramatists. In Germany, Gryphius hammered out *Carolus Stuardus* (1649), a play drawing (like *Perkin Warbeck*) upon memories of *Richard II*, in which Charles compares his death to that of Christ in a Passion Play. The English author of the anonymous, and un-performed, *Famous Tragedy of Charles I* (1649), a man closer to the pain of the event, could not bring himself to represent the king himself – any more than those dramatists writing before the death of Elizabeth could put the Tudors on the stage. He contented himself with a spectacular revelation of the king's mutilated body in the last scene, a discovery in the tradition of Hieronymo's revelation of his murdered son in *The Spanish Tragedy* (1587). Charles I had liked plays, even if he expected them to keep their place. He would perhaps have smiled wryly at this last coming together of Stuart history and its mirror image on the stage.

Medicinable tragedy: the structure of *Samson Agonistes* and seventeenth-century psychopathology

MARY ANN RADZINOWICZ

When Milton first thought of writing a play about Samson, and entered in the Trinity Manuscript the five subjects, 'Samson pursophorus or Hybristes, or Samson marrying or in Ramath Lechi. Jud. 15. Dagonalia. Jud. 16,' his 'foreconceit' differed considerably from the tragedy that we know. The entry in the Trinity Manuscript was made between 1640 and 1642.[1] By this date Milton had written *Comus*, had returned to England from his 'Grand Tour' during which he met the sacred dramatist Bartolommei, had revised his tribute to Shakespeare, and discussed the nature and scope of drama in *The Reason of Church Government*.[2] Had Milton written a tragedy based upon the themes cited from Judges at once, the protagonist would have been arsonous or proud Samson, canny or vengeful Samson, or violent Samson the scourge of God; he would not have been Samson *agonistes*. The mimesis would have been of parts of the Samson fable which either do not enter the play Milton ultimately wrote between 1667 and 1671 or enter it only in brief recapitulation of past action. The theme, the structure and the tragic effect would have differed from those of the achieved tragedy.

None of the plots noted from Judges 15 and 16 provide the action for *Samson Agonistes*; they supply only regretful flashbacks. The Chorus early on grieves at Samson's present hopeless position by remembering warlike 'Samson . . . in Ramath Lechi'; Samson refers to his marrying from policy the woman of Timna, the only wife specified in the Bible; he laments his previous 'hybris'; and he prophesies a Dagonalia when the God of Israel 'will arise and his great name assert'. These references exhaust Judges 15 and 16. Although *Samson Agonistes* opens recalling the ascent of an angel in flames and closes celebrating a phoenix reborn from flames, it does not mention Samson pursophorus, igniting the foxes' tails to burn the Philistine's standing corn. Scripture gives no authority for Samson's three confrontations with first his father Manoa, then his wife Dalila and finally his enemy Harapha. Manoa disappears from Judges after eating honey from the lion's carcass, is not reported to have visited Samson, lamented his blinding or capture, planned his ransom or arranged to bury him. Dalila was Samson's harlot; nor does the Bible record that from whatever motive she went down to Gaza to speak to him and in the event exult over him. Of Harapha or other Philistine champion, Scripture makes no mention.

If neither protagonist nor action, still less would theme, structure or tragic effect as the young Milton understood them resemble the actual theme, structure or tragic effect of *Samson Agonistes*. In *Comus* the Elder Brother's description of the self-destruction of evil and the immutable benevolence of nature suggests the meaning Milton would have given to a Samson play whose subject was the liberating activity of the protagonist against the settled malice of the Philistines. *The Reason of Church Government* (1642) gives evidence of the young Milton's conceptions both of tragic theme and of structure. Of theme he wrote, 'Lastly whatsoever . . . hath passion or admiration in all the changes of that which is call'd fortune from without, or the wily suttleties and refluxes of mans thought from within, all these things with a solid and treatable smoothness to paint out.'[3] A tragedy considers what 'erring men call Chance' or what 'is call'd fortune from without' and shows it powerless against good. Milton's mature sense of tragic theme is as yet only hinted at in 'the wily suttleties and refluxes of mans thought from within'. Concerning structure, he thought that plays shaping truths 'doctrinal and exemplary to a Nation' should follow Greek or Biblical patterns, the 'Dramatick constitutions, wherein Sophocles and Euripides raigne' or 'the Apocalyps of Saint John . . . a high and stately Tragedy, shutting up and intermingling her solemn Scenes and Acts with a sevenfold Chorus of halleluja's and harping symphonies'.[4]

Outlines in the Trinity Manuscript clearly show what in 1640–2 Milton meant by tragic structure: a first act of exposition or a 'prologue' delivered by a speaker other than the protagonist was followed by a choral commentary; a second act of complication with dominant roles assigned to allegorical abstract characters was completed by a second choral 'symphony'; a third act of apparent resolution was again largely reported and again marked off by a third chorus or philosophical comment; a fourth act of further complication was likewise followed by a chorus; and a fifth act of resolution or a 'catastrophe' concluded with a final chorus. In drafting the tragedy 'Paradise Lost', he listed five acts and five choruses, assigned to abstract characters such as Justice, Mercy, Wisdom, or Heavenly Love, the task of reporting action, and placed human persons on stage to be talked at, talked around, and finally talked about as conclusive moral examples. Evidently Milton then conceived of structure as the externalising of educative experiences through the interwoven commentary of chorus and ideal voices. The tragic structure of *Samson Agonistes* is similar only in so far as it is composed of 'acts' with separating choruses.

The young Milton thought that the effect of tragedy was purgative and educative. As an 'interpreter and relater of the best and sagest things', the poet's cathartic role was 'to allay the perturbations of the mind'. His educative role in 'teaching over the whole book of sanctity and vertue through all the instances of example' was to show 'the paths of honesty and good life . . . both easy and pleasant'. Milton recommended that the reformed state offer to the people 'at set and solemn Paneguries, in Theaters, porches or what other place both recreation and instruction'. Right example would inspire the imitation of virtuous action, delight would encourage it, and the allaying or purging of the passions would enable it. 'Of . . . Tragedy' (the preface to *Samson Agonistes*) repeats Milton's earlier emphasis upon the purgative and exemplary effects of tragedy. But catharsis, 'said by Aristotle to be of power by raising pity and fear, or terror, to purge the mind of these and such like passions', is now expounded by Milton in new ways. Catharsis is made to work therapeutically, as in physic 'things of melancholic hue and quality are us'd against melancholy, sowr against sowr, salt to remove salt humours'. A strong audience involvement is asserted: a mimesis of passions on stage will arouse in the audience passionate sympathy, increased understanding and a strengthened mind.

Protagonist, action, theme, structure and tragic effect bore changed meanings to Milton by the time he came to write his tragedy of psychological change, *Samson Agonistes*. My purpose in this essay will not be to account for the changes through an examination of Milton's work in the intervening years, for I have written elsewhere on that subject,[5] but rather to relate *Samson Agonistes* as an affective tragedy dramatising the self-healing ability of the human mind, to contemporary shifts in attitude towards structure, tragic effect and psychological health. I aim to show that *Samson Agonistes* is a 'medicinable tragedy', that its protagonist is depicted in the light of seventeenth-century attitudes toward melancholy, that its structure imitates the cure of a disturbed mind through the recognition and reintegration of its conflicting passions, that its theme is the difficult, tragic but life-affirming possibility of human change, and that its tragic

effect is the alteration of the sensibility of the audience. It is not my purpose to claim that this exhausts the interest of a play full of political,
ethical and religious insight but to pay tribute to Muriel Bradbrook by
drawing out in relation to *Samson Agonistes* the implications of a section of
her finely speculative book, *English Dramatic Form.*[6]

Professor Bradbrook in the chapter of 'Part I: A Psychological Theory of
Drama' entitled 'The Inner and the Outer Drama' makes two points helpful in reading *Samson Agonistes*, the first being protagonist-centred, the
second audience-centred. She thinks that the cast of a play is composed of
individuals each of whom constitutes an 'inner society' of selves and
satellite selves; among these individuals is created an 'outer society'. She
further considers that by imaginative participation in the inner and outer
societies of the play members of an audience may come to rebalance and
integrate their own inner society, strengthened thereby for a better role in
their own outer society. Professor Bradrook's psychological theory of
drama is a modern interpretation of tragic effect and one may ask whether
such a view of tragic effect was ever consciously held by major tragedians
of the past. I shall show that it was held by Milton. The dynamic interaction Professor Bradbrook describes is present in *Samson Agonistes*. I shall
show that Milton's concept of affective tragedy takes shape in conformity
not only to new understandings of human psychology in his day but also in
conformity to new dramatic theories. The Aristotelian–Sidneian concept
of tragedy gave way in the lifetime of Milton to a Cornelian–Drydenic
concept, in which psychological effect was quite as important as moral
example. *Samson Agonistes* participates in this change and is not only the
last English Renaissance tragedy but also the first Restoration or 'modern'
tragedy.

TRAGIC EFFECT: RENAISSANCE TO NEO-CLASSICISM

Agreement is general that as a critic Milton was conservative, a man of the
Renaissance and not a new man of the Restoration.[7] That as a practising
tragedian he was so clearly an 'ancient' has been disputed,[8] but his disdain
for the newfangled was marked and his desire to recover ancient liberties
and restore ancient excellences strong, and these backward-looking forces
are given clear expression in 'Of . . . Tragedy'. The essay commends
tragedy 'as it was anciently compos'd', announces *Samson Agonistes* 'coming forth after the antient manner', deplores the current taste for 'intermixing Comic stuff with Tragic sadness and gravity; or of introducing

trivial and vulgar persons', disapproves of 'what among us passes for best', considers 'Aeschulus, Sophocles, and Euripides... unequall'd yet by any', and promises to follow 'the Antients and Italians . . . as of much more authority and fame' than the English, the French and the moderns. So precise and emphatic are these points, so hostile to Neander's contrary formulations in *An Essay of Dramatic Poesy* published three years before *Samson Agonistes* to which 'Of . . . Tragedy' replies, that they have been taken to overrule any suggestion that Milton's concept of tragedy looks forward as well as backward, it being forgotten that in his post-*Samson Agonistes* criticism, Dryden himself was to abandon his defence of tragi-comedy, to criticise multiple plotting as 'wholly Gothic' and the admixture of compassion and mirth as 'an unnatural mingle', and in *All for Love*, *Aureng-Zebe* and *Oedipus* to echo *Samson Agonistes* again and again.[9] Nevertheless, while 'Of . . . Tragedy' takes up from classical and Renaissance sources the interrelated topics of the imitations of the passions, their catharsis in characters and audience, and the disposition of the fable (or structure) to achieve affective tempering, Milton gives to each of these subjects a characteristically independent treatment, which reflects and predicts the temper of Restoration tragic irony as much as it builds on that of the Renaissance.

The title page of *Samson Agonistes* gives a quotation from Aristotle in Greek and in Latin, '*Tragoedia est imitatio actionis seriae, etc per misericordiam et metum perficiens talium*'. At the beginning of the preface Milton translates the last phrase, 'to be of power by raising pity and fear, or terror, to purge the mind of those and such like passions', and he glosses the translation, 'that is to temper and reduce [the passions] to just measure with a kind of delight, stirred up by reading or seeing those passions well imitated'. The gloss contains slight but significant additions to the classical text: 'to purge *the mind*', 'and *such like* passions', 'to *temper* . . . to *just measure*', and '*delight stirred up*'. These additions relate to several commonly debated Renaissance issues: are the passions aroused, expelled or tempered; are they something harmful to be got rid of or are they neutral forces capable of purification; are they present in protagonist or audience or both; and finally are pity and terror aroused to combat pity and terror or to combat other more harmful emotions; does catharsis apply only to pity and terror, does it exclude pity and terror or does it include them among a variety of mental perturbations?[10]

On the nature of the passions, the preface is consistent with Milton's view in *Areopagitica*, 'wherefore did [God] creat passions within us, pleasure round about us, but that these rightly temper'd are the very ingredients of vertu', and with Christ's dismissal of the stoic ethic in *Paradise Regained* as a 'vain boast'. The passions, together with the humours that influence them, are definitive of human nature and the material both of sin and morality, sickness and health. Milton's medical analogy immediately follows his moral gloss: 'for so in Physic things of melancholic hue and quality are us'd against melancholy . . .' A man without humours is a corpse, without passions a machine; not the extirpation but the integration of the passions heals the soul.

In rejecting extirpative catharsis in favour of moderative catharsis, Milton takes a position not invariably but frequently taken in the Renaissance, the position of Piccolomini, Guarini and Heinsius for example.[11] It is a position which carries the day in the Restoration. Dryden defines the 'end or scope of tragedy' as 'to *rectify* or purge' the passions, makes Lisideius gloss Aristotle on catharsis as 'to *beget* admiration, compassion or concernment', and praises the moderns over the ancients for their affective power: 'The plays of the Ancients are more correctly Plotted, ours are more beautifully written; and if we can *raise* Passions as high on worse Foundations, it shows our Genius in Tragedy is greater'.[12] Rymer translates Rapin making the same point: 'Tragedy . . . *rectifies the passions, by the passions* themselves'. Although to some Restoration theorists moderative purgation meant little more than that tragedy calmed the passions by exercising and exhausting them, to more it meant that tragedy effected a change in the emotional constitution itself and that is Milton's view.[13]

Milton's wording implies a double catharsis: the passions are to be well imitated as they are aroused and moderated in the protagonist, thereby arousing and moderating them with the effect of delight in the audience. This view was possible but not invariable in the Renaissance and came to dominate neo-classical criticism. Sidney considered that the effect of seeing the passions well imitated was not to raise and temper them in the audience but rather to encourage the audience to draw intellectual conclusions from the example offered, and to attempt its own imitation of virtue. Admiration in Sidney teaches and is not expected to alter the mind.[14] When Restoration criticism unanimously insists upon the necessity of poetic justice, it would apparently posit a disjunction between the passions of characters and the meditations of the audience; while characters feel and receive their just deserts, audiences think.[15] Nonetheless the terms 'admiration' and 'concernment' are used by Restoration critics to describe an interactive double catharsis. Dryden defines the 'objects of a tragedy' as 'to stir up a pleasing admiration and concernment' and causes Neander to hold that 'to affect the soul, and excite the passions, and above all to move admiration . . . is the delight of serious plays;' he means that the audience identifies with the characters and sympathetically shares their emotions. He notes, 'the passions . . . always move, and therefore consequently please; for without motion there can be no delight, which cannot be considered but as an active passion'. The process of sympathetic interaction between character and audience supplies *Alexander's Feast* with its dynamics, Alexander 'Revolving in his *alter'd* soul | The various turns of chance below' as Timotheus performs.[16]

Both Renaissance and neo-classical dramatic critics asked which of the passions tragedy was to purge, purify or temper. Agreement amongst Renaissance critics was not general. Piccolomini, Castelvetro and Guarini took Milton's position that tragedy moderated pity and terror by arousing pity and terror against such critics as Maggi.[17] In the Restoration Milton's position became the only possible position and Wasserman remarks, 'That the major function of a tragedy is to produce some kind of beneficial effect upon the spectator through the excitation of pity and fear, was, of course, the central tenet of eighteenth-century dramatic theory'. Milton's extension of the passions to include 'those . . . and such like passions' can be found in some Renaissance critics; it was the position overwhelmingly taken by the Restoration. Dryden, for example, wrote: 'If then the Encouragement of Virtue, and Discouragement of Vice, be the proper End of Poetry in Tragedy: Pity and Terror, tho' good Means, are not the only: For all the Passions in their turns are to be set in Ferment; as Joy, Anger, Love, Fear, are to be used as the Poet's common Places; and a general Concernment for the principal Actors is to be rais'd. . . .'[18]

The second part of Milton's preface is devoted to dramatic structure and that, like the treatment of mimesis and catharsis, looks backward to Renaissance criticism and forward to Restoration criticism while having its own distinctive emphasis. Milton there identifies 'style', 'uniformity' (or thematic coherence), and 'plot' as the three constituent elements of tragedy; he defines plot to distinguish it from fable or action and to interpret it as dramatic structure; and he declares that these three aspects of drama are to be regulated by two principles, decorum and verisimilitude. Decorum is the dominant Renaissance concept of continued use to Restoration critics; verisimilitude is a newer concept debated more fully in the Restoration than in the Renaissance. Characteristically Milton mingles both. He had touched on both before writing 'Of . . . Tragedy'. In

The Reason of Church Government he questioned 'whether the rules of Aristotle . . . are strictly to be kept, or nature to be follow'd, which in them that know art, and use judgement is no transgression, but an inriching of art'. The following of nature rather than rules in the structuring of a play implies regard for verisimilitude. He had also noted that the 'main consistence of a true poem' is 'the choys of such persons as they ought to introduce, and what is morall and decent to each'. Decency in the choice and speech of characters is decorum.

Renaissance criticism is rich in discussions of decorum, the place accorded it being as pre-eminent as in the young Milton where it is 'the grand master peece to be observ'd'.[19] Renaissance decorum is the propriety with which a genre, its characters and actions, its style in narration and dialogue, and its parts and the whole are all fitted to each other. It is commended in every discussion of poetry or tragedy. The concept becomes limited to subject-decorum and character-decorum in the Restoration, to the selective representation of a serious subject and the choice of characters and their language fitting that subject. Hobbes objects, on the grounds of decorum, to imputing inappropriate vices to great persons or using humble language in court scenes; Dryden gives to Neander important concessions about the 'correctness' of Jonson and the value of excluding 'what is either incredible or undecent'. But the theoretical centre of interest for the Restoration shifted from decorum to verisimilitude.

The Renaissance had, of course, a good deal to say about verisimilitude.[20] Its theorists conceded that truth was the goal of imitation and that verisimilitude might be consonant with invention. Yet just as the consideration of the balance between form and content and its connection with decorum was a distinctive contribution of the Renaissance to criticism, so the consideration of the representation of the passions by non-literal imitation and its connection with verisimilitude was a distinctive contribution of the Restoration to criticism. Rapin had said, 'it is the admirable Intrigue, the surprising and wonderful Events, the extraordinary Incident that makes the Beauty of a Tragedy; it is the Discourses when they are *Natural* and Passionate'. Dryden was of the same mind. Empathy with characters established through the verisimilitude, the naturalness and passion of their words in interchange with each other, was an essential aspect of tragic effect; in turn that had implications for structure. The Restoration dramatist devised for his character-centred drama a serial episodic plot, a succession of moments of passionate involvement in a

central character, an interweaving of the main plot conveying this arousal
of passion with a sub-plot augmenting it or relieving it through variety.
The concentration upon character revealed in discourse was a concentration upon the psychological significance of the hero. The psychological
portraiture of Dryden and other serious Restoration dramatists tended so
much to exceed the 'natural' in pursuit of the 'passionate' that a special
critical argument became necessary about the status of non-literal representation. Dryden did not merely assert that 'the spirit of man cannot be
satisfied but with truth, or at least verisimility; and a poem is to contain, if
not "true narratives" yet "narratives like the true ones"', he further argued
that a serious play imitated nature, 'but 'tis nature wrought up to a higher
pitch', 'a Play . . . to be like Nature, is to be set about it'.[21]

Defending verisimilitude, Milton does not take part in the Restoration
discussion of raised, as against natural imitation. Defending decorum, he
does not confine himself to the Renaissance consideration of fitting the
decent to the moral. Rather he couples verisimilitude and decorum as twin
rules in style, uniformity and structure. His doubling is not a tautology.
Dramatic structure must answer to both truth and art. Decorum forbids
'intermixing comic stuff', 'introducing trivial and vulgar persons', requires
'the whole Drama be found not produc't beyond the fifth Act' and
involves 'the circumscription of time'. Verisimilitude requires a structure
which mimes the dynamics of the human psyche. Thus the argument which
Milton supplied for *Samson Agonistes* specifies the central action in introspective and affective terms: 'Samson . . . comes forth to sit and bemoan';
he is 'visited by . . . the Chorus . . . to comfort him'; Manoa 'endeavours
the like' but 'yet more troubles him'; he is 'visited by other persons', the
last being 'a publick Officer'. Milton does not summarise the encounters
with Dalila or Harapha, but he reports those with Manoa and the officer to
draw attention to the sequence of natural passions in Samson. When the
Officer requires Samson to go with him 'to shew his strength to the
Philistines', Samson 'at first refuses' but then 'perswaded inwardly' that
the command 'was from God', he 'yields'. Manoa 'returns full of joyful
hope' to 'procure e're long his Sons deliverance'. Suddenly 'an Ebrew
comes in haste confusedly at first; and afterward more distinctly relating
the Catastrophe', 'Wherewith the Tragedy ends'. It is verisimilitude to
inner psychology which is shown to structure the action in the Argument
and Milton gives his readers a preview of the play in terms not of its action
but of the passions of its protagonist.

When in the dedication of *All for Love* Dryden paid tribute to his patron in the words 'you have wrought out yourself a way to glory, by those very means that were design'd for your destruction', he pointed toward a character type and a theme not only persistent in his own plays but similar to those of Milton.[22] Both define heroic grandeur as self-conquest and creativity as built from the destructive and discordant elements of the personality itself. The resemblance of Dryden's Antony to Milton's Samson has often been remarked.[23] Quite as striking are the resemblances between *Aureng-Zebe* and *Samson Agonistes*, and between *Oedipus* and *Samson Agonistes*. The preface to *Oedipus* links the depiction of such an heroic type to the problem of structure, comparing Corneille and Seneca to their disadvantage with Sophocles. From the opening speech of Diocles predicting 'Our bodies, cast into some common pit', to Creon's denunciation of Eurydice as a woman indifferent to 'merit' but 'caught by outward form', to Tiresias's entrance pleading 'A little farther; yet a little farther . . . / Conduct my weary steps . . . Now stay/Methinks I draw more open vital air'; to the Priests of the People discerning in Thebes 'A midnight silence at the noon of day', the parts of *Oedipus* written by Dryden show how far he found in Milton's Samson a better guide to the expression of tragic passion than he found in Corneille or Seneca. Milton's structure imitates the readjustment of the disintegrative forces within his protagonist in confrontation with opposing characters who mirror the discordant elements in his own psyche, until by a free choice he can discard the incompatible elements in himself even at the expense of his life. This is the structural pattern which also supplies the main plot line in Dryden's greatest heroic tragedies, diffused by strictly Restoration tastes which Dryden himself deplored. In the Preface to *Oedipus*, Dryden criticises Corneille's play on the grounds of decorum of character and of structure. Of the protagonist, he writes, 'The truth is, [Corneille] miserably failed in the character of his hero: if he desired that Oedipus should be pitied, he should have made him a better man'; of the action, he says, 'All we could gather out of Corneille was, that an episode must be, but not his way'. He criticises Seneca's play on the ground of verisimilitude: 'Seneca . . . as if there were no such thing as nature to be minded in a play is always running after pompous expressions, pointed sentences, and philosophical notions, more proper for the study than the stage'. Discarding both Corneille and Seneca as models, therefore, and turning back to Sophocles, 'admirable everywhere', Dryden describes the structural pattern of the classical theatre: 'in every act a single scene (or two at most), which manage the business of the play; and after that succeeds the chorus, which commonly takes up more time in singing than there has been employed in speaking. The principal person appears almost constantly through the play; but the inferior parts seldom above once in the whole tragedy'. He opposes to it the structural pattern of his own stage: 'We are obliged never to lose any considerable character which we have once presented . . . we must form an under-plot of second persons, which must be depending on the first; and their bywalks must be like those in a labyrinth, which all of them lead into the great parterre'. And finally Dryden weighs Athenian against Restoration practice: 'Perhaps after all, if we could think so, the ancient method, as it is the easiest, is also the most natural, and the best. For variety, as it is managed, is too often subject to breed distraction; and while we would please too many ways, for want of art in the conduct, we please in none'.[24]

In the play *Oedipus* Dryden did not use the 'natural' structure of inner psychological verisimilitude rather than the distractingly varied structure of contemporary taste. His concessive 'most natural and the best', however, is made in unmistakably affective and character-dominant terms, the same guides to plotting and tragic effect as Milton endorsed in 'Of . . . Tragedy' and did use in his play. Dryden is critical of two aspects of Athenian convention: the protracted commentary of a detached Chorus and the singly appearing character. The Trinity Manuscript plan for a tragedy 'Paradise Lost' adopted both conventions, *Samson Agonistes* neither. The structure of *Samson Agonistes* places the three characters who but once confront Samson in a chain of continuous references, uses one of them – Manoa – together with the Chorus as agents in a sub-plot depending upon the protagonist and so mediates between the ancient and the modern practice, adapts the Chorus to a cathartic function by constituting it as a physician-character required by the tragic experience of its patient to learn to heal itself, and while classically keeping its principal person continually on stage modernly undertakes to look directly into his mind as it struggles for self-mastery. The drama is modern in mirroring changed views of tragic effect and tragic structure. It is also modern in its treatment of melancholy, the destructive temperamental affliction with which it deals.

MELANCHOLY, RENAISSANCE TO RESTORATION

It is a critical commonplace that Samson begins in despair and ends in faith, and that his personal regeneration constitutes the 'middle' of *Samson Agonistes*, which Dr Johnson could not find. What Samson conquered in himself was a complex of inner pressures and responses which Milton's own times diagnosed and treated as 'melancholy'. Young Milton wrote of 'divinest' melancholy in *Il Penseroso* and banished 'loathed' melancholy in *L'Allegro*. The paired poems contrast two psychological states familiar in Renaissance medicine, literature and iconography.[25] The prefatory poem to Robert Burton's *Anatomy of Melancholy* is but one of many similar contrasting studies in mirth and melancholy. Burton's 'sour . . . melancholy' is the pathological state produced in the 'brooding darkness' of Milton's poem. Both *L'Allegro* and *Il Penseroso* extol the power of drama to raise the emotions each treats, 'Jonsons learned sock . . . sweetest Shakespeare fancies childe' for joy and 'Gorgeous Tragedy' for meditative elevation. Anxiety, grief, and melancholy were regular themes in Renaissance tragedy. Milton's familiarity with Burton, with Joseph Hall, with Shakespeare, Marston and Renaissance studies of suicidal despair is also well known. What I would like to show in this section is the availability to Milton of a view of melancholy which he used to depict Samson's grief and of the beginnings of a changed attitude towards the disease which he reflected in Samson's regeneration. Elizabethan studies of melancholy connected that disorder with a sense that the times were out of joint. The fearfulness of the melancholic was linked to his perception of rapid and undirected cultural change sweeping away the values in his universe and leaving him a powerless and alienated victim of destructive uncertainty. Time was his enemy for it deprived him of social support and personal security. In the course of *Samson Agonistes* the protagonist is cured of despair in a process which also alters his sense of the meaning of time and change and his purposive role within it. While melancholy did not vanish as a literary theme after 1660, it appeared in a new guise, reshaped as a consequence of reshaped attitudes towards mental health and change in the Restoration.

Neither medical nor scientific works of Milton's day were primary sources for his treatment of Samson as a melancholic. The insight into Samson's psychology derives from Milton's intuitive understanding of the human heart, from his reflection, from his reading of the poets and dramatists and not the physiologists and physicians. Milton treats melancholy as a qualitative and subjective phenomenon and not simply as a fixed condition caused by humoral imbalance. He depicts a personality whose moods are not in his own control and whose inner perturbations, fluctuating among shame, anger, suspicion, desire for revenge, guilt, anxiety, alienation and deadly inertia, are brought under his own control by being externalised in others where they can be confronted. The portrait of melancholy in Samson is an active developing portrait which feels as real and contemporary to us as the humorous melancholic Morose, for example, feels distant and inhuman, requiring Dryden's over-assertive defence that Jonson drew Morose 'actually acquainted with such a person', and relied upon his 'knowledge and observation of particular persons'. Milton's specifically medical knowledge, in the preface and the drama, is conventional and backward looking; what is not backward looking but forward looking is Milton's grasp of the psychological dynamics in Samson's suffering.

Milton's widow testified that his favourite poets were Spenser, Shakespeare and Cowley. The nature of the changing view of melancholy which Milton mirrors can be suggested by contrasting Spenser's Despair with Cowley's self-portrait in 'The Complaint' and portrait of maddened Saul in *Davideis*. Despair's dwelling is rendered in literal and allegorical form; 'an hollow cave . . . Dark, dolefull, drearie, like a greedie grave' is surmounted by 'the ghastly Owle, Shrieking his balefull note' set in a landscape of fruitless and leafless tree trunks clinging to ragged rocks. His appearance is emblematic: disordered, long and unbound locks of hair hang about his rounded shoulders and obscure his face; his eyes are hollow and 'deadly dull'; his clothing, ragged. His argument is the 'almightie doom' which limits life, the 'strong necessitie' and the 'destinie' ordaining death to all men, the wrong turns taken which heap up man's 'huge iniquitie/ Against the day of wrath'. He displays to the Red Cross Knight a picture of 'the damned ghosts, that do in torments wail'; and the fear of damnation and inevitability of death drive the Red Cross Knight to the brink of suicide until Una intervenes with the only reliable cure for melancholy,

> In heauenly mercie hast thou not a part?
> Why shouldst thou then despeire, that chosen art?
> Where justice growes, there growes eke greater grace,
> The which doth quench the brond of hellish smart
> And that accurst hand-writing doth deface.   (1.ix.53)

Spenser concludes with a Calvinistic moral comment in his own voice, 'If any strength we haue, it is to ill,/ But all the good is Gods, both power and will'.

'The Melancholy Cowley' in 'The Complaint', however, presents an imaginary despair in an introspective 'deep Vision's intellectual scene'; his landscape of the mind has the usual painted scenes of melancholy, 'black Yew's unlucky green', 'the mourning Willow's careful gray' but they are props 'to his closed sight' in 'Lands of Vision'. In his imagination is enacted a masque-dialogue: his Muse upbraids him for his uncreativeness and taunts him with having been busy at Court and got nothing for his pains, the 'dull work of [his] unweildly Plough' failing to thrive in 'a hard and barren Season'. But 'raising his thoughtful head / The Melancholy Cowley said' that his uncreativeness sprang from too much imagination or the Muse herself who slackened 'all [his] Nerves of Industrie', yet he hoped for patience like that of his king and at length recognition from him. This picture of melancholy as uncreativeness, vain imagining, an introspective personality not sinful but potentially curable is a changed conception. Similarly, in *Davideis* Cowley presents Envy appearing in a dream to Saul 'Dead in this sleep' and inciting him to madness and rage so that 'the infected King leapt from his bed amaz'd', seeing 'piec'd up shapes' in his room 'which fear / And his distracted Fancy painted there'. David is sent for to the King 'raging in a Fit', 'which does no cure but sacred tunes admit'; his 'soft musick did appease / Th'obscure fantastick rage of Saul's disease'. Cowley follows the picture of Saul's rage with a 'digression concerning music' explaining the psychology of aesthetic experience, the tempering or harmonising of the poet or musician in imitation of 'the eternal Minds Poetique Thought' creating a 'sympathy' in the auditor which 'tun'd the harsh disorders' of the soul. In a learned footnote to this digression Cowley cites the 'explication of the reason of these cures' given by 'Magicians . . . Platoniques . . . Rabbies' and others, dismisses them as unscientific ('these, and many Sympathetical experiments are so false, that I wonder at the negligence or impudence of the Relators') and offers his own 'true natural reasons' for believing that art can be beneficial to the nervously diseased: 'in the same manner as Musical sounds move the outward air, so that does the Inward, and that the Spirits, and they the Humours (which are the seat of Disease) by Condensation, Rarefaction, Dissipation, or Expulsion of Vapours, and by Vertue of that Sympathy of Proportion'. My point is not that we should take this science very seriously or believe that it is totally new but rather that it implies a doctrine of medical double catharsis as surely as does Dryden's *Alexander's Feast* (the first cure instanced in Cowley's footnote is Timotheus's cure of Alexander). Furthermore, as one might anticipate in the poet whose pindaric ode 'Upon Dr Harvey' praised Harvey for being open to 'the young Practice of New life' and curing 'Th'Art of Curing', it offers a psychodynamic explanation of a nervous sensibility in place of a discussion of disease as sin and its treatment as grace. No more are melancholy and enraged men to be expelled from human society than the emotions or passions are to be expelled from the individual soul; art itself by the controlled immersion of the auditor in his destructive impulses so that they may be faced and rebalanced prompts a hopeful therapeutic alliance between the artist physician and the reader patient.

Milton's companion poems contain a virtual catalogue of the commonest traits of pathological melancholy depicted in Renaissance painting, drama and expository prose, many of which look back to Spenser.[26] Melancholy is associated with darkness and night 'of blackest midnight born', with solitude and retreat 'som uncouth cell', with a dark visage 'Ore laid with black staid Wisdoms hue', with a deadened spirit 'Forget thy self to Marble', with downcast and sightless eyes 'With a sad Leaden downward cast', with self-neglect and a careless appearance 'As ragged as thy locks', with loneliness and alienation 'in Stygian cave forlorn', with hallucinatory and obsessive imaginings ''Mongst horrid shapes, and shrieks, and sights unholy', with horror and hatred projected or transferred to nature itself 'the night raven sings', and with restlessness and sleeplessness 'Lamp at midnight hour'. Within the companion poems Milton transforms pathological melancholy into a contemplative benign self-awareness, suggested by the very act of naming the second poem *Il Penseroso* and not *Il Melancolico*; he uses melancholy to drive out melancholy so that the mood of *Il Penseroso* is neither diseased nor tragic. The numerous eighteenth-century poems which derive from it likewise treat melancholy as a pleasantly ambiguous self-conscious sense of sweet sadness.

Drawing 'loathed melancholy', Milton depicts Samson in his opening soliloquy as a thought-tormented man, self-absorbed in his anguish of mind, anxious, fatigued and self-critical. His posture is that of the conventional melancholic – the drooping head, the neglected dress, the idle hand. His self-diagnosis communicating his insomnia, his paranoiac fear of the approach of others, is given in the metaphor of living death, 'My self, my Sepulcher, a moving Grave'; the Chorus complements this by the metaphor of double enslavement 'Thy Bondage . . . lost Sight, Prison within Prison'. The thoughts which torture Samson are thoughts contrasting what might have been and what is now, thoughts of the frustration of his gifts, his creativity in bonds. Samson's mental state is suggestively communicated by clusters of Shakespearean echoes. Like Macbeth threatened with becoming 'the shew and gaze o'th'time', Samson feels himself 'made of my Enemies the scorn and gaze'; like Antony as 'plated Mars', before Samson's fall 'old Warriors turn'd thir plated backs under his heel'; like the false favourites of Richard II 'snakes, in my heart-blood warm'd, that sting my heart', his false wife drew Samson to destruction when she became 'a pois'nous bosom snake'; Samson, echoing Othello, 'loved [Dalila] too well . . . could deny her nothing'. The imagery of disease runs as constantly in the thoughts of Samson as in the thoughts of Hamlet; both are paralysed as the play opens; both express self-revulsion, grief and a desire for death; the vanity of human life, its impermanence and instability wounds both; both have had assigned them public roles involving the purification or liberation of the state and private passions inimical to those roles; both doubt their power to act. As a young poet Milton praised Shakespeare for his verisimilitude as opposed to decorum: his numbers were 'easie', they shamed 'slow-endeavouring art' by making 'deep impression' on 'each heart', bereaving the auditor of the use of his own 'fancy' through the superiority of Shakespeare's imaginative penetration into the human psyche; they produced 'wonder and astonishment'.

If Samson's melancholy pain takes resonance from Shakespeare's intuitive understanding of the nature of man, it also resembles the religious melancholy Burton diagnosed. Burton himself used Samson conventionally as an instance of love melancholy and not religious melancholy. He lamented 'Samson and Dalilah's embracings', noted 'Samson's strength enervated' by love, his enslavement to Dalila 'unbefitting [his] gravity and person', the 'infinite mischiefs' that attended his love. Elsewhere Burton drew conventional morals from the Samson fable: he described 'Sampson's hair' as a vain gift; referred to Samson's size and strength as conducing to self-love, pride and vainglory which he thought contributory causes of melancholy; adjudged his voluntary death an innocent and not guilty suicide, and cited Samson's abstemiousness as a remedy against discontent at one's poverty. Burton thought, however, that every man contained irrational mental perturbations. All 'men [are] born from mushrooms, or else they fetch their pedigree from those that were struck by Samson with the jawbone of an ass; or from Deucalion and Pyrrha's stones . . . stoney-hearted, and savour too much of the stock'.[27] Milton's imagery and analysis of Samson's wounded conscience, unquiet mind, weariness with his life, hopelessness of forgiveness, temptation to murmur against God and suicidal self-loathing resembles Burton's unconventional analysis of religious rather than love melancholy. For the cure of that disease, Burton wrote, 'they take a wrong course that think to overcome this feral passion by sole physic; and they are as much out, that think to work this effect by good advice alone'. Burton's 'sole physic' usually looks scientifically backward to a tradition to be superseded; his 'good advice' is of the future and bears resemblance to Samson's cure.

Because of the pervasiveness of melancholy, Burton undertook to 'anatomize this humour of melancholy, through all his parts and species . . . to show the causes, symptoms and several cures of it'. Melancholy was 'so universal a malady, an epidemical disease, that so often, so much crucifies the body and mind' that it required methodical study. For this purpose he adopted the 'assumed habit and name' of Democritus to pursue the study 'as if from some high place above you all . . . A mere spectator of other men's fortunes and adventures'. Yet Burton himself was scarcely a mere spectator. Prompted to write by his own depressive illness – 'for I had . . . a kind of imposthume in my head', Burton was both obsessed by his theme and determined to give his own feelings release, 'one must needs scratch where it itches'. He busied himself to avoid the idleness which he saw both as symptom and cause of pathological melancholy, 'I write of melancholy, by being busy to avoid melancholy'. In choosing the persona of the mocking philosopher Democritus, he deliberately eschewed a tragic mask; his self-analysis would be sceptical and comic. *The Anatomy of Melancholy* was clearly a work of self-therapy. But with characteristic intuition, Burton was aware that not only was he himself the doctor and the patient, the subject and the analyst, the 'spectator' and the actor in the disease at the heart of his book, so also was his reader, 'Thou thyself art the subject of my discourse'. His book would be good medicine for every man by preventing idleness and isolation. It would be good medicine by driving melancholy away through the sympathetic immersion in melancholy itself, by arousing the passions in a controlled situation where they could be safely faced. Burton's conclusion about the human condition was that objectively it was incurable: 'there is no remedy, it may not be redressed . . . it is a thing so difficult, and far beyond Hercules' labour to perform'. His hope remained, however, to offer to himself and to others the good medicine of inner consolation: 'I have no more to say. *His sanam mentem Democritus*, I can only wish myself and them a good physician, and all of us a better mind'. Where it was impossible to do more than imagine or fantasise a better life, Burton resorted to wishing for and striving for a better mind in man. His own suggestions for the reform of society were embedded in 'an Utopia of mine own, a New Atlantis, a poetical common-wealth of mine own' in *The Anatomy*, consciously devised as a vain empire 'to satisfy and please myself', located in *Terra Australia Incognita*, in which anyone might buy a share 'for so much money as Cardan allows an astrologer for casting a nativity'. Significantly it would contain 'hospitals of all kinds, for children, orphans, old folks, sick men, madmen . . . for all those who stand in need'. So deep-seated in the very frame of man himself was the anguish of mind Burton experienced and everywhere met that even in Utopia its sufferers would need succour.

Burton's 'science' is not only an amalgam of medicine and morality, compassion and sceptical fatalism, it is also an amalgam of ancient learning and modern thought. Most looks backward to the Galenic tradition of the four humours and their inherent substantial qualities, the imbalance among which caused melancholy. When Burton discusses the 'rectification' of air, diet and the like, his 'cures' depend upon quantitative transactions among real substances: bloodletting, purgation and the like to diminish bile, 'alteratives' or drugs to strengthen the other humours. Side by side with the conventional wisdom in Burton, however, exists a new wisdom. Burton is aware of breaking new ground while consistently unwilling to relinquish the traditional, and nowhere more plainly than in his discussion of religious melancholy. Burton's perception in himself and others of the phenomena of sadness, self-torment and anguish arising from a sense of guilt and personal unworthiness shades away at a number of points from the ancient wisdom. The interaction of body and soul through humours and animal spirits ceases to preoccupy him and he turns instead to melancholy as a nervous disorder. His descriptions focus on the perceptions of the melancholic and not the causal humours; he observes in himself and others purely psychological phenomena. Their treatment, the gift of a 'better mind' is a qualitative matter involving interaction with others and self-analysis.[28]

Burton himself would have been as unaware as would Milton of a shift toward subsequent concepts of melancholy. Nonetheless both perceived melancholy as a psychological state. The religious melancholic is consoled in Burton's analysis by two kinds of comments. To him Burton gives words about God's grace which sound like the words that Spenser gave to Una. Burton there writes no longer like the mocking–self-mocking Democritus Jr, but like any seventeenth-century clerk in holy orders addressing a grieved sinner. God will cure his religious melancholy by grace. But then comes the shift and the second sort of help which Burton offers, where once more his voice is the voice of Democritus Jr, both detached and self-analytic. God will give grace, doubtless in his own millennial time, but meanwhile, 'comfort thyself with other men's misfortunes'. To those who torture themselves with thinking 'Why doth He not make us all good, able sound? Why makes He . . . this earth itself the muck-hill of the world, a prison, an house of correction', Burton says, 'no man living is free from such thoughts . . . the most divine spirits have been tempted in some sort . . . they would fain think otherwise if they could . . . be not overmuch troubled and dismayed with such kind of suggestions . . . because they are not thy personal sins . . . all [are] so molested and distempered'. The afflicted are to discover in their affliction their identity with others; the same cast of characters – the same harsh judge, tender-minded penitent, stubborn self-defender, reluctant self-loather – enacts the same drama in every soul; all consciences contain 'a continual testor to give in evidence, to empound a jury to examine us, to cry guilty, a persecutor with hue and cry to follow, an apparitor to summon us, a bailiff to carry us, a serjeant to arrest, an attorney to plead against us, a gaoler to torment, a judge to condemn, still accusing, denouncing, torturing and molesting'.[29] Help is to come from the consideration of the sheer humanity of this nervous trouble; each must 'By all honest recreation refresh and recreat his distressed soul'; to each is given the advice, 'Be not solitary, be not idle'.

A clear chain of conventional traditional medical wisdom about melancholy runs through *Samson Agonistes* and constitutes one kind of good medicine in the play. Running parallel to it is an emergent psychological wisdom of an intuitively observed sort and this constitutes another kind of good medicine. The ensuing section will look at both. Medicine provides an over-arching metaphorical structure for the drama: Samson is ill with despair at the outset of the play, he believes his condition 'immedicable' and his plight 'remediless'. He is cured by the medicine of Providence which arranges the educative experience of his tragic existence so that he is purged of melancholy by the experience of melancholy-engendering tragedy. The remedy offered him is the medicine of understanding his experience. God like a tragic poet tempers Samson's passions by means of the tragic passions themselves; his cure culminates in 'calm of mind'.

SAMSON'S ROLE AND CURE: HIS INNER AND OUTER SOCIETIES

The anguish of Samson's mind, alone and dark in the morning sunlight on the day the Philistines will dedicate to drunken exulting in their bloody god who has delivered their enemy into slavery to them, is a complex anguish. The tormented protagonist is not, and does not feel himself to be, a single person. His mind contains an inner society. While he consciously contrasts a former with a present person, 'what once I was and what am now', he also constitutes himself into subject and object, his own judge and plaintiff. Samson's self-contemptuous words,

> Promise was that I
> Should Israel from Philistian yoke deliver;
> Ask for this great Deliverer now, and find him
> Eyeless in Gaza at the Mill with slaves,

divide him into an 'I' who protects its vulnerable selfhood by condemning a 'him' who shares his soul and is the object of his scorn. From the very beginning Samson assumes full responsibility for his state and asserts a singleness of personality: he is one guilty self, 'whom have I to complain of but my self'. But he indulges the irresponsible and incompatible emotions of vengeance, self-pity and complaint under the veil of condemning them. He 'correctly' judges his own case: God gave him extraordinary power 'Heav'n-gifted strength' and designed him for 'great exploits' which he would have performed 'but through mine own default'. Yet he cannot prevent himself from devaluing the gift and diminishing his God: 'God, when he gave me strength, to shew withal / How slight the gift was, hung it in my Hair'. He goes further; not only was the gift dubious, the giver of specious gifts withheld consolation for its loss and had the power to bestow better: blind Samson is denied the 'various objects of delight' which might have eased his grief; sight could have been 'as feeling through all parts diffus'd'. Absorbed in his inner society, Samson paranoiacally fears outer society. 'The tread of many feet stearing this way' must be the tread of 'enemies'.

Samson's outer society consists of his 'friends and neighbors', his 'reverend Sire', his 'wife, [his] Traytress', and the 'Giant Harapha of Gath'. A number of critics have equated these persons with the several tendencies against which Samson must struggle in himself and I shall not rehearse their identifications. It is the originality and psychological profundity of Milton to have drawn them as Samson's *alter egos*, at once selves defining themselves objectively in relation to Samson and also parallel selves to aspects of Samson's conflicting and discordant sense of self. The large movement of the drama enacts the conversion of Samson's divided self into a coherent self, his passions tempered and balanced. That is a movement from the self-definition of 'My self, my Sepulcher, a moving Grave' to the self-definition of 'My self? my conscience and internal peace'. Milton places Samson in the company of the Chorus, men who have come to offer him balm to 'swage the tumours of his mind'. Before these counsellors identify themselves to him, they comment on the change in Samson. Their comments also signal the divisions into subject and object within the protagonist: he is 'by himself given over'; he is 'The Dungeon of him self'; he used to be one who 'weaponless himself / Made arms ridiculous' but now he is 'The rarer example' of one 'from the top of wondrous glory . . . To lowest pitch of abject fortune . . . fallen'. When they make themselves known to Samson, he enters into a therapeutic relation-ship with them and his self-definition of his melancholy state begins its alteration. Samson himself sees that he sees more clearly in their company: 'Your coming, Friends, revives me'. He reflects his clearer vision by a more 'correct' version of his case: 'Immeasurable strength . . . [and] wisdom nothing more then mean . . . These two proportioned ill drove me transverse'. The interaction between Samson and the Chorus not only alters Samson's mood and enables growth, it also affects the Chorus, who progressively change the meanings they infer from his case-history as they sympathetically advise him. Their initial judgement that he is 'example' and 'mirror' of 'our fickle state' is continually modified until at the close he is 'faithful Champion'.

The first exchange between Samson and the Chorus sets the stage for each of the three ensuing encounters with members of his outer society who mirror aspects of his unbalanced inner society. 'Irresistible Samson' who fought weaponlessly and made the conventional military hero look foolish will encounter in Harapha a final opportunity to define heroism. The love-melancholic Samson is given patronising and kindly-meant advice by the Chorus: 'wisest Men / Have err'd, and by bad women been deceived / Deject not then so overmuch thy self'. Samson must face the true imbalances in his nature, not just his felt imbalance between wisdom and strength. He answers the Chorus with integrity: 'of what now I suffer / She was not the prime cause, but I myself'. She is not, however, a 'specious Monster' outside Samson; she is a persistent trigger for Dalila-like res-ponses inside Samson, as he will confess to Manoa in acknowledging that 'foul effeminacy held me yok't / Her Bond-slave', the so-called effeminacy being his and not hers. And meantime in pitting his 'intimate impulse' against the approval of his 'Parents', Samson sets the stage for confronting the legalism and scepticism he and his father share in the Manoa episode.

The Chorus approves of Samson's firm statements of responsibility. It answers him in the opening episode in a way which both slightly shifts

Samson's mood by encouraging him and also challenges him by coming closer to the problem at the core of his grief. That problem is, can Samson change and grow, or can there be any further role in existence for which he can make himself adequate, or as he puts it, 'To what can I be useful, wherein serve / My Nation, and the work from Heav'n impos'd?' The Chorus gives Samson mood-altering confidence and then asks him to confront a new problem:

> In seeking just occasion to provoke
> The Philistine, thy Countries Enemy,
> Thou never wast remiss, I bear thee witness:
> Yet Israel still serves with all his Sons.

The persistence of this supportive-challenging pattern in the Chorus can be seen in its praise of Samson's temperance in repressing 'desire of wine' evoking his question 'What avail'd this temperance, not compleat'; its defining the Timnian bride's 'Paranymph' as 'worthless to thee compar'd' before Harapha arrives to question whether 'Thy appearance answers loud report'; its congratulating Samson on deflating Harapha to 'less unconsci'nable strides and lower looks' but then noting 'and yet perhaps more trouble is behind'.

Along the way toward self-conquest and the re-definition of his role, Samson must understand the true limits of his responsibility; he must know of what he is 'sole Author . . . sole Cause'. The Chorus likened him to Atlas 'whom the Gentiles feign to bear up Heav'n' but they see him 'with languish't head unprop't'. Since he cannot carry even his head upright, if he feels responsible for bearing the whole universe on his shoulders, it is a sign of potential recovery in Samson that he resists the Chorus's implicit imputation of Israel's enslavement to himself: 'That fault I take not on me, but transfer / On Israel's Governours'. God bears up heaven: Israel's leaders guide Israel; Samson is responsible for his own guilt not all guilt. Samson narrates one of many little plays within the play in circumscribing his responsibility to a possible human role. Israel's governors were present at a dumb-show 'seeing those great acts which God had done / Singly by me'; they beheld a drama in which Samson's 'deeds themselves, though mute, spoke loud the dooer'; the heads of tribe 'would not . . . notice'; they did not applaud but 'heaped ingratitude' on him. The Chorus draws the correct conclusion from this psycho-drama: Samson is an example not now of how the mighty fall, but of how the good leader is not followed and Samson concurs 'Of such examples add me to the roul'. The first episode ends with God responsible for regulating the universe and Samson for obeying God's Laws and the Chorus patly observes, '[He] made our Laws to bind us, not himself'.

Samson's second encounter is with his *alter ego* and father Manoa. Samson has felt Manoa's anxious doubting legalism within his own psyche. Manoa's arrival outside Samson is felt as a presence inside Samson, 'Ay me, another inward grief awak't'. Manoa expresses as his own sense of pain just the complex of anguishing thoughts felt by Samson when alone: the contrast between his son's past power and present impotence is painfully repeated (in ironic prolepsis of the bout with Harapha), 'Himself an Army, now unequal match / To save himself against a coward armed'; the shame of publicly disappointed promise is enunciated, 'I gain'd a Son as all Men hail'd me happy; Who would now be a Father in my stead'; and the gift of a son and God the giver of specious gifts both diminished, 'Why [do God's] gifts . . . giv'n with solemn hand / As Graces, draw / a Scorpions tail behind?' Samson meets his father's expressions of self-pity and reproach of God steadily, 'Nothing of all these evils hath befall'n me / But justly; I myself have brought them on'. He had been 'warn'd by oft experience' of the 'contempt' with which Dalila 'sought to make [him] Traytor to himself'; nonetheless he yielded; but he sees his present 'base degree . . . is not yet so base / As was my former servitude ignoble'. This sense of proportion and perspective is realistic and honest; Samson has conquered one aspect of his divided soul and Manoa acknowledges Samson's responsibility: 'True, and thou bear'st . . . the burden of that fault'. What he cannot conquer is Manoa's reflection of his own despair of God and sense of inadequacy and shame:

> Dagon shall be magnifi'd . . .
> Which to have come to pass by means of thee,
> Samson, of all thy sufferings think the heaviest,
> Of all reproach the most with shame that ever
> Could have befall'n thee and thy Fathers house.

Samson makes a good beginning in facing this when he accepts for himself the 'shame and sorrow / The anguish of my Soul' and distinguishes the burden of his remorse from the burden of being God's only support. God will be God: 'He . . . thus provok't / . . . will arise and his great name assert'. The good beginning drains away, however, when Manoa seeks to suggest the corollary that Samson should go on being Samson, 'as for life / To what end should I seek it'. He sees his condition as 'immedicable', his evils 'remediless' and his future as immutable, 'reserv'd alive to be repeated / The subject of . . . cruelty, or scorn'.

Milton secures verisimilitude in the structure of his tragedy by various devices which show the inner and outer societies in Samson. One recurrent device by which we look into Samson's psyche is the embedded play within the play. Samson as 'sole Author' narrates to Manoa, for example, a drama of his marriage, conveying action ('thrice she assay'd', 'thrice I turn'd to sport'), stage directions ('with flattering prayers and sighs', 'with blandish parlies', 'when men seek most repose and rest'), and moral theme ('servil mind . . . servil punishment'). The objectification acts as a re-encounter with destructive moods in which they can be mastered. A second recurrent device is debate. The *alter ego* expresses Samson's own mood, he listens and answers, there ensues an effect upon the *alter ego* as well as upon Samson. Manoa, for example, is visibly cheered by Samson's affirming God's omnipotence 'With cause this hope relieves thee, and these words, / I as a Prophecy receive'. Thus cheered, he turns to the amelioration of Samson's state: 'Thou must not in the mean while here forget / Lie . . . miserable', the Philistines may release him since 'no more canst thou do them harm'. Samson more than concurs with Manoa's sense of his own impotence; he can only 'sit idle on the household hearth'. God is truly God but Samson acted 'like a petty God . . . admir'd of all and dreaded' and is now 'ridiculous'. Only 'oft-invocated death' can bring 'the welcome end of all [his] pains'. Continuing the naturalistic debate, Manoa shrewdly glances at Samson's motives in desiring death, 'Who self-rigorous chooses death as due' may be perhaps 'over-just', 'self-displeased / For self-offence more then for God offended'. His son's desire for death may have a simple medical explanation. It may proceed 'From anguish of the mind and humours black / That mingle with . . . fancy'; he should 'be calm and healing words from these . . . friends admit'. In debate Manoa affords Samson an opportunity to re-examine his attitude toward himself, and the audience an insight into the stages of the re-examination. A final device of structural verisimilitude is the soliloquy or self-communion. When Manoa leaves the stage, Samson speaks a second lyrical stasimon of exacerbated grief, at first picking up the current medical lore in Manoa's words; his griefs are a 'lingering disease' like 'wounds' that 'ranckle, and fester, and gangrene, / To black mortification'; his thoughts 'raise dire inflammation'; his torment finds a secret passage 'to th'inmost mind' and preys on it 'As on entrails, joints, and limbs, / With answerable pain'; 'no cooling herb / Or medicinal liquor . . . Nor breath or vernal air' can heal his internal disorder. Samson expresses his mental suffering in current physiological and psychological terms, terms which would have been understood several centuries earlier. This older wisdom exists side by side with newer insights in the drama.[30] One of these is reflected in the attitude toward change. At present the bitterest of Samson's griefs is the memory of what he has been and is now. Change is only loss to Samson; further change is not to be imagined; he is helpless, his loss is 'irreparable'. Only oblivion can bring to a halt the repetition of fall in him.

Manoa asked Samson to hear the comforting words of the Chorus. Those friends begin confidently enough 'Extolling Patience as the truest fortitude' but come quickly upon the difficulty of helping 'th'afflicted in his pangs' if their good words are 'of dissonant mood from his complaint' and he feels no 'source of consolation . . . secret refreshings' from 'within' or 'above'. Their sympathy for Samson creates in fact a reverse energy; rather than calming him, they feed his loss and pain. They question the 'contrarious' behaviour of God who throws his servants lower than he did 'exalt them high'; they pray for a 'peaceful end' to his 'state calamitous'. The answer to their prayer for peace is the arrival of Dalila, an encounter with yet another of Samson's passionate impulses.

Lying under the intellectual debate of Samson and Dalila is a further confrontation of self and *alter ego*. Intellectually Samson articulates thoughts which defuse Dalila's power over him; psychologically he does not re-enact old impulses. As they meet Dalila defines her sense of self; 'conjugal affection' prompted her to conquer womanly 'fear and timorous doubt' and come to 'appease[his] mind' and offer 'amends . . . recompense'. Samson defines himself 'to Ages an example' of all decent men who if they forgive false wives are re-entangled and rejects her self-image. When Dalila repeats her self-image – she was weak but loving – she extends it to embrace Samson as well; he was as frail as she in trusting to 'womans frailty'; 'Let weakness then with weakness come to parl / So near related, or *the same kind*, / Thine forgive mine'. Samson rejects her identification of their selves: 'I to my self was false e're thou to me', and declines to forgive either of them their separate weaknesses: 'Such pardon therefore as I give my folly / Take to thy wicked deed'. He is 'impartial, self-severe, inexorable' to both self and Dalila. Renewing the assault, Dalila turns toward Samson another of her selves, an heroic self, facing sieges 'which might have aw'd the best resolv'd of men' and deciding that 'to the public good' her 'private respects' must yield. Higher duty demanded the sacrifice of love. Dalila's earlier self-exculpation, that she desired Samson 'whole to my self, unhazarded abroad', awakened Samson's shameful recognition of his own impulses in the description and he comes to grips with that before deflating her false heroism. He loved her 'as too well [she knew], / Too well . . . who could deny [her] nothing'; but as he was not her enemy, it was not heroic to betray him. Dalila reverts to her first suggestion with the deadly hint that Samson is his own worst enemy – 'nor still insist / To afflict thy self in vain'; if Samson will forgive her, she will console him: 'Life yet hath many solaces' and she can offer 'redoubl'd love and care'. Samson finds the power to sever himself from her, 'Thou and I long since are twain'; he declines her 'fair enchanted cup, and warbling charms' because they 'no more on me have power, their force is null'd'; and he deliberately revalues her luxurious household, 'This Gaol I count the house of Liberty / To thine'. Samson's violent urge to murder, to 'tear [Dalila] joint by joint' when she asks to 'approach . . . and touch' him is a frightening reminder of how deep-seated was the passion which he has faced. Since self-acceptance and renewed confidence must accompany his reintegration, however, Samson's next words, 'At distance I forgive thee, go with that', are reassuring. He had undertaken to forgive her as he forgave his own folly; that forgiveness now has come.

The episode concludes with two further instances of Milton's intuitive penetration into the human heart – with relapses, that is, in both Dalila and Samson. Dalila expresses her complacent self-approval: wondering 'why do I humble thus my self', she does not 'disapprove my own concernments', she likes her own lot and leaves Samson to his. Her relapse is final; there can be no change in Dalila. Samson relapses into thinking 'God sent her to debase me / And aggravate my folly'; that is a temporary recoil into exhaustion, self-severity and wounded pride. The Chorus appears to understand the dynamics of the scene: 'beauty, though injurious, hath strange power . . . nor can be easily Repuls't, without much inward passion felt / And secret sting of amorous remorse'. Their subsequent generalisations about how to deal with women are no more than seventeenth-century marriage guidance.

Harapha arrives before Samson claiming a kind of identity with him: 'we might have tri'd / Each others force in camp or listed field'. The presumed identity is one of occupation, strength and pride. Harapha desires the 'glory of Prowess' which would have been his in mastering Samson. Samson, however, masters Harapha in mastering his own vainglory, violence and pride. He defeats the dandiacal giant by relying not on his own power but on his trust in God. The test is 'whose God is strongest' and not whose arm. Samson has finally put his trust where it can safely be put. He was 'to do [his] part from Heav'n assign'd'; he was 'disabl'd' by his 'known offence'; he does not 'despair . . . of [God's] final pardon', because God is always 'gracious to readmit the suppliant'. Neither Samson's compulsive Nazarite observances, nor his personal prowess but God's nature limits human responsibility, removes guilt, regulates purposive change.

Milton tells the rest of Samson's story swiftly. The choral commiseration – 'This Idols day hath bin to thee no day of rest, / Labouring thy mind / More than the working day thy hands' – underlines the dramatic structure he has adopted. Samson's 'labour of mind' has restored balance to his mind. Now threatened from without by an Officer who warns, 'Regard thy self', Samson unequivocally states his integrity: 'My self? my conscience and internal peace'. At first rejecting the demand of the Officer that he enter a 'place abominable' to a Nazarite, the new Samson who does not maintain his identity by ritual observances thinks again, 'God may dispense with [such rites] for some important cause'. He feels 'rousing motions' in himself and he accompanies the Officer. The changeability of men does not render him fearful; he accepts it relaxedly, 'And for a life who will not change his purpose / (So mutable are all the ways of men)'. He leaves his friends taking thought of them: 'Brethren farewell, your company along I will not wish' lest the exasperated Philistines harm them. He departs in the determination to be worthy of 'Our God, our Law, my Nation, or my self'. Samson once divided is now Samson himself; he quits 'himself like Samson'.

When the process of tempering in Samson is done, there remains to complete the double catharsis by dramatising it in an on-stage audience for the sake of an off-stage audience. The inner society of Samson is drawn together into a whole; he acts for the help of an outer society which also must discover the positive value in change. For this Milton has recourse again to the device of a play within the play at which the on-stage characters conceive themselves an audience. The Messenger confronts Manoa and the Chorus with an account of a drama which he himself saw enacted, a drama Manoa asserts 'No Preface needs'. The 'horrid' spectacle the Messenger saw 'pursues' him as a 'dire imagination'. For the audience of Manoa and the Chorus he sets the stage, the 'spacious Theatre', the 'seats' under the vaulted roof where the 'Lords and each degree' sat, 'the banks and scaffolds' under the open sky for the vulgar 'throng'. He describes the entrance of Samson 'in state Livery', the accompaniment of 'pipes and timbrels', the parade of his military guard. He relates Samson's feats of a first 'act', his withdrawal to the pillar-supported wings 'for intermission sake', his thoughtful silence, and then his speech, rendered in direct discourse. Samson's words continue the metaphor of the play: he has provided 'wonder . . . delight' and will now add a second 'act' 'As with amaze shall strike all who behold'. Finally the Messenger brings down the theatre 'Upon the heads of all who sate below', Samson destroyed in their midst; 'The vulgar only scap'd who stood without'.

The staging of the catastrophe prompts responses of the on-stage audience to direct those of Milton's readers. They pass through a response to tragedy which is therapeutic to them. The Messenger has given them an imitation of the passions in the Philistines and Samson, the 'hearts' of the Philistines filled with 'mirth, high chear and wine', filling the air with their shouts 'clamouring thir god with praise', Samson's stillness and harmonious control. He has placed before them the complicity of the Philistines in their own destruction and Samson's consent to his destiny. They exhibit the natural effect of great tragedy and wonderingly view Samson victorious 'self-killed / Not willingly' and the Philistines violently lost in self-induced ruin. The second semi-chorus continues the response they have been guided towards; in contrast to the wild Philistines, Samson displays to them the true and delightful energy of revival, the re-flourishing of a man whose inward eyes were illuminated. Manoa is the final commentator on the drama re-staged for him and his comment reflects his own catharsis of doubts and anxieties into a clear sense of 'what may quiet us in a death so noble'. The final quatrain of the choral *nunc dimittis* attributes the beneficient action of the tragedy to God, viewing him metaphorically as the tragic poet who can restore to his creatures the delight in his dramatic universe which sends them again into their own creative lives: 'With new acquist of true experience from this great event, / with peace and consolation . . . all passion spent'.

During Milton's life-time changes occurred in the understanding of melancholy, in the definition of tragic effect and in the formulation of the principle of dramatic verisimilitude. The play *Samson Agonistes* mirrors these changes. Milton devised a dramatic structure incorporating an imitation of the passions and their changes within the principal person by projecting his inner state on to other persons in detached episodes of cumulative force. He portrayed a protagonist afflicted with melancholy and doubting his own power to change. He allayed the protagonist's melancholy by plunging him into his destructive passions and forcing their confrontation. Milton, the balancing and integrating of the protagonist accomplished in his catharsis, then extended catharsis a stage further. Defining it as applying both to on-stage characters and off-stage audience, he made use of a double circle in plot structure to place the off-stage audience as it were on-stage, calling attention to the complexity of the imaginative effort involved by repeated use of the play within the play. The result was 'medicinable tragedy', a psycho-aesthetic theory of tragedy made functional in one of the great tragic poems of our culture, a play looking forward in time as well as drawing on the finest insights and arts of the past.

Exotick but rational entertainments: the English dramatick operas

RICHARD LUCKETT

Masquerades and Operas is hardly Hogarth's best engraving, but it must nevertheless compel the attention of the student of the operatic stage. A wheelbarrow, heaped with the classics of English dramatic literature, is pushed by a coster-woman who cries 'Waste Paper for Shops'; around her the unheeding crowds mill at the doors of Heidegger's Masquerade, and of *Harlequin Dr Faustus*. Sound triumphs over sense, and the consequence of the national infatuation with the lyric drama is the impoverishment of the legitimate theatre – impoverishment material as well as spiritual, for on Heidegger's show cloth we see the Earl of Peterborough and two fellow grandees begging the singer Cuzzoni to accept a mere £8,000. Hogarth's plate is dated February 1724, but it aptly stands for views expressed before and after its making, by critics as diverse as Dennis and Addison, Cibber and Pope, Chesterfield and Johnson.[1] Johnson summed up the matter in his life of John Hughes (1781): the Italian opera, he wrote, was 'an exotick and irrational entertainment, which has been always combated, and always has prevailed'. Yet even the critics of opera experienced its lure: Dennis wrote the libretto for *Rinaldo and Armida*, and Addison that for *Rosamond* (a text praised by Johnson); Cibber incorporated a masque and much incidental music into *Love's Last Shift*; Pope contributed to two of Handel's libretti, whilst several of his friends were prominent in their support of opera; Lord Chesterfield was once a Director of the Royal Academy of Music (established under royal protection to promote opera); Johnson himself in the *Dictionary* offered an alternative definition and this, since it derived from Dryden's preface to *Albion and Albanius*, even suggested critical propriety: 'An *Opera* is a Poetical tale, or Fiction, represented by Vocal and Instrumental Musick, adorn'd with Scenes, Machines, and Dancing'.

In some ways Johnson's terse observation in the life of Hughes is not so
far removed from the *Dictionary* definition; Dryden anticipated and par-
ried the charge of irrationality with his use of 'poetic', of 'representation'
and of 'adornment', but he could scarcely deny that opera was exotic. Yet
the differences between the views are revealing, and the proleptic refuta-
tion of irrationality is in itself of considerable significance. Opera was
innately 'exotick' since it was not an indigenous form; but the particular
exoticism of Italian opera, the sense in which it was actively foreign, lay in
its use of a language incomprehensible to the generality of theatre-goers.
John Hughes had believed that 'the English language might be very happily
adapted to musick', and Dr Johnson, concurring with the principle of
intelligibility which informed this belief, seized the opportunity to launch
his barb. This was directed, not at opera at large, but at *Italian* opera; it
summed up a tradition of opposition, which had begun with antipathy,
not to musical drama, but to the use of a foreign language on the English
stage. Dennis, Addison and Pope had each attempted to contribute to
English opera, only traducing the form after their endeavours had failed
and Italian opera had won the day. Steele, Gay and Smollett were similarly
embroiled, and similarly disenchanted. Italian opera held the boards
throughout the eighteenth century, surviving the collapse of managements
and the premature waning of seasons, the incursions of ballad opera and
oratorio. Singers grew rich on it, instrumentalists made a steady living,
even the managements often avoided a loss: the losers, financially, were the
guarantors, yet fresh support came forward as decade followed decade. It
is all the more curious, then, to reflect that there was once a viable English
opera, distinctive in its form, successful on the stage, and that during the
forty years of its existence only a handful of foreign operas reached London.
This English Restoration opera was not 'English opera' in the sense that
Addison or Hughes understood the term: opera with English words, but
employing an Italian musical idiom and Italian dramaturgical conventions.
Restoration opera involved spoken dialogue, which was never a feature of
Italian opera; and it made extensive use of choruses and dances, which were
seldom employed in Italian operas after 1660, except on festal occasions.
The immediate models of English Restoration opera were French, and
though in this respect it might be thought doubly exotic, since French opera
stemmed from an Italian root, I shall try to show that, paradoxically, these
models made seventeenth-century English opera a more truly national form
than any strict imitation of Italian practice would have done. The French
origins were known to one or two eighteenth-century writers including

Addison: James Grassineau, in his *Musical Dictionary* (1740), observes that 'The *Opera's* we derive from the *French*, they from the *Italian*'. But this insight was not shared by the men immediately involved in promoting English opera in the eighteenth century, and their adherence to the Italian model both frustrated their own schemes and doomed the earlier tradition of English opera to its prolonged decline in the debased form of pantomime.

The English musical dramas produced between 1670 and 1710 have been variously called 'dramatick operas', 'semi-operas' and 'ambigue entertainments'. The last was Roger North's expression, and is critical rather than descriptive, matching in this respect his much quoted dictum that 'some come for the play and hate the musick, others come onely for the musick, and the drama is pennance to them, and scarce any are well reconciled to both'.[2] North may have accurately represented the feelings of the cognoscenti in the audience, but there is evidence that dramatick opera (which is surely the best of the contemporary names) met with an enthusiastic popular response. John Downes, in his *Roscius Anglicanus*, notices all the principal examples: the Dorset Garden *Macbeth* (1673) was 'Excellently perform'd', and 'being in the nature of an Opera, it Recompenc'd double the Expence'; in Shadwell's *The Tempest* (1674) everything was 'perform'd . . . so Admirably well, that not any succeeding Opera got more Money'; *Psyche* (1675) cost over £800 for scenes alone, yet 'prov'd very Beneficial to the Company'; *Circe* (1677), also, 'answer'd the Expectation of the Company'. *Albion and Albanius* (1685), on the other hand, failed: 'it was perform'd but six times, which not Answering half the Charge they were at, Involv'd the Company very much in Debt'. This disappointment Downes attributes to the alarm created by Monmouth's landing, but a contemporary satire suggests that neither words nor music pleased. Since *Albion and Albanius* was a through-composed work rather than a dramatick opera its failure does not compromise the argument, though Downes's information is valuable because it emphasises the high risks (and thus the high expectations) involved in such productions.[3] The losses induced caution, no operas being given until 1690 when *Dioclesian* 'gratify'd the Expectation of Court and City'; presumably it showed a profit, since the company was emboldened to venture on *King Arthur* (1692) which 'being well perform'd, 'twas very Gainful to the Company'. This success prompted Betterton to mount *The Fairy Queen* (1692, revised 1693) with its 'Scenes, Machines and Decorations, all most profusely set off', though, sadly, 'the Expences in setting it out being so great, the Company got very little by it'.

After this Downes records no more dramatick opera until 1705. This is mainly because his account concerns the fortunes of Betterton's company, to which he was prompter, and Betterton seems for a time to have concentrated on self-contained 'masques' within plays; nevertheless one exception to this policy, Dennis's *Rinaldo and Armida*, deserved mention, though it was not a financial success. In the meantime a whole series of dramatick operas graced the rival Drury Lane, and these must have proved reasonably profitable. The first, which followed close on the break up of the United Company in 1695, was *The Indian Queen*, and here Gildon provides an appropriately Downesian note: 'formerly Acted with general Applause, at the Theatre Royal, but now turn'd into an Opera, and many times of late represented at the same Theatre, with the like Success'.[4] When Betterton returned to dramatick opera it was with Lord Lansdowne's *The British Enchanters* (another text praised by Johnson), an entertainment 'very Exquisitely done, especially the Singing Part; making Love the *Acme* of all Terrestrial Bliss: Which infinitely arrided both Sexes, and pleas'd the Town as well as any *English* Modern Opera'.[5] The last noteworthy dramatick opera brings the tale almost full circle, for it was a version of *The Tempest* given at Drury Lane in 1712; the music for this, by John Weldon, has often been attributed to Henry Purcell.

This record of success is the more significant since, in the first decade of the Restoration, a prestigious attempt to establish Italian opera had come to nothing. The patents for both London theatres (as also for Ogilby's Dublin theatre) permitted 'tragedies, comedies, plays, operas, musick, scenes, and all other entertainments of the stage whatsoever' to be 'shewed and presented'. The inclusive wording cannot be taken as evidence of a special intention to produce opera; in October 1660 a privilege was granted to Giulio Gentileschi to establish an Italian opera in London: that it was never implemented may have been due to representations by Davenant and Killigrew, but the fact that it was drawn up indicates that they had no immediate plans for opera. Sir William Davenant, who presented opera with some success under the Commonwealth, had done so for special reasons; after the Restoration, though he produced plays with a good deal of music in them, he reformed *The Siege of Rhodes* into a 'just drama', and produced no new opera.[6] But Thomas Killigrew had definite operatic ambitions, as we know from entries in Pepys's diary. On 2 August 1664 Pepys, who chanced to sit next to Killigrew at the playhouse, learned of his plan to set up a 'Nursery' where, besides plays by fledgling actors, Killigrew would mount four operas every year, for six weeks at a time, with 'the best Scenes and Machines, the best Musique, and everything as

Magnificent as is in Christendome; and to that end hath sent for voices and painters and other persons from Italy'. By 1667 Killigrew had not yet accomplished this: on 12 February Pepys recorded a visit to Lord Brouncker's house, 'there to hear some Italian Musique; and here we met Tom Killigrew, Sir Rob. Murray, and the Italian Seignor Baptista – who hath composed a play in Italian for the Opera which T. Killigrew doth intend to have up . . . [Baptista] is the poet as well as the Musician, which is very much'. On this occasion Killigrew talked at length of his devotion to music, his endeavour 'in the last King's time and in this, to introduce good Musique', and his achievements in gathering 'nine Italians from several Courts in Christendome to come to make a consort for the King'. Fuller details of Killigrew's 'Quire of Italians' may be garnered from the State Papers, for rather than employ the musicians himself he apparently persuaded Charles to establish a King's Italian Musick. Arlington, as Secretary of State, took in hand formal arrangements for the new establishment; Sir Bernard Gascoyne, as envoy in Tuscany, recruited singers. On 7 June 1664 Gascoyne reported to Arlington that, besides a musician already arrived in England, he had found a 'Eunuche of 16 years of age' with an excellent voice, and also a girl singer; he hoped that the king would receive them and 'send away those Francemen that not worth a fiddelstick'.[7] By 1666 the Italian Musick was complete, with Vicenzo Albrici, a pupil of Carissimi latterly in royal employ at Dresden, as Master; his brother and sister were also given positions. The nine Italians mentioned by Killigrew can all be identified, though it is not always clear which of the posts they filled: the establishment comprised two women singers (presumably sopranos), two castrati, one tenor, one bass, the Albrici brothers as composers, and finally 'the poet' – who seems certain to have been Draghi. At £200 a year the basic stipend for each post was as much as that of the Master of the King's Musick.[8]

This expensive ensemble was used in several ways, for it helped provide music in the Queen's Chapel, and it entertained king and queen in their apartments. But the provision for the 'poet' confirms what we are told by Pepys: that it was originally anticipated that the Italian Musick would present opera, though this can never have been its sole object. Yet the only trustworthy evidence that the Italian Musick ever appeared on stage concerns Carissimi's serenata *I Naviganti*, sung 'at a Muster of Voices in the Theater at White Hall'. This is not an opera, and Roger North explains how Charles 'had a fancy for a comparison to hear the singers of the severall nations, German, Spanish, Italian, French, and English, performe upon the stage at Whitehall'; the affair hardly rates as a stage performance in the normal sense.[9] The Italians took part in the Queen's Ballet given in February 1671, but in conjunction with the King's and the Queen's Musicks; again, it was certainly not an opera that was given. The '*Italian Opera* in musique, the first that had ben in *England* of this kind' seen by Evelyn on 5 January 1674 remains an enigma, but it is most likely that it was a rehearsal of Cambert's *Ariane* – a French, not Italian, work.[10] Equally enigmatic is the late seventeenth-century English version of Cavalli's *Erismena*; this survives in score, and is remarkable testimony to a serious interest in Italian opera, but if it was performed it is unlikely to have been given by the Italian Musick, who did not sing in English.[11] The version of *Erismena* stands with Richard Fleckno's two libretti, *Ariadne Deserted . . . Apted for Recitative Musick* (1654), and *The Marriage of Oceanus and Brittania* (1659) (for both of which he composed music, now lost), as evidence of an English and probably amateur interest in Italian opera, which did not have direct consequences for the professional stage.[12]

Italian opera, despite substantial patronage, established no perceptible foothold on the English stage until the first decade of the eighteenth century. French opera was more successful, reaching the stage three times between 1660 and 1700. Perrin and Cambert's *Ariane* was given at Drury Lane in 1674, Mme La Roche Guilhen's *Rare en tout* (a *comédie-ballet* rather than a true opera) at court in May 1677, and Lully's *Cadmus et Hermione* at Dorset Garden in February 1686.[13] In addition there appear to have been private or amateur performances of works which, if not properly operas, were at least conceived in terms of the stage: Grabu's *Pastoralle* (1684) and an *Idylle* and *Prologue* with words and music by St Evremond are examples.[14] Yet the scale of activity is not as extensive as might at first seem the case, and this is particularly evident when it is considered in relation to royal patronage of French music. As early as December 1661 John Bannister had been sent into France on 'Special Service' which involved learning about developments in musical practice. On his return he was rapidly promoted to lead the royal band of violins, itself modelled on Louis XIV's *grande bande des vingt-quatre Violons*. Bannister was followed into France by the young Pelham Humfrey who returned in 1667 'an absolute Monsieur'. A separate establishment for the King's French Musick was formally created on 29 July 1663, whilst the Queen Mother continued to maintain French musicians of her own. Antoni Robert served in both Henrietta's Musick and Charles's (English) Musick; he was also a senior member of the Corporation of Musicians. The French

Musick suffered by the rise of the Italian Musick and was disbanded late in 1666. Nevertheless the singer Desgranges was kept, but on the English establishment, and his appointment reveals a new tendency: the extensive employment of Frenchmen in the English Musick.[15] This is borne out by the appointment of Louis Grabu to the mastership of the Private Musick on 24 November 1666. Grabu was eventually dismissed from this post, probably in the summer of 1674. But in March that year he had succeeded in mounting Cambert's *Ariane*, with a new prologue in honour of the marriage of the Duke of York with Mary of Modena, first at court and then – presumably with Killigrew's collaboration – at Drury Lane. Little is known of this production: the singers and dancers appear to have been French; the 'Royal Academy of Musick', to which the performance is credited in the libretto, has left no traces, and seems to have been more a hope than an institution (an impression which is substantiated by the exceptionally mendicant dedication to the king). In the event Charles did not 'deign own' the Academy, and perhaps Grabu's temerity contributed to his downfall. Nonetheless, French musicians continued to be taken into royal employ, particularly players of woodwind, of which the construction and technique had recently been revolutionised in Paris. Though the music for *Calisto* was by an Englishman, Staggins, it was Robert Cambert who took charge of the performance. *Rare en tout* was the work of a visiting company (though members of the King's Musick, directed by James Paisible, made up the band); Peregrine Bertie recorded of the 1686 *Cadmus* that it was 'acted by none but French'. Grabu's association with the stage increased after his dismissal from the King's Musick, and culminated in *Albion and Albanius*; apart from his *Pastoralle*, however, he set English words and provided entirely conventional incidental music for English plays.

Taken all in all it is not a remarkable record; the success of French opera is a relative matter, signifying because the Italian enterprise failed so utterly, but not comparable with the native achievement. The two productions in public theatres seem to have evoked very little interest, despite the careful provision of a translation of the *Ariane* libretto.[16] We can trace enthusiasm for French opera in English circles: St Evremond obtained the latest airs through friends such as the Comte de Lionne, received reports of recent productions from d'Hervart, the banker, and referred in a letter to Lord Montagu to episodes in Lully's *Acis et Galatée* and *Roland*; the allusions suggest that Montagu and his musical friends would have known the works, and it may have been the same group which heard St Evremond's own semi-dramatic compositions. Etherege, disconsolate in Pontine

Ratisbon, was grateful that three of his household were skilled in music; he had, besides 'all the Operas', a correspondent at Paris who sent him new works.[17] Both Etherege and St Evremond were friendly with James Paisible, a French musician in Charles's service whose doings afforded amusement to Henry Saville and the Earl of Rochester. Rochester retained a French boy, Baptiste; the youth's singing was celebrated and in demand at court. Samuel Pepys's domestic musician arranged songs from Lully's operas for his master. The Amsterdam publisher Pointel issued, in the late 1680s, collections of opera songs by Lully; these he provided with English titles, presumably because he had hopes for an English market, though in the event it must have disappointed him.[18] The taste for French music (and this includes opera) looks in the end to have been a coterie affair; the coterie may have been influential in a number of ways, but it could not convert a broader public to undiluted French music, and probably had no wish to do so. It is only when we consider the effects of French music and opera as they were modified by local circumstance that a different picture begins to emerge.

At first glance it is easy to see dramatick opera as an indigenous growth. A sense of the importance of music in Jacobean and Caroline theatre, an awareness of the artistry and ingenuity devoted to the masque before the civil wars, a knowledge of Davenant's activities during the interregnum – all these suggest a steady development of music in the theatre, and ulti-mately of musical theatre. It could be argued that *The Tempest* in its original form, by its use of masque and song, points inexorably to its eventual apotheosis as a dramatick opera. In the 1690s critics certainly felt that, after the Restoration, 'the Play-house Musick improved Yearly', and they drew this into their proposition that sound was now triumphing over sense.[19] *The Rehearsal* (1671), with its castigation of the 'interlarding' of plays with 'Songs, Ghosts and Idols' for the sake of the receipts, and its parodies of recitative and fanciful dancing, is a demonstration that all the elements of dramatick opera could exist, yet without that crystallisation of the concept of 'opera' which is implicit in Downes's account having taken place.

The process is worth considering. Both 'masque' and 'opera' were words used very loosely in England. A masque might mean a court masque, a mumming, a ball, a revel, a musical interlude in a play, or a tableau in a pageant. *The Siege of Rhodes*, confidently asserted by the author of the preface to *The Fairy Queen* to be 'the first *Opera* we ever had in England', was termed on its title-page 'a Representation by the Art of Prospective in Scenes, And the Story sung in *Recitative* Musick'. But in the Stationers' Register it is 'a maske', and in the Davenant folio of 1673 it follows on from the three masque texts there printed. To Pepys it was 'the Opera', and the posthumous attribution to Davenant of the definition of 'opera' offered in Blount's *Glossographia* (the definition appears in all editions, the attribution only in the fifth) shows how the playwright had become associated with the term. Crowne's *Calisto* (1675), designated a 'Masque' on its title, and performed, not by professionals in a theatre open to a paying public, but 'at Court . . . by Persons of Great Quality', could nevertheless be referred to by contemporaries as a 'Play and an Opera', whilst its form displayed the direct influence of the French *pastorale* and *tragédie à machines*. In his dedication and preface Crowne resolutely called *Calisto* an 'Entertainment', and Miss Boswell has pointed out that the work was termed 'by Evelyn first a comedy and then a pastoral, by the Clerk of the Kitchen a ball, and by the tailors a masquerade'.[20] The word 'opera' is itself almost as widespread in its application as 'masque'. Both Dryden and Downes on occasion used it to describe works primarily remarkable for elaborate scenes and machines, though they generally gave the word its more customary sense. Perhaps the best comment is the caustic remark by a contemporary annotator of the English translation of Raguenet's *Comparison between the French and Italian Musick* (1709). The translator had inserted the disparaging observation that 'some years ago, they gave the Name of Opera to all those Plays here in *London* as had any Musical Dialogues intermix'd with the Scenes', and this prompted the annotator to enquire 'why not as well as all the Italians give it to a dozen sonatas or setts of Tunes'.[21]

Yet when Locke published his music from *Psyche* and *The Tempest* as *The English Opera* (1675) he was conscious of a precise meaning for his title, and conscious also that his fellow composers might 'stumble' at it, since his 'English' opera, for all that it employed a diversity of musical forms such as had never yet been presented in England, was not all sung. Two factors, in Locke's view, justified his use of 'opera'. The first was his extensive involvement with projects 'of this kind' – a reference, it must be presumed, to his contributions to *Cupid and Death*, *The Siege of Rhodes*, Stapleton's tragi-comedy *The Step-Mother*, Settle's *Empress of Morocco*, and probably other works besides. The second was Shadwell's view, reported by Locke, 'that though *Italy* was and is the great Academy of the World for that Science and way of Entertainment, *England* is not'; consequently Shadwell saw to it that *Psyche* was 'mix't . . . with interlocutions, as more proper to our Genious'. Locke's appeal to his earlier involvement with theatrical music is significant, for though *Psyche* in one way develops out of his earlier work, in another it remains quite distinct. It is recognisably by the same man who wrote the earlier dramatic music, yet in organisation and atmosphere it is different, and this has its consequences for the musical style. The most extensive of Locke's previous dramatic compositions was *Cupid and Death*: the libretto of the 1653 version describes this as a 'Masque', whilst that of the 1659 revision calls it a 'Private Entertainment'. But the autograph title of Locke's score for the 1659 performance designates it a 'Morall representation'. It is a description that admirably suits the work, and indicates the way in which its tone remains characteristic of Jacobean and Caroline masque (meaning, in this instance, court masque): that is, it remains didactic and emblematic. *Psyche*, for all that it has its didactic and emblematic elements, is essentially different. It is so by virtue of the intention and ordering of the text, which deploys fabulous material for emotive ends, the object being the evocation and modulation of feeling. Shadwell is quite explicit about this intention in his preface: 'the great Design', he tells his readers, 'was to entertain the Town with variety of Musick, curious Dancing, splendid Scenes and Machines', and in achieving this he felt his own musical knowledge and experience to be of great importance.

The avowedly emotive object of *Psyche*, and the vital part played by the idea of 'admiration' in its scheme, differentiates it sharply enough from Locke's previous enterprises, and in itself justifies the new name; for *Psyche* is not masque, not play with music, but something else again: a play conditioned by music and conditional upon music. It has the same kind of emphasis that emerges, in another way, from the first page of the libretto for Shadwell's opera version of *The Tempest*: 'The Front of the Stage is opened, and the Band of 24 Violins, with the Harpsicals and Theorbo's which accompany the Voices, are plac'd between the Pit and the Stage. While the Overture is playing, the Curtain rises . . .' The music contains the words, where once the words contained the music. Though it would be foolish to deny that both *Psyche* and the operatic *Tempest* (particularly the latter) possess characteristics shared by the masque, and by the play with music, what remains much more remarkable is the way in which they both conform, in organization and atmosphere, to a pattern that is standard for the next forty years.

It is Shadwell's preface to *Psyche* that, once again, vouchsafes an explanation. Shadwell concludes by acknowledging that 'in those Things that concern the Ornament or Decoration of the Play, the great Industry and Care of Mr. *Betterton* ought to be remember'd, at whose desire I wrote upon this Subject'. Dryden, in the preface to *Albion and Albanius*, offers a similar tribute: 'The Descriptions of the Scenes, and other Decorations of the Stage, I had from Mr. *Betterton*, who has spar'd neither for Industry nor Cost, to make this Entertainment perfect, nor for Invention of the Ornaments to beautifie it'. Granville's *British Enchanters*, its author tells us, was 'the first essay of a very infant Muse, rather as a taste at such hours as were free from other exercises, than any way meant for public entertainment: but Mr. Betterton, having had a casual sight of it many years after it was written, begged it for the stage, where it found so favourable a reception as to have an uninterrupted run of at least forty days'. Roger North was confident in his assertion that 'Mr. Betterton who was the cheif ingineer of the stage, contrived a sort of plays, which were called Operas but had bin more properly styled Semioperas, for they consisted of half Musick, and half Drama'. North attributed the responsibility for dramatick opera solely to Betterton, and felt strongly enough to tax him with it in conversation.[22] The extent to which dramatick opera was Bettertonian opera does not seem to have been fully understood by theatre historians, although it provides the only adequate explanation for the stability of the form, a stability that must otherwise seem extraordinary.

We have seen how Shadwell held that all-sung opera was alien to the English genius; precisely the same thought lies behind the statement by the author of an essay in *The Gentleman's Journal* for January 1692 that though 'Other Nations bestow the name of Opera only on such Plays whereof every word is sung . . . experience hath taught us that our English genius will not rellish that perpetual Singing'. This essay (possibly by P. A. Motteux) was in part publicity for *The Fairy Queen*, where the same theme is touched on in the preface, as it is also by Dryden in his preface to *Albion and Albanius*. Dryden (who must be taken to refer to his original plan for combining *Albion and Albanius* and *King Arthur*) is at pains to establish the genre by means of examples; he describes dramatick opera as 'of the Nature of *The Tempest*', which he associates with 'some Pieces that follow'd' in the employment of a distinctive and distinctively English form. Lansdowne, in the preface to *The British Enchanters*, which is the fullest and best exposition of the form, is clear that in English opera (as opposed to French or Italian) the dialogue should be spoken: 'If the numbers are of themselves harmonious, there will be no need of music to set them off: a good verse, well pronounced, is in itself musical; and speech is certainly more natural for discourse than singing'.

This notion has nothing arcane about it; the surprising thing is that it is so often repeated, but if we accept it as a proposition advanced by Betterton the repetition becomes natural. It recurs in company with another assertion: that opera demands patronage beyond the means of players and private persons, and that English opera is restricted by its poor economic circumstances. The players did not let the audience forget this, announcing in the prologue to Shadwell's *The Tempest* that:

> Wee, as the ffathers of the Stage have said,
> To treat you here a vast expense have made.

Thereafter the theme is recurrent, harked on in prefaces and prologues, recalled by the memorialists of the stage. When we find Betterton himself, in speaking Dryden's prologue to *King Arthur*, expressing this hope for patronage, we are driven to realise to what an extent dramatick opera depended on those assessments of what audiences wanted, and what funds would bear, that only a man of his experience could command. For in reality the plea is less a real hope for patronage than a boast, emphasising all that has been accomplished without royal or aristocratic bounty, and the boast can also be taken as a statement about the nature of dramatick opera.

Betterton's early association with Davenant is well-known, but, despite Colley Cibber's contrary belief, Davenant seems to have lost interest in opera after the Restoration; it was Killigrew who tried to explore that direction. Only after Davenant's death in 1668 does the Duke's Company commence its series of dramatick operas; Betterton's rise to a position of predominance within the company seems to have been a necessary precondition. If we knew precisely when it was that Betterton was sent by Charles II to France to study the staging of opera we might have a clearer sense of another necessary precondition. It would be foolish to presume that Betterton was alone in his knowledge of French operatic experiments, since there are significant indications that this was not the case. Dryden, for instance, quotes (inaccurately) from Benserade's *Ballet de la nuit* (1653) in the *Essay of Dramatic Poesie*. If this is unexpected the treatment accorded to Corneille in the early Restoration theatre is even more remarkable. Each act of Katherine Phillips's translation of *Pompey* concludes with a musical interlude; for the London production in 1663 John Bannister, just returned from France, composed the songs and act tunes.[23] When Charles Cotton translated *Horace* in 1665 he added songs and choruses to each act; in the preface to the published version he points out that these are his original work. In 1668 Mrs Phillips's posthumous version of the same play, completed by Denham, was given at court by amateurs (it was also performed professionally); Evelyn noted that "twixt each act [there was] a Masque & *Antique*: daunced . . .' Though not all of the Restoration versions of Corneille acquired musical interludes the tendency to expand his plays in this way is noteworthy, both because it offered a logical format that was employed with some deliberation in later works (the libretto of *Calisto* promises 'The late Masque . . . With the Prologue, and the Songs betwixt the Acts'; the book of Lee's *Theodosius* appeared in 1680 'with the Musick betwixt the Acts'), and because the principle conforms to a remark of Corneille's recorded by St Evremond in a letter of 1675, but presumably circulated by him long before that. What Corneille had proposed was that 'the words of a song should . . . comment on what has gone before, and be, so to speak, an expression of the spirit of each act. In this way it would resemble the Greek Chorus, and bring ideas together instead of scattering them'.[24] The notion seems to be much better realised in these English versions of Corneille than in any of his own plays with music.

It is pertinent to consider whether St Evremond himself might have exercised an influence upon dramatick opera, for it is in the 1670s, the formative period, that we encounter references to the problem of opera in his letters, and St Evremond's circle, for all that it was a coterie, comprehended members of the nobility who were intermittently involved in theatrical affairs. In some respects St Evremond's views on opera, as expressed in his letter to the Duke of Buckingham, provide a warrant for dramatick opera. He dislikes recitative, which 'has neither the charm of singing, nor the agreeable energy of speech', yet he finds song justified in scenes of ritual and invocation, and of love. Sung prologues are legitimate, as also are *intermedes* and epilogues (there is thus no real contradiction involved in St Evremond's composition of such pieces). These opinions could be taken to provide a *rationale* for dramatick opera. Yet, though he records having seen 'plays in England, wherein there is a great deal of musick', and in a letter to the Duchess Mazarin of 1676 makes reference to the 'passionate songs at the Opera' which they have heard, there is no evidence that he took any favourable note of semi-opera. This is not surprising, partly because St Evremond remained so utterly oblivious, throughout his many years in England, to all manifestations of native art, and partly because all his feelings about opera are subordinate to his overwhelming conviction that the form can never do because, though the whole might seem wonderful, 'it must be granted . . . that this wonderful is very tedious'. To St Evremond the aesthetic of astonishment and delight was fundamentally defective. If the English dramatick operas which St Evremond knew had proposed other ends than these it is conceivable (if not likely) that he might have become interested; but both Shadwell (in the preface to *Psyche*) and Crowne (in the preface to *Calisto*) deprecate their works in terms of the aesthetic that St Evremond found so restricting. It is as though they would have agreed with St Evremond about the problems of all-sung opera, yet were unaware that what they were writing in any way differed from the through-composed type; the possible advantages of the English form were not admitted. The same tendency can be seen in Dryden's preface to *Albion and Albanius* (which must also be regarded as in some measure a preface to *King Arthur*), where matters are made no simpler by the evident influence of St Evremond's letter to Buckingham.

St Evremond's views on opera did not go unchallenged. Ferrand Spence attacked them in the dissertation prefixed to his translation of St Evremond's *Miscellanea*, which included the letter on opera. His attack is particularly important in that he sought to defend the actors who had mounted *Albion and Albanius* at such vast expense, some of whom 'of *Eminent judgment* and *sense*' Spence was '*proud* to call my *Friends*'. His observation that the '*general* design' of the opera 'is but as yet in a *State* of *Probation*' suggests he might have preferred to justify the work as it was planned, and not as it was produced.[25] But this does not make his remarks the less cogent. That opera is not dull is proved, he claims, by experience. If the argument about lack of matter for the intellect is valid, then music itself would be intolerable. But if music is defensible, then so is opera, more particularly as the arbitrary distinction between emotion and intellect, implicit in the division of sound and sense, is a false dichotomy. Operas must be judged for what they are: the breaking of the unities can be a virtue, and the appeal to the senses is fundamental to the design. Fair criticism of opera is impossible unless these postulates are understood.

Spence's declaration of allegiance provides some warrant for our treating his opinions, which must have been most welcome to Betterton and the actors, as the Theatre's reply to the Critics. His views also serve to emphasise the ambivalence of Dryden's position, for Spence warmly praises Dryden's versification, and quotes part of his preface with approval, whilst silently but firmly disregarding much else that Dryden advances. Betterton himself, for all his wide culture (to which the sale-catalogue of his art collection and library testifies), seems never to have troubled to be his own spokesman; even when North challenged him he answered briefly and allusively. We must presume him to have seen the operas as their own justification – perhaps the only proper attitude, however unhelpful to the historian. But we should not be surprised that it was to Betterton that Etherege addressed his letter from Ratisbon, enquiring after music, nor that it was Betterton who chose Purcell to set *Dioclesian* and thus paved the way for the composer's collaboration with Dryden on *King Arthur*. We move into the realm of speculation if we ask to what extent he had a hand in *The Fairy Queen*, though the enquiry becomes worthwhile when we examine the episode of the drunken poet, inserted into Act I for the 1693 revival. Who was it who grafted a song from Lyly's *Six Court Comedies* (1632; the song, which first appears in this edition, is not necessarily by Lyly) to a scene which, in its musical and dramatic organisation, derives from the *Ballet des nations* composed by Lully for *Le bourgeois gentilhomme* (Chambord, October 1670)? Betterton is certainly the best candidate.[26]

Since we do not know when Betterton went to Paris it would be as foolish to make exclusive claims in the small instance of this scene from *The Fairy Queen* as to make similar assertions about his more general function as a propagator of French examples. That French influence was pervasive in operatic affairs, we can see from the two surviving English chamber operas; Blow's *Venus and Adonis* (1682?) is in form a miniature Lullian opera, with a prologue and three acts; Purcell's *Dido and Aeneas* (1689?) is constructed on the same model, though this is obscured by its survival only in an incomplete form, as adapted for playhouse interlude performance in the first decade of the eighteenth century. It is not possible to date the first performances of either *Ariane* or Shadwell's *Tempest* with sufficient confidence to be sure which came first, but it is clear that they were in some sense in competition, and thus that the knowledge necessary to mount an English counterblast to French opera had reached England in advance of French opera itself. For *Psyche* Locke, whose colleagues in the Queen's Musick were Italians, and whose references in his preface were to Italian practice, produced a score far more French than Italian; and this was entirely appropriate for a work modelled, however distantly, on Quinault and Lully's *comédie-ballet* of 1671.

But if Betterton's part was not exclusive it was nevertheless decisive for the history of dramatick opera. The voice-production and delivery characteristic of the Restoration stage has occasioned both contemporary and modern comment. The 'Musical Cadence in speaking' known to every worthwhile player is referred to in the preface to *The Fairy Queen*; long afterwards Richard Cumberland recounted how in his youth he had listened while an actress of a generation trained in Betterton's theatre 'sung, or rather recitatived' her lines, and all the accounts of Betterton stress this aspect of his technique. Whenever it was that Betterton went to France, it was certainly before Lully finally managed to consolidate his monopoly of opera. The distinctive feature of French opera, in the period between the end of the Fronde and the issue, in 1672, of the *lettres patentes* granting Lully sole control of the *Académie royale de musique*, was its experimental quality. The object of the experimentation was the creation of the appropriate national form for opera. When Lully finally established that form he did not do so merely by the exercise of an unparalleled artistic despotism: the foundation of his achievement was the moulding of his own distinctive style of recitative, and this style, according to Lecerf de La Viéville, was based on the declamation of the great actress Marie de Champmeslé. If we allow Betterton the intelligence that all we know suggests him to have possessed, then two points emerge: first, that French opera, precisely because it was national and arrived at through the radical adaptation of a foreign form, could never be exported *tout court*; second, that the device of Lullian recitative, which in essence energises the French language by giving it the emphatic accents that can only be artificially imposed, is largely redundant in the case of a language as rich in accentual stress as English. So considered dramatick opera can be seen as having its own basis in criticism, and it is not surprising to find the broad lines of the thesis stated in the preface to *The British Enchanters*, a work which owed its staging to Betterton's initiative.

The argument about opera was far from simple. There was, for example, an international debate, lasting through the seventeenth century and beyond, which greatly influenced feelings on the subject, whilst never receiving systematic exposition. It concerned the classical origins of opera and the assumption, by its Italian pioneers, that classical tragedy was all sung. This opinion, and the classical warrant for opera that it implied, was rejected by French critics such as Boileau and St Evremond, as also by Milton in England. Dryden evaded the matter, but English criticism seems to have agreed with St Evremond's view that only the choruses of classical tragedy were sung. Both Jeremy Collier and George Adams, the translator of Sophocles (1729), held this view: when Gilbert West suggested the opposite, and even proposed an analogy with Italian opera in his translation of *Iphigenia in Tauris* (1749), he did so in the expectation that most of his readers would be outraged by the suggestion. Thus opera was swept into the battle between the ancients and the moderns, but with the complication that it might be defended or attacked from either position; this greatly hindered clear statement of the real issues.[27] It is not surprising, then, that dramatick opera failed to leave any deep impression on contemporary criticism, and must today be recreated, insofar as we wish to understand its principles, from the texts and from fragmentary observations.

If this account is somewhere near the truth, then the death of the form becomes explicable. Several factors, as we would expect, contributed: the triumph, in the first decade of the eighteenth century, of the Italian taste in music, the decline (emphasised by a state of war) of enthusiasm for things French, and the construction of Vanbrugh's cavernous Queen's Theatre, so bad for spoken drama, but in size akin to the large Italian theatres, and having an acoustic responsive to trained Italian voices. The decline in the importance and relative wealth of the crown meant that no state institution for the training of English singers could be founded, whilst the old informal relationships between the King's Musick, the Chapel Royal and Cathedral choirs, and the theatres, were also destroyed by the altered status of the monarchy. In the fluctuating system of subscription finance it was more practical to buy in ready trained (and hence Italian speaking) singers; the castrati provide the extreme illustration. Henry Carey put the whole position in a couplet when he made his *beau* lament that: 'Without Farrinelli the Op'ra must fall,/ So I'll fling up my ticket, and not pay the call.' Subscription finance made managements pay less attention to popular demands for intelligibility, and more to the competitive instincts and technical demands of the cognoscenti, who contributed a disproportionate amount of the theatres' steady income. But above all it was the death of Betterton, who uniquely possessed the imagination, the knowledge and the managerial ability to fuse together the various parts of a successful dramatick opera, that brought about the end of the form.

The easiest modern justification for dramatick opera is that it was the occasion for much of Henry Purcell's greatest music. But, with the notable exception of Mr Roger Savage, no recent critic has been willing to treat the integrity of the operas as a significant matter: the typical assumption is that they were 'vehicles' for Purcell's music.[28] Save for P. A. Motteux's brief references in *The Gentleman's Journal* and for some ambiguous observations by Dennis, the only contemporary comment against which this assumption can be tested has been that provided by Roger North. If other criticisms had survived, North's remarks might not have acquired the definitive status that they are so often allowed today. In this situation any views that diverge from North's are worth taking seriously, and this makes it the more disappointing that the annotator of the copy of Raguenet's *Comparison* now in the Cambridge University Library cannot be identified.[29] He was a man of mordant wit, who had travelled in France and Italy, had apparently met Corelli, had heard performances of works by Stradella and Alessandro Scarlatti, and besides an extensive knowledge of music, possessed sufficient learning to discuss Dr Wallis's commentary on Ptolemy. His views are more informed and perceptive than either those of Raguenet, or of the translator who appended to the *Comparison* its extensive footnotes and the *Critical Discourse upon Opera's in England*. The particular interest that this annotator has for us is his forthright enthusiasm for 'the opera[s] . . . wee had of Mr Purcell's', and his distaste for the London audiences of the new century, who 'did not stick to commend Arsinoe above Poor mr Henry Purcels Performances'. Of Italian opera he observes: 'I have seen much Italian musick. And in all that wch ever came or coud come to mr Purcells Sight I never saw anything but what I coud have matchd wth something of his as good att least'. He sees no reason why an English opera is an impossibility, nor why plays with spoken dialogues should not be called operas; and it is clear that he considers England to have had an opera, superior to anything that has reached the stage recently, at least as good as the best of Italian opera, and in some respects, such as choruses 'of 5 or 6 parts finely managed Such as one might name 20 of Mr Harry Purcels', clearly better. The annotations may be casual and unconsidered, but they are a remarkable demonstration that Purcell's operas (and hence Betterton's operas) could be apprehended as unified and consequential works, and that there were informed spectators ready to accept them on these terms.

An examination of the works set by Purcell (*Dioclesian*, *King Arthur*, *The Fairy Queen*, and *The Indian Queen* as completed by his brother Daniel) confirms that dramatick opera was not merely an extension of the resources of the legitimate stage. The musical amplification was also a conditioning, restricting the possible range of subjects and dominant moods, though the author or adaptor of a dramatick opera continued to enjoy a greater freedom than the poet of a libretto that was to be all sung. This comparative restriction might also create its own intensity. That is what seems to happen in *King Arthur* and *The Fairy Queen*, where the celebration of community (or patriotism), and of love, provide the essential themes. In neither opera does virtuosity, or sheer sensation, or even spectacle, predominate. Their virtues are accessible to, and in no way contemptible to, the admirers of the finest legitimate drama. They were the product of real insight into the nature and possibility of a native opera, both despite and because of the fact that they were profoundly influenced by French models. Above all they show the importance of an active intelligence in the theatre, accepting and modifying the facts of popular taste. It was the absence of any comparable intelligence and purpose, even more than the absence of Henry Purcell, that eventually cleared the way for Hogarth's coster-woman and her shameful barrow.

The significance of Gay's drama

HOWARD ERSKINE-HILL

John Gay's comedy *The Distress'd Wife* is the last and least-known of his full-length plays. Among those but once reprinted since the eighteenth century, it is a useful vantage-point from which to view Gay's dramatic achievement. The great original success of *The Beggar's Opera*, and continuing attention paid it in our time, have obscured the interest of the other plays, the relation of these to the *Opera*, and the larger significance of the canon.[1] I want to consider these matters, and to convey to the reader the experimental combination of forms, idioms and attitudes, and the humour and humanity, to be found in most of Gay's work for the theatre.

Gay wrote just two plays which espoused the formal dramatic orthodoxies of his time: his blank verse tragedy *The Captives* (1724) and *The Distress'd Wife* (written but probably not completed in his last years, and published in 1743). Only in the latter did Gay ever practise the form of the so-called Restoration comedy of manners. Yet this form was the most prominent and successful in Gay's lifetime; it had the approval of the great Congreve, had been flexibly adapted by Farquhar to the rendering of provincial life, and, stylised as it may seem to us with the hindsight of the eighteenth-and nineteenth-century novel, it was the literary realism of its age.[2] In *The Distress'd Wife*, as in other plays in the tradition of the comedy of manners, the language of the drama has a plausible relation with its fiction, judged by realist criteria. A terse, pointed and mainly polite prose is to be found in much of Gay's drama, but only here would it have been accepted by a contemporary audience as approximately the idiom they might hear in the specified setting.

The Distress'd Wife throws into relief the non-realist origins of all Gay's earlier drama. If we look at the earliest, *The Mohocks. A Tragi-Comical*

Farce (1712), we infer from the subtitle an attraction towards parodic form.
Indeed the farce comprises three kinds of literary language, of which the
least conspicuous, the idiom of *beau* Gentle ('I vow and protest Gentlemen,
I just now came from my Lady *Pride*'s in the City' 1.ii.181–2[3]), derives
from the fopling figures of the comedy of manners. Most conspicuous is
the mock-epic manner of the Mohocks themselves, a seemingly innocent
amalgam of the more elevated blank verse of Milton and Dryden, interspersed with Rochesterian echoes:

> Thus far our Riots with Success are crown'd,
> Have found no stop, or what they found o'ercame;
> In vain th' embattell'd Watch in deep array,
> Against our Rage oppose their lifted Poles . . .
>
> May constant Impotence attend his Lust;
> May the dull Slave be bigotted to Virtue;
> And tread no more the pleasing Paths of Vice   (1.i.1–4, 51–3)

High style goes with high-handedness and licence, homely with the
humble and lawful. But the latter idiom, like the Mohocks' in 1.i, under-
goes extreme exaggeration, and Gay goes to school to Shakespeare (not for
the last time in his plays) to strike the right note of lubberly yet warm
farce. Dogberry, Verges and the Watch, and the mechanicals of *A Midsummer Night's Dream*, are all suggested by Gay's Watch, while Peter
Cloudy is allowed one near-Falstaffian moment:

d'ye see, Mr. Constable, here is this Pole, Mr. Constable – I'll engage that this Pole –
Mr. Constable, if it takes a *Mohock* in the right Place – it shall knock him down as flat
as a Flounder, Mr. Constable — Pole is the word, Sir — I, one Night, Mr. Constable,
clap'd my Back against the Watch-house, and kept nine *Mohocks*, with their Swords
drawn, at Pole's length, broke three of their Heads, knock'd down four, and trim'd the
Jackets of the other six.   (1.ii.93–8)[4]

Each kind of language is exaggerated so as to make us aware, not just of
a social decorum of high and low styles, but of the problem of style itself;
it is as if the boldly discrepant styles of *1* and *2 Henry IV*, or Dryden's *Don
Sebastian*, have been drawn, in comic game, so far apart that each questions
not only the others but itself. In this respect *The Mohocks* derives not
from the relatively mimetic mode of the comedy of manners, but the
critical farce of Buckingham's *Rehearsal*. Yet with a difference. The manner
of Buckingham's Bayes is reductive farce, while Gay's first scene enters
with verve into the vein it mocks: mock-epic to Buckingham's burlesque.
Buckingham's commentators are terse and dry compared with the child-
like muddling of Gay's Watch. And while in *The Rehearsal* Bayes is hardly

received into the gentlemanly milieu of Smith and Johnson, the Mohocks
are eventually assimilated into the ignominious deference of the Watch.
The movement of the piece is one of descent from the high style and
pretensions of the Mohocks in 1.1 to the point at the end where the
Emperor declares (aside): 'Faith, 'tis high time for us to sneak off' (1.iii.108).
The Mohocks is in this way similar to *Mac Flecknoe* or Rochester's *Disabled
Debauchee*: all three works have a calculated movement from high to low,
and from it their, admittedly various, comedy in large measure arises.

But the movement of the piece focuses on something not yet mentioned:
on sex – on the intent of the Mohocks to ravish, cuckold and castrate, and
on the happy survival of Joan and Peter Cloudy's marriage. The warm and
virtuous bawdry of Peter's plea to Abaddon:

> my Ears or my Nose is wholly at your Worship's
> Service; but pray, good, dear, loving Sir, don't
> let poor *Gillian* lose her only Comfort   (1.ii.141–3)

may suggest a *double entendre* in Gillian (Joan's) later reproach that Peter
'throws away upon two Wenches in one Night, [*Weeping*] what with good
Huswifery would have satisfied his poor Wife for a Fortnight' (1.iii.102–4),
and certainly constitutes the prosperous outcome of the piece. The bubble
of high language and high action has been pricked; the Mohocks fall to
fearful and undignified men, like the Watch; Peter and Joan are intact;
and the final dance concludes the comic form of the farce.

The happy note of *The Mohocks* is maintained in the intrigue and disguise
of Gay's next play, *The Wife of Bath* (1713). But this is comedy of intrigue
and disguise with a difference. While in his Prologue Gay insists that men
and women in Chaucer's day were not more innocent than those of his own
time – 'They knew the World as well as You and I' – his play differs from
any contemporary model. It ignores realistic illusion by presenting itself
happening, as it were, in the interstices of the famous *Canterbury Tales*, in
an inn on the pilgrims' road to Canterbury. It is avowedly 'literary' in the
sense that it offers the audience the pleasure of seeing on stage characters
such as the Franklin and the Wife of Bath.[5] The poet Chaucer himself
appears in the intrigue, where he uses his poetic skills to gain the woman
of his choice. And though the style of the play is certainly more homo-
geneous than the contrasting exaggerations in *The Mohocks*, there are
within it very sharply distinct idioms of both prose and verse.

The fopling type is again the most obvious connection with seventeenth-
century comedy, and it is in relation to this type that the varieties of the

rest of the play are best displayed. The idiom of the poetaster Frank Doggrell is effectively juxtaposed with the blunt English bawdry of the Wife of Bath and the distinctly pre-Waller lyricism of Chaucer. Doggrell is the successor of *beau* Gentle and the speaker of the most self-consciously polite and modern idiom of the play:

My Name is originally of *French* Extraction, and is written with a D, and an Apostrophe – as much as to say, *De Ogrelle*, which was the antique Residence of my Ancestors. (p. 2)

At the end of the play, tricked into marriage with a woman's woman, he becomes the frank Doggrell he has always resisted being. The Wife of Bath can then exclaim that his new wife's 'Great Uncle, in the Fifty Ninth Degree, was Groom of the Privy Stool to *William* the Conqueror – ha, ha, ha – ' (p. 62).

This contrast, within the range of Restoration comedy, is the basis for others best demonstrated from the characteristic lyrics of the play. Here is the vein of the sophisticated D'Ogrelle (read aloud by Chaucer in a bored voice):

> STANZAS, *upon a Fair Lady making me Happy.*
> Ye Gods! did Jove e'er taste such Charms,
> When prest in fair Alcmena's Arms,
> O ye Immortal Pow'rs . . .

Dogg. Hold, hold, Sir, – Mark the Harmony, Sir; – and the easie Cadence that falls through the whole Stanza. (p. 45)

Here is the Wife of Bath: 'The Maiden and the Batchelor,/Pardie . . . are simple Elves' (p. 27); or again:

> There was a Swain full fair,
> Was tripping it over the Grass,
> And there he spy'd with her Nut-brown Hair,
> A Pretty tight Country Lass.
> Fair Damsel, says he,
> With an Air brisk and free . . . (p. 55)

And here is the lyric incantation of Chaucer the feigned Magus:

> Swiftly, swiftly haste away,
> And my inverted Wand obey:
> Let no hurly-burly rise;
> Nor Storms the Face of Heav'n disguise;
> Let the Winds in silence lye,
> Nor dreadful Lightnings streak the Skye . . . (p. 39)

These are more various literary idioms than simply rude and polite. The polite Restoration is assimilated into the vein of Doggrell, and Gay uses his medieval setting to tap different and older literary sources (in Chaucer's lines we may note the Shakespearean 'hurly-burly' and faint reminiscence of the Dirge in *Cymbeline*) by means of which the polite is placed. Different styles almost seem to call themselves in question, and not only through song. Even that prose which, with greater or lesser degree of bluntness or affectation, is the shared idiom of most characters becomes comically problematic when spoken by Canterbury pilgrims:

Myrtilla. Love naturally flows into Poetry. I admire, Sir, that your Muse was never so
    obliging as to throw away a few tender things upon the Lady to whom you
    are so generous as to bestow your Heart.

Chaucer. Really, Madam, I never write Elegy.   (p. 47)

It would have sounded quite different in the milieu of *The Distress'd Wife*.

   The Wife of Bath has been regularly dismissed.[6] It has been said that Doggrell is a mere mouthpiece for Gay; how can this be true of a character whose affectation the comedy progressively deflates? It has been said that most of the figures are *roles* not personalities; by this criterion much early Shakespearean and Jonsonian comedy could be condemned. It has been said that its plot is 'broken-backed', the interest 'continually divided between the Florinda-Merit and Chaucer-Myrtilla episodes'.[7] It has indeed a double and not very streamlined plot, but intrigue and disguise bring the two parts farcically together. Thus Doggrell, pressed but unwilling to marry Florinda (who prefers Merit), pays court to Myrtilla (who is about to take the veil). Lured into thinking he has enjoyed a liaison with Myrtilla (it was the Wife of Bath disguised as a nun), he is further tricked into the belief that he has achieved clandestine marriage with Myrtilla (it was Myrtilla's maid disguised as a nun). Chaucer wins Myrtilla through disguise as an astrologer. It may be seen that Doggrell and the Wife of Bath, one as gull and the other as plotter, bring together the two strands of the play. It can also be seen that their liaison formally joins the downright and the affected in idiom and outlook, as we find when she asks him next morning how he got on:

Dogg. Ah, Madam, – the most lovely of her Sex! kind, tender and obliging! – to find her
    pretty Lips the very Fountain of Wit, threw me in a perfect Extasie; – Harmony
    dwells in her Voice, and *Zephyrs* wanton in her Breath

Wife. Was you thereabouts my Man of Might, – 'twas I advised you, my Lad . . . a
    rare Pupil i'fackins! – Her Breath sweet as balmy *Zephyrs*! 'Slidikins, – I begin to
    think my self young again –   (p. 54)

This comedy of juxtaposition is admirably built up to the successful theatre of the conclusion. Doggrell, still congratulating himself on his good fortune, resolves to keep cool in the face of Franklin's wrath – 'I'll hum a Tune, and receive the Storm with all the Patience of an ancient Philosopher'. He hums a very Popean pastoral while Franklin rages up and down:

Dogg. Fa, la, la, la . . .
　　　For *Damon* stay'd; – *Damon* the loveliest Swain;
Frank. Bred up a Child under my own Wing, as a Body might say –
Dogg. And she the fairest Nymph of all the Plain.
Frank. Mad! stark staring Mad! – Why *Frank*, Sirrah
Dogg. Thus she complains, while all the Feather'd Throng,
Frank. Death, and Confusion!　　　　　　　　　　　　　　　　　(pp. 59–61)

Doggrell doubly invites his come-uppance when he warns the Wife not to be familiar with his spouse (the maid Busy) and thus learns the latter's true identity:

Dogg. Oh most egregious Error! Embarrass'd with a Chamber-maid, when I bid fair
　　　for a Countess!
Frank. Dal te ral, tal lal [*Sings*]　　　　　　　　　　　　　　　　(p. 62)

Doggrell's glittering bubble is burst, and Franklin can sing his 'Dal te ral' to D'Ogrelle's earlier 'Fa, la, la'.

The play concludes in reconciliation. Jack hath his Jill. Merit wins Florinda, Chaucer Myrtilla, Doggrell, reconciled to Busy, can congratulate Chaucer, and the Wife seems likely to marry Franklin: 'Give me thy Hand then, old *Nestor* – I will defy the World to shew another such like Couple, in the decline of their Age. Ours is a meer *Italian* Autumn, that even excells the Spring in its variety of Beauty' (p. 63). In this atmosphere 'all turn Mediators' and the comedy ends with a dance more inclusive than *The Mohocks*'. But again the comic form has been a process of deflation. Again (though to a lesser degree) the drama has been rich in linguistic contrast, though too happy to scourge fools out of their humour. Doggrell loses Myrtilla but not his *beau* idiom, and the play, self-consciously literary as it is, manages to slip free from the patterns of Restoration comedy (which it nevertheless makes use of in part) and sail simply towards a sweeter final reconciliation than any other drama by Gay.

The pastoral mode in *The Mohocks* was the confused prose of the Watch. This was succeeded in *The Wife of Bath* by that of Franklin's servants Anthony and William (ii.i), but another version of pastoral in the play was the strain of Doggrell's Popean eclogue in iv.iii. That couplet vein, considerably fraught with workaday particulars and earnest incongruity, becomes the chief mode of Gay's next play, *The What D'Ye Call It : A Tragi-Comi-Pastoral Farce* (1715). Again it is worth pausing upon the title. *What D'Ye Call It* comments wittily on the subtitle – what indeed ? – but also alludes to Shakespeare. It carries *As You Like It* and . . . *What You Will* a step further (as Mr P. E. Lewis has pointed out), while the sub-title reminds us of *Hamlet* (II.ii.424–30). Parodic sophistication is thus announced more conspicuously than before, and this is further stressed by the way the couplet vein of the play itself is set off by the more or less realistic rustic prose of a substantial induction. Alerted by Gay's Preface (lines 111–14) we easily connect Gay's rustics preparing their play with the mechanicals in *A Midsummer Night's Dream* (see III.i.195 for the probable source of Gay's Peascod). In a sense the real pastoral of the play is the induction, contrasting almost as strongly with the verse of the play itself as the prose of the Watch contrasted with the hyperbolical vein of the Mohocks. We are again alerted to the relative arbitrariness of literary forms and decorums.

The induction also makes it clear that the play is a piece to order. As Sir Roger demands of his steward: 'And is the play as I order'd it, both a Tragedy and a Comedy ? I would have it a Pastoral too; and if you could make it a Farce, so much the better – and what if you crown'd all with a spice of your Opera ?' (lines 43–7). Sir Roger is the strongest link between induction and play, since his role as master is the same in each. He has ordered: now he can preside. By Sir Roger's 'hint' the play has so fitted the parts to his own tenants that 'ev'ry man talks in his own way!' (lines 53–5). He, Sir Humphry and Justice Statute sit at the table throughout the first act (perhaps throughout the play) with pipes, tobacco and tankard, and, appropriately enough, never speak without drinking. Their mastery gives them the advantage of being inside and outside the action at the same time; they propose for themselves the best of both worlds, with claret into the bargain.

The couplet vein of *The What D'Ye Call It* is quite remarkable. It has astonishing pace and verve; Gay deploys it in expressive variety of form and tone with the brilliance of a virtuoso, and a very notable subtlety of effect. Its most conspicuous feature, burlesque, is indeed responsible for some of the funniest moments, but the laughter is not dismissive. There are points when Popean pastoral is allowed its overt emotion:

KITTY

Dear happy Fields, farewell; ye Flocks, and you
Sweet Meadows . . .   (II.viii.1–2)

When she turns to her rake, 'Companion of my Cares', anyone familiar with Gay's age of burlesque and mock-epic prepares to laugh at the low and ludicrous to come; yet what follows is not simply funny:

> 'Tis to thy Help I owe this Hat and Gown;
> On thee I've lean'd, forgetful of my Work,
> While *Tom* gaz'd on me, propt upon his Fork.   (II.viii.6–8)

We have only to compare this with Pope's burlesque of Ambrose Phillips in *Guardian* 40 to realise that Gay's humour does not preclude a real pathos in Kitty's artless literalism, which also has the merit of giving us a precise picture. When, in the next line, a more elevated note is regained –

> Farewel, farewel; for all thy Task is o'er –

rake, hat, gown and fork are taken up by the emotive pastoral vein to which they delicately lend substance.

Or let us look at the most famous and funny burlesque moment, brilliantly successful on the stage: Timothy Peascod's dying speech as he prepares to be shot for desertion. The literary joke comes over first as the couplet rhetoric ('O Fellow-Soldiers, Countrymen and Friends' II.i.5) plunges on into artless detail:

> I play'd at Nine-pins first in Sermon time:
> I robb'd the Parson's Orchard next; and then
> (For which I pray Forgiveness) stole – a Hen.

(But these crimes are not merely low and ludicrous if we remember eighteenth-century penalties.)

> I. COUNTRYMAN.
>
> Come, 'tis no time to talk. –
>
> II. COUNTRYMAN.
>
> – – – – – – – – – – – – – – – – – Repent thine Ill,
> And Pray in this good Book. – [*Gives him a Book.*]
>
> PEASCOD.
>
> – – – – – – – – – – – – – – – I will, I will.
> Lend me thy Handkercher – *The Pilgrim's Pro* [*Reads and weeps.*]
> (I cannot see for Tears) *Pro – Progress –* Oh!
> *– The Pilgrim's Progress – Eighth – Edi -t- on*
> *Lon-don-prin-ted – for – Ni-cho-las Bod-ding-ton*
> *With new ad-di-tions never made before.*
> – Oh! 'tis so moving, I can read no more.   [*Drops the Book.*]
>
> (II.i.12–14, 21–30)

I have spoken of Kitty's artless literalism; here we have literalism specific-ally pointed. What is it that we laugh at? Certainly the banal details of the imprint and the idea that Tim should call them moving. But we see that in this situation anything would move him; he weeps really for his own death. To do this is not purely risible by any means. Gay has used the exaggerations of farce to create a most peculiar blend of hilarity and pity. At the same time the buoyant song of the couplets, every sob in place, runs its course like a nimble athlete taking each obstacle in his stride to complete his lap. Altogether a strange sense of the separateness of the constituent elements is achieved: printed object distinct from the emotions it appears to evoke, pity distinct from laughter, couplet-form distinct from potential disorder of laughter or tears. This is highly sophisticated and self-conscious farce. It warrants every term of the subtitle.

Sir Roger, however, wanted not merely a tragi-comi-pastoral farce, but 'a spice of your Opera' as well. Here too Gay keeps the promise of his induction. In II.viii Mrs Bicknell, playing Kitty, sung the ballad ''Twas when the seas were roaring' which Gay also published separately, and which Handel may already have set. It is the climax of Gay's lyric performance in the drama. Kitty's situation is first intimated in the induction ('Ay, I have felt Squire *Thomas*'s love to my cost'); in the play itself, in ways we have already seen, her situation is lyrically if humorously expounded, but in the ballad it is raised to a pure lyric intensity. This is another of Gay's salient formalistic contrasts, and may be thought to bring farcical rusticity to the brink of the tragic:

> All melancholy lying,
>   Thus wail'd she for her dear;
> Repay'd each blast with sighing,
>   Each billow with a tear;
> When, o'er the white wave stooping,
>   His floating corpse she spy'd;
> Then like a lily drooping,
>   She bow'd her head, and dy'd.   (II.viii.55–62)

Not without its own exaggeration, this operatic moment effectively puts Kitty beyond the reach of patronising laughter. (Her final lines in this scene seem to me to be funny in a purely 'literary' way – parodying Belvidira's madness at the end of *Venice Preserved* – and not to affect her status as a dramatic figure.)

One of the effects of Gay's writing is that we sympathise with as well as laugh at the rustics.[8] This is endorsed by the speech Gay liked enough to copy out and send to Parnell on 29 January 1715 ('O Tyrant Justices . . .')[9] and indeed by the structure of the play as a whole. Like *The Beggar's*

Opera, The What D'Ye Call It is suddenly checked before the end: its fictionality is suspended, 'what's our Play at a stand?' and the parson refuses to mount Sir Roger's 'stage *pro tempore*' to marry Kitty and Filbert. Hurried parleying induces him to marry the two in the parlour – 'So natural!' as the unsuspecting Sir Roger says – and thus the play is turned against the despotic patron who had ordered tragedy, comedy, pastoral and farce altogether, yet also a drama so like the existing order of things that each could talk in his own way. Kitty, the steward's daughter, whom Squire Thomas had seduced in real life, but who was only to be married to him (playing Thomas Filbert) in fiction, is now by the contrivance of the steward married to him in fact. Thus art turns unexpectedly on the patron; it refuses to be both acceptably fictional and acceptably factual: conscious of fact, it turns back upon fact to rectify it, and thus paradoxically vindicates its independence as fiction. Like *The Wife of Bath*, *The What D'Ye Call It* ends with marriage, here promoted by that 'plaguy dangerous thing' a stage play, but the concluding dance excludes Sir Roger who has stormed off in a passion.

The What D'Ye Call It was Gay's first stage success. We know something of how it was played and what people thought. Gay considered it to be 'out of the way of the Common Taste of the Town' (Gay to Caryll, 3 March 1715) and at first it bewildered. Some could sit through a performance and still not agree with the majority that it was meant to be funny. Pope's anecdote about the deaf Henry Cromwell who, 'hearing none of the words and seeing the action to be tragical, was much astonished to find the audience laugh' tells us that the play was performed in tragic manner, at least in part, as the frontispiece to the editions (insufficient evidence on its own) also suggests.[10] Gay himself was especially pleased with the performances of Penkethman as Peascod, Mrs Bicknell as Kitty and Miss Younger as the little girl Joyce. It is probable that the overall theatrical effect was mock-heroic, not burlesque, and that manner and gesture remained dignified even when the words were low. Some of the surreal touches – the chorus of sighs and groans, and the ghost of the unborn child – would not of course have been so apparent to the audience as to the reader. One way and another the play made people uneasy; they felt it was getting at something but didn't know what. Griffin and Theobald read it as a 'jest upon the tragic poets'; others, noting the authorship, thought it a 'satire on the late war' (the impressment of country folk for military service).[11] Each response holds a part of the truth, but the brilliance of Gay's achievement lies most in his having evolved from a hint in *Hamlet* a dramatic structure which dissolves the hierarchy of dramatic forms, disorients by making its audience sympathise where they also ridicule, and, integrally with these effects, promotes a most unhierarchical marriage.

Griffin and Theobald thought Pope had a hand in *The What D'Ye Call It*, and a phrase in one of Gay's letters suggests some assistance from Pope and Arbuthnot.[12] With his next play, *Three Hours After Marriage* (1717) they certainly assisted, and were regarded and lampooned as confederates. With Cibber playing Plotwell, Penkethman Underplot and Mrs Bicknell Phoebe Clinket, *Three Hours* was performed on seven consecutive nights at Drury Lane to a tumultuous and controversial reception. On the second night, as a 'neutral' member of the audience recorded, 'the play was acted like a ship tost in a tempest'; the evidence is, however, that by the time Cibber got the play withdrawn the favourable party was prevailing, and general applause being given.[13] While there were extrinsic reasons for the play's excited and in part hostile reception, there were intrinsic ones also, for the play is perhaps the most avant-garde comedy of eighteenth-century England.

Gay called *The What D'Ye Call It* a farce, but *Three Hours* a comedy.[14] The later play has not less of the absurd than the former, yet the designation reliably suggests a close relation with seventeenth-century comedy. It is in that pattern that the play seems to be set at the start, and to focus on the hasty marriage of a woman of the town to the elderly doctor and collector Fossile, a figure descended from Congreve's Foresight, and probably a lampoon on the contemporary Dr Woodward. Stock expectations concerning young wives, old husbands and prolific cuckoldry have been aroused when Phoebe Clinket, Fossile's niece and a poetess, enters, pens stuck in her hair, and preceded by her maid bearing a writing desk on her back. The first lines she recites concern the imminent death of Nature (p. 5), and proceed, as Ian Donaldson rightly observes, to deploy an image from Horace's *De Arte Poetica* and Ovid's *Metamorphoses* traditionally associated with natural confusion and literary enormity. Pope was later to give the allusion brilliant setting in *The Dunciad*.[15] 'A rare Affected Creature' (as Mrs Townley calls her), Phoebe is an extension of the Doggrell figure into the realms of near-fantasy. The juxtaposition of a standard comedy-of-manners setting with (as it turns out) a tragedy on *The Universal Deluge* is the first of the surreal effects of this drama.

The recitation of *The Universal Deluge* is next mingled, in most effective stage farce, with the efforts of Plotwell and Mrs Townley to communicate surreptitiously with one another under cover of reciting their parts:

Town. [As Pyrrha]   Thou seest me now sail'd from my former Lodgings
                       Beneath a Husband's Ark . . .
Plotw. [As Deucalion] Through all the Town with Diligent Enquiries, I sought my
                       Pyrrha –
Clink.   Beyond all Patience! the Part, Sir, lies before you; you are never
                       to perplex the *Drama* with Speeches *Extempore.*
Plotw.   Madam, 'tis what the top-Players often do.   (p. 16)

The comedy works outwards from the intermingling of two orders of fiction (Deucalion's Flood unnervingly penetrating the world of Townley and Plotwell) to reflect upon the relation of fiction and fact. The whole sequence is working up to the open recognition that it is Colley Cibber, a 'top-Player', who is thus made to admit his own practice. The audience, having perceived that the part of Deucalion really discloses Plotwell, suddenly sees that the part of Plotwell really discloses Cibber, there on the stage playing Plotwell playing Deucalion. In this way the drama comically explores the very idea of dramatic fictions.

In the admirable scene that follows, the tragedy, now feigned to have been written by Plotwell lest its female authorship inhibit its reception, is submitted for the approval of Sir Tremendous (Dennis) and two players. Its opening (Phoebe Clinket now reads) discloses an immense flood with cattle and men swimming, steeples rising above the waters and 'with Men and Women perching on their Weather-Cocks'. Sir Tremendous perceives an improbability:

Sir Trem. Begging your Pardon, Sir, I believe it can be proved, that Weather-cocks are
            of a modern Invention.   (p. 21)

As anachronism after anachronism is excised (to the protests of Phoebe that 'Were the Play mine, you should gash my Flesh, . . . any thing sooner than scratch my Play' p. 22) the pace madly accelerates:

Sir Trem. Such Stuff! [*strikes out.*] abominable! [*strikes out.*] most execrable!
1st Play. This Thought must out.
2nd Play. Madam, with Submission, this Metaphor.
1st Play. This whole Speech.
Sir Trem. The Fable!
Clink.   To you I answer –
Sir Trem. The Diction!
Clink.   And to you – Ah, hold, hold – I'm butcher'd, I'm massacred. For Mercy's
            Sake! murder, murder! ah   [*faints.*]   (p. 24)

The sequence farcically asks the question: what is a play? Everything is struck *out*. What can be left? Only a metaphysical emptiness. But the play has no existence outside the disordered imagination of its author, hence the propriety of her fainting at the moment she does. The scene, with a kind of *Alice Through the Looking Glass* logic, comically exposes the notions of dramatic '*Vray-semblance*' and neo-classical regularity.

A later scene, the most celebrated or notorious of the play, is even richer in farcical humour and sophisticated literary awareness. Here Plotwell and Underplot woo Mrs Townley, the first disguised as a Mummy, the second as an Alligator:

Plotw.   Thus trav'ling far from his *Egyptian* Tomb,
           Thy *Antony* salutes his *Cleopatra* . . .
           [*Underplot in the Alligator crawls forward, then rises up and embraces her.*]
Under.   Thus Jove within the *Serpent*'s scaly Folds,
           Twin'd round the Macedonian Queen.
Townley Ah!   [*shrieks.*]
Plotw.   Fear not, Madam. This is my evil Genius *Underplot* that still haunts me. How
           the Devil got you here?   (pp. 58–9)

As in the earlier scene, the pace soon accelerates to what F. W. Bateson has well called 'a crescendo of absurdity'[16]:

Plotw.   Madam, I am a Human Creature. Taste my Balsamick Kiss.
Under.   A Lover in Swaddling-Clouts! What is his Kiss, to my Embrace?
Plotw.   Look upon me, Madam. See how I am embroider'd with Hieroglyphicks.
Under.   Consider my beautiful Row of Teeth.
Plotw.   My Balmy Breath.
Under.   The strong joints of my Back.
Plotw.   My erect Stature.
Under.   My long Tail.
Townley Such a Contest of Beauty! How shall I decide it?   (p. 60)

In this scene Gay is closer to Jonsonian comedy (we may remember Volpone rising from his bed to woo Celia, and the uncasing of Sir Politic Would-Be) than in any other of his plays. The logic in the fantasy works wonderfully, the two disguises expressing different amorous advantages, Plotwell having the sweet kiss, the erect stature and the embroidered garb, Underplot the embrace, the strong back and the long tail. Plotwell is the polite lover, Underplot the bawdy seducer. The names of the two lovers convey not only different roles within dramatic fictions, but different aspects of them; here again the drama thinks about the composition of dramas. The Mummy has the conventional stiffness and sweetness of the overplot, the Alligator the underplot's propensity to rise vigorously from below and carry away the interest. (The farce is so fertile here that when, on the fourth night of performance, Penkethman playing Underplot fell backwards into the Mummy-case and got stuck, the audience may have seen some point in it; certainly the fifth-night audience demanded a repetition.[17])

Gay brought this stage *Dunciad* to resolution with perhaps the most adroit and suggestive of all his concluding reconciliations. Mrs Townley is reclaimed by a previous husband; Fossile who desired posterity without a wife, can keep her baby. Phoebe Clinket, in a beautifully conventional end-of-comedy speech, puts it thus:

Clink. Uncle, by this Day's Adventure, every one has got something. Lieutenant
    Bengall has got his Wife again. You a fine Child; and I a Plot for a Comedy; and
    I'll this Moment set about it.   (p. 80)

What will this comedy be like? Very much, no doubt, like what the audience has just seen. Thus the fantasies of *Three Hours After Marriage. A Comedy* bend back to link with the fantasies of *The Universal Deluge. A Tragedy*, like a serpent biting its own tail. If, before, we thought the mad imagination of Phoebe Clinket was 'placed' in the play, Gay in the concluding lines removes that assurance. Have we not, perhaps, been witnessing her new comedy?

Gay's next two dramas mark a break from the sophisticated literary combinations we have been exploring. *Dione. A Pastoral Tragedy* (published in 1720 but never performed) is straightforward in a way the earlier plays are not. 'Pastoral Tragedy' has, of course, none of the comic paradox of the subtitles of *The Mohocks* or *The What D'Ye Call It*, and works entirely within one literary mode: the pastoral eclogue in couplets, expanded in such a way as to comprise a sustained action. The skilful and often moving quality of the verse has often been noted. *The Captives* (1724), a relative success in the theatre, is in some ways similar. Written in the muted and flexible blank verse deriving from *All For Love, The Mourning Bride* and *Cato*, this tragedy never questions its own conventions by combination or contrast. In one important respect, however, these two plays mark an advance on what has gone before, and a development to be sustained in Gay's future drama. While the dramatic figures of the earlier plays were on a diminutive scale, capable of being easily manipulated into ingenious and surprising patterns by the dramatist, the chief figures of *Dione* and *The Captives* are on a full human scale, and are sufficiently sustained in a single dramatic mode as to induce a measure of identification on the part of the audience. Dione in particular, who has the cruelly ambiguous role of Viola in *Twelfth Night* – disguised as a man commissioned to woo for another the man she is herself in love with – certainly invites this interest, while in *The Captives* something of the same is true of the imprisoned prince Sophernes, his wife Cylene, and Phraortes the king. It is further notable that both these plays are studies of fidelity in love. In *The Captives*, too, it is corruption in high places that menaces a fidelity which could survive even military defeat and capture. Gay has built up the sketchy magistrates of *The Mohocks*, and the petty but believable tyrant Sir Roger in *The What D'Ye Call It*, into the figure of Phraortes the gullible though good king. Perhaps for the first time in Gay's drama, certainly the last, authority effectively aids fidelity.

In several ways, then, these little-known plays point ahead to the best known. To turn from *The Captives* to *The Beggar's Opera* (1728) is by no means to be returned simply to the manner of the experimental farces and comedies, for the human scale is maintained, as is the preoccupation with fidelity. Yet *The Beggar's Opera* is a return to a mixed dramatic form. And here it is necessary to affirm what is perhaps still a minority view about the *Opera*, expressed by Bertrand Bronson in what seems to me the best criticism we have on a drama by Gay.[18] 'There is little probability that Gay intended a serious attack on Italian opera ... *The Beggar's Opera* may more properly be regarded as a testimonial to the strength of opera's appeal to John Gay's imagination than as a deliberate attempt to ridicule it out of existence'. This makes sense if we remember *The What D'Ye Call It*. The farce became operatic when Kitty sang '"Twas when the seas were roaring', which Handel set. (The setting is used again in the *Opera*, II.ix.) The effect of that song was to set Kitty's experience in a new light, to release from a diminutive and sometimes ridiculous figure a lyrical emotion which the structure of the drama could not otherwise have conveyed. If it mocked operatic form it did so in a context where every dramatic form was mocked. The life of *The Beggar's Opera* lies also in its deployment of contrasting but equally valid and equally questionable modes. It does not follow *The Rehearsal* in mocking one mode to endorse another.

This point may be referred to the parting of Polly and Macheath at the end of Act I. While many of the airs are taken from high opera, Purcell, Handel, Buononcini and others, these settings happen to be popular. But when Macheath sings:

> Were I laid on Greenland's Coast,
> And in my Arms embrac'd my Lass;
> Warm amidst eternal Frost,
> Too soon the Half Year's Night would pass   (I.xiii.31–4)

it is not apparent that the choice of 'Over the Hills and far away' is ridiculing either Italian operatic form, operatic form, or the reality of the lovers' emotion. It may, certainly, be building on the English Dramatic Operas to create a more popular English operatic mode than had existed before: that is to claim something different. In this instance the poetry too – 'Warm amidst eternal Frost' – has an affirmative intensity denied by the terse, polished, worldly idiom of Macheath's preceding prose: 'You might sooner tear a Pension out of the Hands of a Courtier, a Fee from a Lawyer, a pretty Woman from a Looking-glass, or any Woman from Quadrille' (I.xiii.27–9). *The Beggar's Opera* is most obviously a mixed form because Gay has abandoned recitative, thus leaving himself free to employ much highly unoperatic colloquialism. Having thus, in the song, established a mode strikingly different from the prose of a cynical world, Gay is able, in Polly's symmetrical response, to hint at a prospect from the world of crime and punishment: transportation:[19]

> Were I sold on *Indian* Soil,
> Soon as the burning Day was clos'd,
> I could mock the sultry Toil . . .   (I.xiii.35–7)

The operatic plighting of troth, and the corrupt world of robbers and receivers, are momentarily held side by side in the song. That is not all. Contemporary responses to Gay's drama show how ready audiences were to detect literary allusion.[20] Bronson's suggestion that this scene remembers the parting of the lovers Floridante and Elmira in Handel's *Floridante* (1721) is eminently plausible, but it is surely clear from the way Gay's scene itself works that it is hardly 'ridiculing it out of existence'.

In *Three Hours After Marriage* we noticed how a part of the comedy arose from the contrast of different levels of fiction with what a historical actor (Cibber) actually did. In the famous quarrel of Polly and Lucy (II.xiii) a similar effect is achieved, if not quite with the outrageous practicality which used the actor in question to admit his own fault on stage. The quarrel in the *Opera* unmistakably alludes to the notorious stage quarrel of the two rival singers Faustina and Cuzzoni, in Buononcini's *Astyanax* (1727). Equally certain is the allusion to Handel's *Alessandro* (1726) which had been written to give each of the two celebrities an equally good part, as Lisaura and Rossane vie with each other for the great conqueror's love. A contemporary witness of the *Opera* detected an allusion to the same *matter*, though in this case in the form of the earlier drama by Lee.[21] Once again three levels of 'reality' play off against one another: Faustina and Cuzzoni, whose real quarrel broke the fiction of *Astyanax*; Polly and Lucy (were Miss Fenton and Miss Egleton really quarrelling, the first audiences could have wondered); and the rival lovers in Handel and Lee, an allusion which, as Bronson observes, 'makes something of an Alexander out of Macheath'.[22]

The relation between prose and song is the whole art of the *Opera*, and is of course far more various than these instances suggest. If its chief feature is the contrast between the prose of familiar corruption – 'Indeed, indeed, Brother, we must punctually pay our Spies, or we shall have no Information' (II.x.39–41) – and the lyric of high intensity or tenderness – the *Twelfth Night*-like vein of 'Love with Youth flies swift away,/ Age is nought but Sorrow' (II.iv.37–8) – there are plenty of songs whose mordant satiric pace reinforces our sense of the world that the prose renders. There are moments too when the roles are reversed, as at that politically crucial point where the buoyant singing about court treachery to the tune of Lillibullero is succeeded by Macheath's ringing avowal: 'But we, Gentlemen, have still Honour enough to break through the Corruptions of the World' (III.iv.6–17). For the moment (it will not be sustained) Macheath has moved into the part of the true patriot, *Craftsman*, or Tory satirist, dedicated to saving his country by bringing down corrupt government.[23]

Perhaps it may be said that while Gay's earlier comedies playfully use different conventions to question and undermine one another, in the *Opera* an equally analytic and experimental skill deploys them to question and make one another good. This may be one mark of the *Opera*'s relatively greater stature. Yet nobody who compares *The What D'Ye Call It* with the *Opera* can fail to see certain formal similarities. In each a 'criminal' about to be executed attempts to face death with courage only to break down (Peascod by attempting to run away, Macheath by drinking until his 'Courage is out'). In each he is confronted by mistress and 'base-born child' – in the *Opera* to an almost farcical degree. In each play the extreme artifice of the main action is thrown into relief through being set in a wider framework – Sir Roger and the steward, the Beggar and the player – and in each case the drama comes to an unexpected yet supremely fit conclusion as inner and outer fictions collide. The conclusion of the *Opera* is problematic in that it is a 'happy' ending in which every problem raised by the drama is conspicuously unsolved. Peachum and Lockit are not 'brought to the gallows', the fate of Polly and Lucy remains in suspense, Macheath sneakingly acknowledging his marriage in an aside to Polly, but putting off its public announcement.

Much recent criticism of Gay has stressed his importance as a social critic and as one of that courageous group of satirists who assailed the Hanoverian court and the Walpole régime. I am far from dissenting from this view, though my present argument has been of a different kind. It is, however, necessary to bring this issue into focus as we turn to Gay's last works for the theatre, *Polly* (published 1729), *Achilles* (1733), *The Distress'd Wife* and *The Rehearsal at Goatham* (published 1754). 'John Gay: Lightweight or Heavyweight?' is a question that has recently been posed.[24] The dichotomy is misleading. It associates 'serious' with the grave, earnest and even ponderous, and links 'entertaining' with the trivial. Gay is a serious critic both of life and art, but what makes his criticism tell is precisely his deft and lighthearted manner. A devastating reflection in the buoyant gaiety of a song, or the turn of a swift sentence – these are his means, but not his only means. His light but mordant touch is the effect also of the protean nature of his dramatic structures. The carefully poised instability of his comic form, as I have tried to display it, lends lightness to his reflections: a moral parallel or a political allusion is suddenly perceived, only to be whisked away as the kaleidoscope of his perspective is deftly thrown into a new configuration.

With *Polly*, however, Gay does move in the direction of a more straight-forward kind of moral play. The action of *Polly* is not fully framed, like that of the *Opera*; it has an induction of Poet and Players but they never reappear at the end. We are thus led into the central fiction, culminating in the execution of Morano (Macheath), and the union of the faithful Polly to the virtuous Indian prince Cawwawkee, as into a truth-telling mode that is never challenged. It is in this respect closer to *The Captives* than *The What D'Ye Call It*, *Three Hours* or the *Opera*. There is good evidence that in *Polly* Gay sought to create a more stable moral fiction than the *Opera*, with a clear and firm conclusion.[25] Polly, virtuous and faithful, true to the now unromantically criminal Macheath to his death, can finally be joined to a virtue worthy of her own. This does not mean, in my view, that *Polly* is drastically inferior to the *Opera*.[26] It is rather a kind of moral *riposte* to the *Opera* and to be judged as such. Macheath is here the criminal hero of unglamorous middle age; not an Alexander of the underworld but the

Antony of an opulent West, Jenny his Cleopatra, tempting him to abandon
the empire of the Indies for love ('Let us seize the ships then, and away for
England' II.ix.58–9). Polly is his suffering Octavia. This parallel, explicit
more than once, is the governing metaphor of the play. The *Opera* gave us
the old world, *Polly* the new; in the *Opera* Polly is threatened with poison-
ing by Lucy, in *Polly* with seduction by Jenny; in the *Opera* suspense over
Macheath's death is ended by a reprieve, in *Polly* by execution; in the
Opera the conclusion is indeterminate, in *Polly* it is clear.

The 1730 revision of *The Wife of Bath* is another sign of Gay's move
away from an experimental, formally self-questioning drama. A full
discussion of the changes would be of interest,[27] but it is clear from the
conversion of Franklin into Plowden, Chaucer into Sir Harry Gauntlet,
and the excision of the more archaic and interesting poetry, such as
Chaucer's spell and the Wife's ballad of love-making, that Gay now
wished to bring his early play closer to the comedy-of-manners form. This
version perhaps deserves Allardyce Nicoll's judgement that *The Wife of
Bath* 'owes more to the dramas of the time of Charles II than to any
others'[28] and is the less interesting for it.

Gay's course towards a plainer moral form of drama is interestingly
complicated by his last opera, *Achilles* (posthumously performed in 1733).
The truth-bearer is now not Dione or Polly in men's clothing but the
youthful Achilles in woman's clothing, placed in that disguise in the
corrupt court of Lycomedes by Thetis, to keep him from the Trojan War.
The form is that of situational farce, the theme fidelity to a purpose.
Achilles is, as it were, the Manly, the Plain Dealer in a world of gossip and
intrigue. And the shock at hearing Gay's polite modern prose in the
mouths of the Canterbury Pilgrims is outdone by the same parlance being
given to a Homeric hero and his divine mother:

Ach. Were I allow'd to follow my Inclinations, what wou'd you have to fear? – I
    shou'd do my Duty, and die with Honour. – Was I to live an Age I cou'd do no
    more.
Thet. You are so very obstinate, that really, Child, there's no enduring you. – Your
    Impatience seems to forget that I am a Goddess . . .   (I.i.52–6)

True to himself, Achilles as Pyrrha gets a court lady with child and
rebuffs with great violence the amorous advances of the king. In a well-
contrived resolution, Ulysses disguised as a merchant precipitates the
definitive betrayal of Achilles's masculine and martial character. The comic
conclusion is a celebration of honesty to Nature –

> Nature breaks forth at the Moment unguarded;
> Through all disguise she herself must betray –   (III.xii.79–80)

the dance celebrates both Achilles' marriage and his departure for the Trojan War, and marks also the fall of the corrupt minister Diphilus whose 'paltry flattery' brought about the king's humiliation at Achilles' hands. The quite *recherché* unrealism of the opera's action lightly and charmingly endorses the heavyweight virtues embodied in Achilles. Though the quality of the songs is notably inferior to those of *The Beggar's Opera* and *Polly*, Gay's third and final opera is a work of real merit, and considerable stage potential.

And so we return to *The Distress'd Wife*, and come to *The Rehearsal at Goatham*. Both plays labour their moral judgement, and while the idea of the latter had possibilities for experimental farce, these are undeveloped in the rough dramatic sketch about the censorship of *Polly* which has come down to us. *The Distress'd Wife* is more considerable, and the first act has an overt moral desperation quite new in the drama of Gay. Viewed as a whole the relative realism of its mode falls into the pattern of a fable of false stewardship and marital betrayal. There is no combination or questioning of modes. Sir Thomas, a country gentleman whose wife entangles him in the web of court deception and connives with his treacherous steward to gamble away his inheritance, struggles to preserve his integrity and be master of his household again. (In the context of the Tory writers' assault on Walpole and Queen Caroline the political implications are reasonably clear)[29] Gay's last plays are serious works at least, and each contains speeches which help us appreciate what is implied in the dazzling formalistic indirection of his earlier drama.

Sir Headstrong. [on the innocent Romantic puppet-show at Goatham]:
> Such audacious Wretches should starve, who, because they are poor, are so insolently honest in every thing they say, that a rich Man cannot enjoy his Property in quiet for 'em.

Pother.   We must keep these Wretches down. 'Tis right to keep Mankind in
Dependance.   (pp. 37–8)

This exchange may stand, in summary, for 'John Gay: Social Critic'.[30] It underlines Gay's true pastoral perspective upon power and wealth, which his plays repeatedly though never steadily or continuously offer their audience. Gay is not proposing an alternate social structure; he may hardly be thought to oppose hierarchy as such, yet no part of the operation of hierarchy escapes his radical mockery and free judgement. But Gay the social critic is part only of Gay the dramatist. Here is the culminating speech of the strong first act of *The Distress'd Wife*, Sir Thomas in soliloquy:

Where shall one look for Honesty? – Who hath it? – Or of what use is it to the Owner? – 'Tis a Restraint upon a Man's Fortune; 'tis a Curb upon Opportunity, and makes either a Publick or private Trust worth nothing. What's its Reward? – Poverty – Is it among the Rich? No. For it never keeps Company with Avarice, Luxury and Extravagance. – Is it among the Vulgar? No. For they act by Imitation – Who can one Trust? – If I trust my servant I tempt him. – If I trust my friend I lose him. – If I trust my Wife, for the quiet of the Family She looks upon it as her Duty to deceive me.

> 'Tis then our selves, who by implicit Trust,
> Tempt Servants, Friends and Wives to be Unjust.   (pp. 21–2)

This is a little more complicated than the exchange from *The Rehearsal at Goatham*. Gay writes here with understanding of a person who cannot relate truth and falsity in a single coherent picture of society. In the Falstaffian self-interrogation on Honesty (cf. the soliloquy on Honour in *1 Henry IV*) there lurks a deeper paradox concerning the complicity of the judging mind in what it judges. The possibility of a moral life seems questioned. The soliloquy asks the question: 'Where shall one look for Honesty?' and touches on the question: 'How shall one look for Truth?' It may be thought that it is dubiety on this score which underlies the formal experimentation, the contrasting and questioning of modes, and the kaleidoscopically shifting perspectives of Gay's best comedy. Far from seeing man in 'One clear, unchanged and universal light' (*An Essay on Criticism*, line 71), these plays are aware that the thing perceived depends on the approach of the perceiver; Kitty in *The What D'Ye Call It* is tragi-comi-pastoral, farcical and operatic. As the genre is applied so the truth will be found. The writer who feels this must, like Gay, seek to construct his plays out of several genres, making them work together while yet letting the audience sense the separateness of the constituent parts, as versions of reality.

Gay stands in a special place in English drama. The sixteenth and seventeenth centuries had exhausted the available dramatic forms, in the sense that an early eighteenth-century dramatist could not but be aware of their full and successful exploitation in the hands of his predecessors. Though the comedy of manners was by no means dead, as the drama of Sheridan, Goldsmith and Boucicault attests, English drama was not to find new forms until the Irish playwrights of the twentieth century. This may account for the restless character of Gay's dramatic achievement – 'Will he, alone, not imitate himself?' asks the Prologue to *Achilles* – and its curious

Janus-faced position. On the one hand it seems *fin-de-siècle*: the amused, sophisticated parody of greater masters, the lively farce after the great century's drama was done. On the other hand, as Gay seems to have recognised, his restless combination of different forms, idioms and subjects was innovatory, and to that extent it is not absurd to detect a modernistic indeterminacy in some of his best drama. Gay was after all one of the Scriblerus Club, whose deep humanistic respect for classical forms combined with an inventively parodistic freedom in their handling to produce *A Tale of a Tub* and *The Dunciad*, those formally problematic and multi-perspectived masterpieces.

I don't wish to weaken a case which may already seem to be verging on the wildly anachronistic, but I suggest that Gay's peculiar dramatic achievement can helpfully be seen in the light of some remarks of Serenus Zeitblom on the early work of Leverkühn in Mann's *Dr Faustus*: '. . . this disillusioned masterpiece . . . already bore within itself the traits of parody and intellectual mockery of art, which . . . so often emerged in a creative and uncanny way . . . All the superficial lot simply called it witty and amusing. In truth parody was here the proud expedient of a great gift threatened with sterility by a combination of scepticism, intellectual reserve, and a sense of the deadly extension of the kingdom of the banal'.[31] Needless to say, Gay is no Leverkühn, Schönberg or Mann. The grandiosity of Zeitblom's formulation is inappropriate to England's least pretentious writer. These qualifications made, Mann's words do, I suggest, help us to recognise something of the larger significance of Gay's theatre, corresponding to the *fin-de-siècle* face of modernism. Gay's gift and situation had something in common with Leverkühn's 'great gift'. But it is to another great twentieth-century German author we must turn for applicable words expressive of the other face of modernism: Brecht developing some remarks on *The Beggar's Opera* and *The Threepenny Opera*. 'The new school of play-writing must systematically see to it that its form includes "experiment". It must be free to use connections on every side; it needs equilibrium and has a tension which governs its component parts and "loads" them against one another'.[32] This well describes some of Brecht's most famous plays (not just *The Threepenny Opera*). It would be a good description of the best drama of Gay. It makes it clear that Brecht did not just find in *The Beggar's Opera* the raw material for a new kind of play. It means rather that, surprising as it may seem, there are some radical affinities between the eighteenth-century and the twentieth-century playwright.

'Coming Wonders': uses of theatre in the Victorian novel

GILLIAN BEER

By the end of the eighteenth century, novelists were moving away from drama as their primary model for presenting behaviour. The increased emphasis on sentiment and consciousness meant that more value was being accorded to the velleities of the inner life than to speech and completed action. The eighteenth century theatre, with its organisation of encounter into scenes, confrontations, debate, is implicit in Fielding's novels. His training as a dramatist shows in his command of dialogue and in his command, too, of that intricate dance of exits and entrances which gives subtlety to his characters' journeyings. Even his own presence as narrator is dramatised. He addresses us, he involves us in 'external dialogue'. He is *embodied*, paradoxically and very thoroughly, in his book. Fielding delighted in the new power that fiction gave him of manifesting himself – a power denied to the dramatist, though enjoyed by the actor. The reader, like the spectator, surveys the scene, weighs the dialogue, quizzically watches the characters.

Richardson in *Clarissa* is a *deus absconditus* who pits two modes of experience against each other – the calculating, organising, stage-managing way of Lovelace to whom all the world's a stage and all the men and women merely players, and the circumspect, suffering inwardness of Clarissa who is manipulated, spontaneous, immersed. Although as Mark Kinkead-Weekes points out in *Samuel Richardson Dramatic Novelist* (1973) Clarissa's language draws on the 'she-tragedies' of the time, her activity in the novel spurns drama. She is at the opposite pole in her integrity from Lovelace's protean capacity for disguise and performance. She seeks to keep, and to sublimate, her self, honing it to perfection, dreading falsity. She lives in her inner life; inaction is for the most part her only possible form of action. So the new territory of the novel is her homeland: unspoken thoughts, wishes never to be discharged, the terrible shores of identity where the self is under threat of erosion from the perpetual activity of others, the equally terrible enclosures where no metaphors can make a bridge between inner experience and outer happening. It's an area that Charlotte Brontë was to explore with peculiar lyricism but for which, as I shall show in my discussion of *Villette*, she re-invoked theatrical experience.

In *Tristram Shandy* the activity of reading becomes a metaphor for the activities of consciousness; any elements of drama, therefore, have become internalised. The reader's medium, as well as the book's topic, is Tristram's streamy associative consciousness. The reader is actor, yes, but he is constantly made aware of his limitations as a performer of another man's consciousness and shown the limits of his imaginative capacities. The book itself is both solid object and assimilated process. The novel of sensibility, which had learnt much from Rousseau and his anti-theatricalism, emphasises the trend to identify fiction's highest values with the inner life. It was a way of claiming authenticity for the novel. Since the novel's verisimilitude must work by means of the reader's inner eye and not through what can be shown, many novelists laid claim to the unapparent as the particular territory of fiction. There was a tendency to align the theatre with what is spectacular, evanescent, illusioned, specious, to repudiate the long-established metaphor of our life as a play. This is not to say that novelists held back from ransacking the drama of the past for material for their plots. The Gothic novelists, in particular, stylise the speech of their characters into patterns drawn from plays and conjure in the reader fore-ordained responses previously created in them by the drama.

Much Victorian fiction is preoccupied with the theme of disillusionment: *Vanity Fair*, *Great Expectations*, *Middlemarch* are three of the greatest examples. One might expect this to lead to a distrust of the theatre though not necessarily of drama read in the closet. To test how far this is true I want to examine some of the uses made of theatre by Victorian novelists, and to consider the ways in which their other great theme – the survival of the individual – is linked to manifestations of theatre. In the course of the argument I shall think about theatricality and role-playing in the Victorian novel as well as drama as written text and theatre performance.

Before going further it is important to establish the distinction between attitudes to the drama of the past and the theatre of the present. Greek tragedy and the Jacobean dramatists are invoked. Sometimes they are used simply in order to provide impressive epigraphs for chapter-headings; more deviously and creatively, the Greek dramatists are implicit in George

Eliot's tracking of the idea of Nemesis in the new guise of positivism, with its emphasis on manifold cause and effect. Design in Victorian fiction tends towards *entrelacement* rather than containment, but the increasingly popular detective-story plot, to be seen in *The Moonstone* or *Felix Holt*, or the latter part of *Bleak House*, continues the structure of reversal, discovery, and the brooding power of Nemesis derived from Greek tragedy. The extent to which Shakespeare was summoned to ennoble or to gild the fiction of the Victorians is too large a topic to be discussed here, but one has only to mention *The Old Curiosity Shop* and *Moby Dick* to indicate the extent and depth of the influence of Shakespearean *language*. And one only has to read Mayhew's interview with the boy reciter of Shakespeare in *London Labour and the London Poor* to understand poignantly the ways in which he entered people's experience. Among French dramatists, Molière, in particular, provided quarry for Dickens and for Meredith.[1] And Ben Jonson, in *Volpone* and *Bartholomew Fair*, offered two dramatic images which were vital and troubling to the Victorians: the hypocrite and the fairground as the world.

Terry Otten in *The Deserted Stage: The Search for Dramatic Form in Nineteenth-Century England* (Athens, Ohio, 1972) suggests that in nineteenth-century poetic drama there was an attempt 'to discover a new expressive form capable of reflecting [the] interest in subjective reality'.

Facing a theatre which afforded no opportunity for experimentation and an audience not interested in serious drama, he could reject the actual stage and compose a closet drama or adjust his play to the demands of the current theatre. Either way he was almost certain to fail, in the first case because he was groping towards an unrealized and untestable stage form, and in the second case because accepted stage practices worked against the new drama of character.   (p. 10)

Robert Langbaum's fine book, *The Poetry of Experience* (1957) tracks one of the pathways that the Victorians sought out for a dramatic experience which cannot find its form within the theatre: speaking of the dramatic monologue he says 'The poetry of experience breaks through the Aristotelian succession of events to achieve the condition of the lyric' (p. 227). The Victorian novel is notable for its expansiveness, its accumulative power, its sense of how things ramify. 'Conclusions are at best negations', wrote George Eliot in a letter of the 1850s. Many novelists exploited the lateral quality of narrative – the way the text spreads out experience and extends relations, instead of coalescing them within a set time span. Such interests take the novel in very different directions from the ideal of the 'well-made' play which became fashionable in mid-nineteenth-century theatre.

Although there was admiration of the great drama of the past, there is no lack of witnesses for the very low regard in which contemporary theatre was held in the intellectual life of the 1830s to 60s.

In 1834 we find F. M. Jones writing *On the Causes of the Decline in the Drama* and in 1853 we reach a pamphlet entitled *A new drama: or we faint!!! decline of the drama!!! review of the actors!!!* reprinted from *Bentley's Monthly Review*. In 1833, Bulwer Lytton, himself to be among the most successful, intelligent and opportunistic of contemporary novelists and dramatists, discussed the state of the theatre in his analysis of the country, *England and the English*:

The two large theatres, having once gorged the public with show, have rendered themselves unfit for dignified comedy and sober entertainments, because they have created a public unfit to relish them. The minor theatres being against the law, few persons of capital have been disposed to embark property in illegal speculations.[2]

In London, legitimate theatre was, at the time he wrote, and for another ten years, still confined to Covent Garden, Drury Lane and the Haymarket. Other theatres were obliged to present only musical entertainment – that is, 'melodrama' –, except for occasional licences. This led to some very ingenious outposts of drama such as the play on horseback at Astley's that Kit and his family visit in *The Old Curiosity Shop*:

Then the play itself! the horses which little Jacob believed from the first to be alive, and the ladies and gentlemen of whose reality he could be by no means persuaded, having never seen or heard anything at all like them – the firing, which made Barbara wink – the forlorn lady, who made her cry – the tyrant, who made her tremble – the man who sung the song with the lady's-maid and danced the chorus, who made her laugh – the pony who reared up on his hind legs when he saw the murderer, and wouldn't hear of walking on all fours again until he was taken into custody – the clown who ventured on such familiarities with the military man in boots – the lady who jumped over the nine-and-twenty ribbons and came down safe upon the horse's back – everything was delightful, splendid, and surprising.   (ch. xxxix)

The reasons behind the system of licensing were political rather than moralistic. Lytton shrewdly points out that it was this absence of current relevance which vitiated the theatre: 'At present the English, instead of finding politics on the stage, find their stage in politics'. There was little that was fresh going on in the theatre and audiences were not accustomed to seek discovery or renewal from the legitimate stage. Instead, they sought representation, and fore-known stylisations. They enjoyed adaptations and revivals. G. H. Lewes put it succinctly: 'That our drama is extinct as literature, our stage in a deplorable state of decline, no one ventures to dispute; but there are two opinions as to whether a revival is possible'.[3]

In *Ranthorpe*, his first novel, written in 1842 and published five years later, Lewes gives a vigorously comic and anxiety-ridden account of a young playwright's experience during the production of his first play, a five-act tragedy entitled 'Quintus Curtius'. After its failure the manager 'resolved never to burn his fingers again with 'that d–d humbug, the legitimate drama', but to spend his money upon spectacles and ballets.[4]

Yet it was possible to see the matter in another light. As Lewes comments in 'Foreign Actors on our Stage': 'The Stage may be in a deplorable condition at present, but the delight in mimic representation is primal and indestructible.' Bulwer Lytton had prophesied that out of melodrama would come the seeds of the new tragedy and Dickens, writing in two early issues of *Household Words* on 'The Amusements of the People' (30 March and 30 April 1850) demonstrated the extent to which the surviving theatre must draw upon the needs and energies of a popular audience:

Joe Whelks, of the New Cut, Lambeth, is not much of a reader, has no great store of books, no very commodious room to read in, no very decided inclination to read, and no power at all of presenting vividly before his mind's eye what he reads about. But put Joe in the gallery of the Victorian Theatre; show him doors in the scene that will open and shut, and that people can get in and out of; tell him a story with these aids, and by the help of live men and women dressed up, confiding to him their innermost secrets in voices audible half a mile off, and Joe will unravel a story through all its entanglements, and sit there as long after midnight as you have anything left to show him . . . Heavily taxed, wholly unassisted by the State, deserted by the gentry and quite unrecognised as a means of public instruction, the higher English drama has declined. Those who would live to please Mr. Whelks, must please Mr. Whelks to live.

There is here an implicit contrast with the situation of the novel reader, who must above all have a power 'of presenting vividly before his mind's eye what he reads about'. The extraordinarily vigorous and detailed scenic representations on the stage were one of the show pieces of the drama. G. H. Lewes's play *The Chain of Events* was ensured success by its realistic representation of a shipwreck. George Eliot saw the production in 1852 before she had met Lewes himself and was shocked by it:

As a series of tableaux I never saw anything to equal it. But to my mind it is execrable moral taste to have a storm and shipwreck with all its horrors on the stage. I could only scream and cover my eyes. It was revolting to hear the cheers and clapping of the audience.[5]

Despite his own early career as a dramatist and drama critic, Lewes continued to feel disaffection from the theatre into the 1860s when he wrote of the deplorable condition of English drama: 'It is the more irritating because never were theatres so flourishing'.[6]

And this was the central anomaly: although drama seemed uncreative, theatres were thriving. Taine commented on the upper class addiction to opera: 'Good society does not patronise the theatre in England, with the exception of the two opera houses, which are luxurious and exotic hot-house flowers'.[7] Dickens quizzically noted the kinship between opera and melodrama: 'When the situations were very strong indeed, they were very like what some favourite situations in the Italian Opera would be to a profoundly deaf spectator . . . So do extremes meet; and so is there some hopeful congeniality between what will excite Mr. Whelks, and what will rouse a Duchess'.[8] The popularity and power of melodrama is one of the most striking aspects of Victorian theatrical life. The staple elements in Victorian theatrical performance were melodrama, translations from the French, and adaptations of novels, – in particular, Dickens's novels. Pantomime and burlesque were especially popular entertainments.

This, then was the situation of the theatre as far as it can be gauged by the not unbiased accounts of contemporaries, most of them aspirant artists or playwrights. Their attitudes are what concern me particularly here. A more detailed account of theatrical conditions at the time will be found in Raymond Williams's essay in this volume. As Henry James enquired, remembering childhood visits to *The Cataract of the Ganges* and other plays: 'How *could* quality of talent consort with so dire an absence of quality in the material offered it? where could such lapses lead but to dust and desolation and what happy instinct not be smothered in an air so dismally non-conducting?'[9] But James's accounts of his theatre visits convey the terror and elation of theatrical experience as well as its absurdity. James greatly wished to become a successful dramatist; he succeeded instead in becoming a great novelist. But like aniseed at the centre, there is a hidden nub of melodrama lodged within many of his fictions.

The plots of Henry James's novels are, indeed, de-constructed melo-dramas. He dislimns the hard outlines of action, the easy probity of our judgement. He wills upon us the lassitude which leads to uncontrollable consequences quite as surely as does energetic action. Spectators take on the status of heroes. But at the base of the fictions remain certain well-known, fore-ordained, vulgar stories of the kind exploited by French dramatists at that time: the young man seduced by the older woman in Paris; the heiress sought falsely for her wealth, the gift of gold which destroys a life. The novels' indirection of method and commentary perform a critique upon such simple melodramatic plots by foregoing apparent meanings and by-passing ready-made judgements. But the plots have a way of surviving – even of re-constituting themselves in the books' conclusions: so, Chad *will* leave Mme de Vionnet; at the end of *The Wings of the Dove* the conniving lovers do find that they have divorced themselves. The rank, epitomising judgements inherent in melodrama seem to be in abeyance, yet they remain in the wings, ready to take their bow at the end.

James was more openly fascinated by theatre than most Victorian novelists –, with the overmastering exception of Dickens to whom I shall turn later in this argument. But Thackeray, who claimed Fielding as his master, made devious use of theatrical models.

POPULAR PERFORMANCE

Punch, you know, sir, is a dramatic performance in two hacts. It's a play, you may say. I don't think it can be called a tragedy hexactly; a drama is what we names it. There is tragic parts, and comic and sentimental parts, too. Some families where I performs will have it most sentimental – in the original style; them families is generally sentimental theirselves. Others is all for the comic, and then I has to kick up all the games I can. To the sentimental folk I am obliged to perform werry steady and werry slow, and leave out all comic words and business. They won't have no ghost, no coffin, and no devil; and that's what I call spiling the performance entirely. It's the march of hintellect wot's a doing all this – it is, sir.   (*London Labour* III, 43–4)

Mayhew's Punch man has no doubt about the value, antiquity, and meaning of his craft. In a very long interview he recounts the ancestry and mystery of Punch and his followers, and the problems of modern performance. His evidence brings out vividly the extent to which theatre in the Victorian age was *street* theatre. Mayhew's taxonomy of street entertainment covers an enormous range of performers such as the 'penny-circus jester' (a model for Thackeray's narrator in *Vanity Fair*), strolling actors and mummers, tight-rope dancers and stilt vaulters, street reciters, and the street fire-king or salamander. One strolling actor told Mayhew: 'There's very few penny gaffs in London where they speak; in fact, I only know one where they do. It ain't allowed by law, and the police are uncommon sewere. They generally play ballets and dumb acting, singing and dancing, and the like'. (III, 139)

The effect of censorship and licensing had been to press Victorian theatre in all its manifestations towards *performance*: realistically painted scenery, opera, and histrionic revivals in the polite theatre; singing, dancing, horseback riding, miming, puppetry, improvisation, in popular performance. (Mayhew's informant also told him that the strolling actors rarely had parts to learn: 'he's supposed to be able to find words capable of illustrating the character; in fact, he has to "gag", that is, make up words.') This is the anarchic, skilful world from which Thackeray draws his images to tumble the pride of his characters, his readers and himself: 'quacks (*other* quacks, plague take them!) bawling in front of their booths'.

When Charlotte Brontë first saw the great actress Rachel she wrote: 'She and Thackeray are the two living beings that have a spell for me in this great London'.[10] Charlotte Brontë's admiration for Thackeray has an element of the magical in it. Perhaps she was drawn to him precisely because of his rejection of the heroic; his refusal to believe much in the power of aspirations. Thackeray, so mordant, so obsequiously constricting to the hubris of the reader, satisfied Charlotte Brontë's dread and dislike of passions run out of control. Thackeray's terrible impartiality creates characters who are like us but whom, in the course of writing the book, Thackeray increasingly comes to see as sharing the hoydenish vitality of puppets. So that in the concluding sentence of *Vanity Fair* which is both plangent and shocking, we find ourselves back in the authoritarian and diminishing world of nursery play: 'Come, children, let us shut up the box and the puppets, for our play is played out'.

The image of the fair draws on *Pilgrim's Progress* but also on Jonson's *Bartholomew Fair*. Thackeray casts himself as preacher, jester, and puppet-master. There is here a suggestion of the paltriness of first causes. If nothing is heroic it may be because the only surviving image of the Maker is the puppeteer. Thackeray is a street performer in the midst of Vanity Fair. In the prologue to the book, 'Before the Curtain', he diminishes his characters by taking away their autonomy. But he does not substitute an all-knowing or all-seeing planner – only the 'Manager of the Performance':

As the Manager of the Performance sits before the curtain on the boards, and looks into the Fair, a feeling of profound melancholy comes over him in his survey of the bustling place. There is a great quantity of eating and drinking, making love and jilting, laughing and the contrary, smoking, cheating, fighting, dancing, and fiddling: there are bullies pushing about, bucks ogling the women, knaves picking pockets, policemen on the look-out, quacks (*other* quacks, plague take them!) bawling in front of their booths, and yokels looking up at the tinselled dancers and poor old rouged tumblers, while the light-fingered folk are operating upon their pockets behind. Yes, this is VANITY FAIR; not a moral place certainly; nor a merry one, though very noisy. Look at the faces of the actors and buffoons when they come off from their business; and Tom Fool washing the paint off his cheeks before he sits down to dinner with his wife and the little Jack Puddings behind the canvas. The curtain will be up presently, and he will be turning over head and heels, and crying, 'How are you?'

The crucial and deliberately debilitating irony of *Vanity Fair* is that what we are shown in the book is *not* Tom Fool or stilt-walkers or tinselled dancers or rouged tumblers but the apparently orderly respectable world of the middle and upper classes where disorder takes place in secret, behind closed doors, not as part of a licensed public display. Hypocrisy cannot be avoided if we would be actors. The reader's assumed social world is transposed, opened as if on a stage, and shown to be as low, as speciously entertaining and as ephemeral as the world of the Fair: 'the whole accompanied by appropriate scenery, and brilliantly illuminated with the Author's own candles'.

At the end of 'Before the Curtain' the imagery of the fair and of stage performance gives way to the image of the puppet show:

The famous little Becky Puppet has been pronounced to be uncommonly flexible in the joints, and lively on the wire: the Amelia Doll, though it has had a smaller circle of admirers, has yet been carved and dressed with the greatest care by the artist: the Dobbin Figure, though apparently clumsy, yet dances in a very amusing and natural manner: the Little Boys' Dance has been liked by some; and please to remark the richly dressed figure of the Wicked Nobleman, on which no expense has been spared, and which Old Nick will fetch away at the end of this singular performance.

Mimesis becomes mimicry. Despite the extraordinary richness and profusion of social life and motivation recorded in the book, it proves that we are all gesture, performance, antics. We are fixed in the endlessly repetitive patterns of melodrama or morality play. The reader is implicated because, as Lewes said in *The Morning Chronicle* (6 March 1848), Thackeray 'indulges in no false sentiment; disturbs you by no ambitious bursts of rhetoric. There is no fustian in him, no glare from the footlights is thrown upon exaggerated distortions of human nature.' Because the people in the book are so amply and unprodigiously described, the book's functional images of fairground, stage, puppet show, playthings, are the more dis-quieting. Teleology is reduced to theatrical metaphor. Instead of rejecting the metaphor of our life as a play, Thackeray shows, with a vengeance, that all his men and women are merely players.

Q. D. Leavis comments on Dickens's use of obtrusively staged scenes, particularly scenes of exposure near the end of his novels, such as the unmasking of Mr Pecksniff: 'the sense of our being not in a realistic novel but in the audience witnessing a traditional scene enacted on the boards is very strong'.[11] The effect, as she suggests, is to delineate what we hold in common. Scenes in which characters conform to their acquired roles and perform their own epitomes can be very comforting. 'Theatrical' behaviour in a novel is often reassuring because it condenses character, reifies it, even. Experience at such moments is already arranged for us, unknown but foreknown. It is both removed and yet fully performed. We think with relief of those scenes in which Thackeray and George Eliot relinquish for a while the niceties of motive, the brooding surveillance of the narrator's voice: the confrontation between Rawdon Crawley and Becky when he finds her with Lord Steyne and knocks him down in *Vanity Fair*, Gwendolen sitting screaming among Mrs Glasher's diamonds in *Daniel Deronda*. Thackeray's narrative irresolution, his refusal to winnow – his habit of forcing us to select among the contrary motives of his people and his way of demonstrating that such selection is fruitless: all these make the reader thirst for expressive action. Such a scene assuages the need for the positive energies of melodrama and its rigid classifications. Similarly, *Daniel Deronda*, which offers a series of dark conundrums concerning the responsibility of the self towards others, achieves and uses in the scene of the diamonds, the expressiveness of opera. Daniel's mother, it will be remembered, proves to have been a great opera singer. Gwendolen wished to be an actress.

Whereas George Eliot and Thackeray are much preoccupied with the process of disillusionment, Dickens, particularly in his early work, is engrossed with the powers which sustain life. For Dickens, the medley of noise, inventiveness, formulaic happening, and high useless skill manifested in popular theatre and entertainment becomes a type of the imagination's survival in the face of industrial and utilitarian pressures.

In 'A Curious Dance round a Curious Tree' Dickens writes of:

that jocund world of Pantomime, where there is no affliction or calamity that leaves the least impression; where a man may tumble into the broken ice, or drive into the kitchen fire, and only be the droller for the accident; where babies may be knocked about and sat upon, or choked with gravy spoons, in the process of feeding, and yet no Coroner be wanted, nor anybody made uncomfortable; where workmen may fall from the top of a house to the bottom, or even from the bottom of a house to the top, and sustain no injury to the brain, need no hospital, leave no young children; where everyone, in short, is so superior to all the accidents of life, though encountering them at every turn, that I suspect this to be the secret (though many persons may not present it to themselves) of the general enjoyment which an audience of vulnerable spectators, liable to pain and sorrow, find in this class of entertainment.[12]

Dickens's style performs the pantomimic process and goes out beyond it to the 'vulnerable spectators, liable to pain and sorrow.' This eloquently comic account bears upon the appeal of Dickens's own fiction. Writing of pantomime in 1817 Leigh Hunt gave an account which brings out the kinship of *organisation* between pantomime and Dickens's early novels:

The three general pleasures of a Pantomime are its bustle, its variety, and its sudden changes. We have already described the increasing vivacity of the music. The stage is never empty or still; either Pantaloon is hobbling about, or somebody is falling flat, or somebody else is receiving an ingenious thump on the face, or the Clown is jolting himself with jaunty dislocations, or Colombine is skimming across like a frightened pigeon, or Harlequin is quivering hither and thither, or gliding out of a window, or slapping something into a metamorphosis. But a Pantomime, at present, is also the best medium for dramatic satire.[13]

The prodigal activity of Dickens's novels comes in part from his animism. He endows objects with life, his language throngs with metaphors of activity, so that even in face of sickness and death, the narrator's inventiveness sustains our sense of life persistently improvising its own survival. Dickens's fascination with the mechanics of theatre has been widely written about.[14] His friendship with Macready meant that he had been present at professional rehearsals during Macready's directorship of Covent Garden. He was an enthusiastic amateur actor and wrote a play himself, *The Frozen Deep*. His public readings of his own novels were necessary financially and emotionally to him, particularly in his later years. He knew the world of theatre and entertainment in many aspects. As the dismal stroller in *Pickwick Papers* remarks: 'To be before the footlights is like sitting at a grand court show, and admiring the silken dresses of the gaudy throng – to be behind them is to be the people who make that finery, uncared for and unknown, and left to sink or swim, to starve or live, as fortune wills it' (ch. III). Bulwer Lytton in *England and the English* complained about the lack of amusements for workers in England: 'Excitement of one sort or the other must be sought for, as a counterpoise to toil; at present the poor find it only in two sources – the conventicle or the alehouse' (p. 34). Dickens in the introductory essay to the first issue of *Household Words* (30 March 1850) puts it more ideally when he sets out the aim of the magazine as being 'to teach the hardest workers at this whirling wheel of toil, that their lot is not necessarily a moody, brutal fact, excluded from the sympathies and graces of imagination'.

For Dickens performance and entertainment have value in themselves. In his early novels actors and entertainers embody a limited but innocent kind of goodness. In *Nicholas Nickleby* the Crummles family, and the troupe of provincial actors are kings in the world of the shabby genteel. Their hypocrisy is self-evident and thus harmless, their theatricality is comfortingly hierarchical and orderly. When Nicholas leaves the company the Crummles family turns out to bid him farewell.

In fact, Mr. Crummles, who could never lose any opportunity for professional display, had turned out for the express purpose of taking a public farewell of Nicholas; and to render it the more imposing, he was now, to that young gentleman's most profound annoyance, inflicting upon him a rapid succession of stage embraces, which, as everybody knows, are performed by the embracer's laying his or her chin on the shoulder of the object of affection, and looking over it. This Mr. Crummles did in the highest style of melodrama, pouring forth at the same time all the most dismal forms of farewell he could think of, out of the stock pieces. Nor was this all, for the elder Master Crummles was going through a similar ceremony with Smike; while Master Percy Crummles, with a very little second-hand camlet cloak, worn theatrically over his left shoulder, stood by, in the attitude of an attendant officer waiting to convey the two victims to the scaffold.

(ch. xxx).

The world of the shabby genteel is inevitably one of acting. All the characters in *Nicholas Nickleby* perform their aspirations, not their actual stations. They all set out to impose upon the world a sense of themselves as they would be, not as they are at present unhappily circumstanced. In order to do this, they compose their behaviour according to the dramatic book of rules. When the news of Mr Lillyvick's marriage reaches the Kenwigs and bereaves them of their 'expectations' they react with an absurd, because learnt and mechanical, display of despair and hysteria:

Mr Kenwigs started from his seat with a petrified stare, caught his second daughter by her flaxen tail, and covered his face with his pocket handkerchief. Morleena fell, all stiff and rigid, into the baby's chair, as she had seen her mother fall when she fainted away, and the two remaining little Kenwigses shrieked in affright.

'My children, my defrauded, swindled infants!' cried Mr. Kenwigs, pulling so hard, in his vehemence, at the flaxen tail of his second-daughter that he lifted her up on tiptoe, and kept her for some seconds in that attitude. 'Villain, ass, traitor!' (ch. xxxvi).

And Mr Crummles shrewdly points out the theatrical elements in Nicholas's behaviour when he is persuading him to act with his company: '"There's genteel comedy in your walk and manner, juvenile tragedy in your eye, and touch-and-go farce in your laugh", said Mr. Vincent Crummles. "You'll do as well as if you had thought of nothing else but the lamps from your birth downwards"' (ch. xxii). In her book, *Theatricality* (1972), Elizabeth Burns offers a useful definition:

'Theatricality' in ordinary life consists in the resort to this special grammar of composed behaviour; it is when we suspect that behaviour is being composed according to this grammar of rhetorical and authenticating conventions that we regard it as theatrical. We feel that we are in the presence of some action which has been devised to transmit beliefs, attitudes and feelings of a kind that the 'composer' wishes us to have.   (p. 33)

The joke about the theatrical behaviour of all the characters in *Nicholas Nickleby* is that they never impose upon us, and rarely on each other. The minor characters are all obsessed with gesture and appearance, with parade. There is a suggestion in Elizabeth Burns's definition that theatricality is essentially a *failed* composition. And it is the improvident energy with which Dickens's people seek to persuade us of their dignity that gives comic pathos to the characters in *Nicholas Nickleby*. Ralph Nickleby is the principal exception. His restraint and composure become as a result far more menacing. In *Nicholas Nickleby* Dickens has shown the way actors can surpass hypocrisy and make a kind of truth out of their social stylisa-tions of behaviour. Hypocrisy becomes a harmless tautology when applied to a troupe like the Crummles. *Nicholas Nickleby* is peopled with the shabby genteel who must live in their pretensions. They are bit-players for tonight, but Hamlet in the wings. Dickens is fascinated by props, gesture, the speech-styles by which people articulate a learnt role, rather than a whole heart. The actors have so thoroughly assimilated stylised speech, gesture, and appearances that an absurd accord has been created: histri-onics and feelings no longer fall apart.

Dickens solves the problem of hypocrisy in relation to actors and the theatre in much the same terms as Browning was to use in *Fifine at the Fair*:

> Is it not just our hate of falsehood, fleetingness,
> And the mere part things play, that constitute express
> The inmost charm of Fifine and all her tribe?
> Actors! We also act, but only they inscribe
> Their style and title so, and preface, only they,
> Performance with 'A lie is all we do or say'.
> Wherein but there can be the attraction, Falsehood's bribe,
> That wins so surely o'er to Fifine and her tribe
> The liking, nay the love of who hate falsehood most,
> Except that these alone of mankind make their boast
> 'Frankly, we simulate'.   (Section LXXXV)

Dickens appreciated the ebullience and formality of the actor's art. Although he emphasised the disparity – the often monstrous gap – between the actor's gestures and the evasive feelings he purports to mimic in his hectoring way, yet he aligns theatre with survival, buoyancy, the life-impulse. It is the prowess of entertainment which is valued, not any commentary that theatre may make on ordinary social experience. As Mayhew's Punch-man comments: 'Punch and preaching is two different creeds – hopposition parties, I may say.'

In Dickens's eyes popular entertainment is innocent because it is pure performance without the will to chide, deceive, or reform. It does not mimic, it manifests: 'the vague smell of horses suggestive of coming wonders; the curtain that hid such gorgeous mysteries . . . Everything was delightful, splendid, and surprising.' The show at Astley's is innocent exhibition – innocent of moral complexity, and of death. *The Old Curiosity Shop* is in some ways a threnody for the passing world of popular fair-ground entertainers: the stilt walkers, wax work displays, and Punch-men are part of a world of performance and open illusion. They *aspire* to drama, true enough:

'I never saw any wax-work, ma'am,' said Nell. 'Is it funnier than Punch?'
'Funnier!' said Mrs. Jarley in a shrill voice. 'It is not funny at all.'
'Oh!' said Nell, with all possible humility.
'It isn't funny at all,' repeated Mrs. Jarley. 'It's calm and – what's that word again – critical? – no – classical, that's it – it's calm and classical. No low beatings and knock-ings about, no jokings and squeakings like your precious Punches, but always the same, with a constantly unchanging air of coldness and gentility; and so like life, that if wax-work only spoke and walked about, you'd hardly know the difference. I won't go so far as to say, that, as it is, I've seen wax-work quite like life, but I've certainly seen some life that was exactly like wax-work.' (ch. XXXVII)

And the kindly Punch-man Short rebukes Mr Codlin for his loss of belief since he took to collecting the money from the audience: 'When you played the ghost in the reg'lar drama in the fairs, you believed in every-thing – except ghosts. But now you're a universal mistruster' (ch. XVI). By the time Mayhew came to collect his interviews, Dickens's renderings of fairground characters had become part of the travellers' own lore – the Punch-man in Mayhew claims to be the original of Dickens's Punch-man. Punch in the book is a kind of shadow-puppet aping the career of Quilp, knocking his wife about, throwing the baby downstairs, prodigal of villainy and like Quilp, reassuringly trapped within his own grotesqueness.

Dick Swiveller is rescued from the triteness of himself, sustained and comically stilted on the language learnt from melodrama and popular song. What at first looks like a delusive and bathetic language allows him to escape the limits of his position and to express his imaginative aspirations. Dick's absurd high language corresponds to his sense of his own worth and the world's marvels. He is not disillusioned – his power of raising actually succeeds in raising the poor little scullery maid whom he names the Marchioness. Through his elaborate game-playing with her, she discovers her own powers and escapes upwards from her cellar. Like Mayhew's boy reciter Dick asserts the value of his experience by endowing it with the patina of theatrical phrases which gives it a gratifying grandeur. Mayhew found the same phenomenon with his boy reciter: 'He had picked up several of the set phrases of theatrical parlance, such as, "But my dream has vanished in air" or "I felt that a blight was on my happiness"; and delivered his words in a romantic tone, as though he fancied he was acting on a stage' (III, 151). The Malthusian idea of the expendable masses is challenged by Dickens's and Mayhew's articulation of individuals. And both of them have a special tenderness for the fantasies with which people sustain their sense of their own uniqueness. Inevitably, such fantasies draw on the formulas of power offered by theatre.

In *Hard Times* Dickens defends the fancy against the encroachments of utilitarianism. He opposes the mechanistic world of hard facts to the dexterities, freedoms and absurdities of Sleary's Horse-riders. Sleary's Horse-Riders combine the slipshod vagrant life of the roads with exact skills, beautiful unuseful arts, the power of making people laugh, of giving pleasure. Their morality is that of good performance. Sissy's father leaves when his act no longer produces laughter. Sissy (or Cecilia to give her her full symbolic name) is the daughter of a dancer and a clown. She knows the nine oils needed to rub away the bruises of the ring; she knows stories of ogres, demons, fairies. She is without illusions about her stage life. Dickens emphasises the familial quality of the group with their strange skills. The warmth and the tarnish, the anti-Malthusian profusion of people, the mess, is set against the bounded, clearcut, *untrue* world of discrete facts. Despite the 'chaste Shakespearean quips and retorts' performed by Signor Jupe, this is the world of entertainment rather than the world of drama.

Dickens, seeking an expression of the imagination to counterpoise utilitarianism, deliberately chooses the tinsel, strangely skilled world of horse-riders, acrobats, clowns, performing dogs. Instead of the moralised world of drama even, we have a group whose morality is simply that of appearances. They are what they seem – not actors, but performers. And in the circumventing way Dickens so often hedges his bets, he makes them more truly part of the world of work than those who despise them as idlers:

'Then', said Mr. Bounderby, with a loud short laugh, 'what the devil do you rub your father with nine oils for?'
'It's what our people always use, sir, when they get any hurts in the ring,' replied the girl... 'They bruise themselves very bad sometimes.'
'Serve 'em right,' said Mr. Bounderby, 'for being idle.'   (ch. v)

Bounderby, the realist, proves to be living a self-gratifying fiction, based on fairy-tale. He claims to have been born in a ditch, deserted by his mother, self-made, and come into his wealth by his own efforts. The story has the shape of fairy-tale. It is false. It is the entertainers who are hard-working and without illusions.

No-one, it proves, can live without fancy – not even Bounderby. The circus offers the exhilaration of fancy realised and surpassed. In Dickens's world jubilant performance assuages cozening and secret dreams. Hypocrisy comes from dreams suppressed. Theatre in all its forms is, for him, dream embodied. More than any other Victorian novelist, Dickens draws upon the theatre's power of *manifestation* in his subject matter, characterisation and in the activities of his style. His style is spectacle. And when he does turn to the theme of disillusionment in *Great Expectations* he gives it lugubriously comic expression in Mr Wopsle's performance as Hamlet.

INTROVERSION AND PERFORMANCE

In his three articles on anti-theatricalism Jonas Barish emphasises the continuity of hostility to theatre from the time of Plato and the Christian fathers down to Gordon Craig.[15] His learned and fascinating account certainly seems to be borne out by attitudes to be found in minor Victorian novelists: 'there was that horrid, sickening, suffocating smell which is inseparable from a theatre. It may seem ridiculous, but to me that smell is always connected with the idea of moral degradation.' Or 'Looked into closely, and under the searching glare of gaslight, what miserable, worn, and ill-grained creatures they seemed! Not all the paint and powder in the world could hide the fact that they were not happy peasantry, but poor, half-starved units of an urban population, who eked out their scanty earnings during the day by equally scanty earnings during the night.[16] Barish sees the 'ontological subversiveness' of acting as one of the principal sources of mistrust. He emphasises that the Romantic insistence upon privacy, integrity and spontaneity, recharged the older Puritan and

theological prejudices against 'show'. Certainly it is true that there seems
to be a belief among many novelists that vivid inner life is threatened by
any demands for 'performance'. George Eliot maintained that exaggerated
contrasts and effects which are accepted as a sort of rapid symbolism by a
theatrical audience are utterly out of place in a fiction. The novel's
medium for translating impulse into event becomes metaphor rather than
gesture.

In 'Anti-theatrical prejudice in the nineteenth century' Barish, like many
previous commentators, turns to *Mansfield Park*. Since *Mansfield Park* is
such a *locus classicus* for discussion of anti-theatricalism in fiction it is
worth considering briefly the extent to which Jane Austen plays on
theatrical experience to gain her effects in that novel. Most commentators,
Barish among them, note the sense of moral and social indecorum generated
by the amateur theatricals. The theatricals are deceitful and collusive at
many levels: because they take place in the absence of the father whom it
is known would disapprove of them, because they allow covert intimacies
to burgeon beneath the façade of acting a part, because they break down
distinctions between family, friends, and acquaintances, giving them the
common intimacy of performance. Fanny retains her integrity throughout
this episode as far as she may by remaining a spectator – a painful role
which forces her to watch the play-within-the-play of Edmund and Mary's
growing friendship.

Jane Austen's use of theatrical metaphor in *Mansfield Park* goes beyond
this episode of amateur dramatics. At Sotherton Fanny is the fixed spectator
while all the other characters pass before her, acting out a highly stylised
dance of exits and entrances, unforeseen couplings, symbolic and stage-
like breachings of conventions by passing through forbidden gates and
winding pathways into the wings. Part of the menace of the theatrical
allusions at Sotherton comes from our knowledge that these are *not* actors:
when they go off-stage they do not doff themselves. The wings here are
neither the void nor eternity, nor leading to the green room, but to other
parts of Sotherton where Fanny and we cannot follow them. Fanny is
'god's spy' because she is static. She perceives patterns that the others
cannot see. We, through her spectator's eyes, perceive the potentialities of
all the relationships as we might do in a theatre, not so much through
dialogue as through such dramatic means as people passing over the stage
and off again. The effect is so unusual in Jane Austen's work that it must
surely be a deliberate allusion to the mechanics of stage-craft – an allusion
which is taken up again in the episode of the amateur dramatics. At the end

of the dramatics Jane Austen moves beyond the sinuous dance of Sheridan-like comedy. She achieves a triumphant and deliberately stagey *coup de théâtre*. Instead of the quarrelsome, fudged, amateur dramatics, we have the reappearance of Sir Thomas Bertram, come like the Commendatore to judge and finish 'My father is come! He is in the hall at this moment!' The end of the chapter and the volume here is the curtain falling on Act I. Jane Austen wittily demonstrates what true theatre can be like.

In *Mansfield Park*, it seems, heroism may consist in taking on the suffering passivity of the spectator who retains his integrity by sitting still, sympathising, but not taking part. But, of course, the spectator is a part of the performance.

No-one saw this more vividly among the Victorians than Charlotte Brontë. In *Villette* she chose as first-person narrator Lucy Snowe, who wishes to remain intact, uninvolved, unmoved. Charlotte Brontë could not take to Jane Austen. When G. H. Lewes urged her to read her she said afterwards that she thought her 'more real than true'. In *Villette* she creates a heroine superficially not unlike Fanny. Outwardly Lucy is helpful, meek, responsible, thoughtful, but whereas Fanny is the very type of romantic impressionability sustained and constrained by moral duty, Lucy at the beginning of the book is a cold recalcitrant rebel, merely curious at other peoples' emotional crises:

When the street-door closed, she dropped on her knees at a chair with a cry – 'Papa!'
It was low and long; a sort of 'Why hast thou forsaken me?' During an ensuing space of some minutes, I perceived she endured agony. . . . Nobody spoke. Mrs. Bretton, being a mother, shed a tear or two. Graham, who was writing, lifted up his eyes and gazed at her. I, Lucy Snowe, was calm. (ch. 11)

A little earlier she says: 'On all occasions of vehement, unrestrained expansion, a sense of disdain or ridicule comes to the weary spectator's relief'. She is determined to ward off the incursions of others' emotions: she dreads 'scenes', display, self presentation, showing off. She dreads the power of theatre. Theatre in this novel marks symbolically the stages of her coming to impassioned life.

The isolation of the self, its inhibition and internal mastery, the impossibility of registering its needs – all these are the topics of Charlotte Brontë's fiction, as they had been of *Clarissa*. But Lucy Snowe's world is frozen. The need to *impose* upon others seems at the furthest extreme from Lucy's secretive, never fully confessional first person voice. Even the reader is flouted, the apparent intimacy of first person narration never borne out, the trust breached by opacities in the narrative, so that we are imprisoned within Lucy without full knowledge of her. Others are intractably present, felt as bulk and weight not malleable to her needs. The shared experience of drama is at the furthest reach from the insights of this narrator who shackles the reader within her partial interpretations which are sometimes paranoid and even hallucinated. But the hermetic self needs the vital contrary of theatrical performance. Lucy Snowe's conception of Truth at the beginning of the book is too constricted and exclusive – a matter of cutting things down to size as Thackeray does in *Vanity Fair*. Three episodes of theatre are used to express her discovery of the *scale* of emotional life.

It was in June 1851 that Charlotte Brontë went to see Rachel perform in London. She saw her as Scribe's *Adrienne Lecouvreur* and as Corneille's Camille in *Les Trois Horaces*. She wrote to Sidney Dobell of her perform-ance as Camille: 'I shall never forget her – She will come to me in sleepless nights again and again'. And to Ellen Nussey: 'On Saturday I went to see and hear Rachel, a wonderful sight, terrible as if the earth had cracked deep at your feet, and revealed a glimpse of hell. I shall never forget it. She made me shudder to the marrow of my bones; in her some fiend has certainly taken up an incarnate home. She is not a woman; she is a snake.'[17] The overwhelming impression that Rachel made on spectators is described again in G. H. Lewes's third chapter of *On Actors and the Art of Acting*: 'Rachel was the panther of the stage with a panther's terrible beauty and undulating grace she moved and stood, glared and sprang. There always seemed something not human about her.' And of her Phèdre: 'What a picture she was as she entered! You felt that she was wasting away under the fire within, that she was standing on the verge of the grave with pallid face, hot eyes, emaciated frame – an awful ghastly apparition.'

In *Villette* Rachel becomes Vashti. On a visit to the theatre Lucy Snowe moves into an ecstasy of dismayed fascination:

For awhile . . . I thought it was only a woman, though a unique woman, who moved in might and grace before this multitude. By-and-by I recognised my mistake. Behold! I found upon her something neither of woman nor of man: in each of her eyes sat a devil. These evil forces bore her through the tragedy, kept up her feeble strength – for she was but a frail creature; and as the action rose and the stir deepened, how wildly they shook her with their passions of the pit.

Lucy Snowe rises and inwardly takes part in this demoniac experience, through orgiastic passages of metaphor: 'The strong magnetism of genius drew my heart out of its wonted orbit; the sunflower turned from the south to a fierce light, not solar – a rushing, red, cometary light – hot on vision and to sensation' (ch. XXIII). Then, in a passage which diagnoses her own ills and what is needed to assuage them, she continues: 'instead of merely irritating imagination with the thought of what *might* be done, at the same time fevering the nerves because it was *not* done, it disclosed power like a deep, swollen winter river'.

Performance, enactment, embodiment, satisfy Lucy because they go beyond the metaphorical which is her usual stylistic means of making connections between herself and the world beyond self. So much so are things made real by this performance, that an actual fire breaks out at the end. Dr John whom Lucy loves, self-abnegatingly, begins to be judged that night for his lack of response to Vashti, his cool 'Hm-m-m'. When the panic breaks he is in command: ' "Lucy will sit still, I know" said he. Yes, thus adjured, I think I would have sat still under a rocking crag: but, indeed, to sit still in actual circumstances was my instinct'. The instinct to sit still remains with Lucy but in that excoriating experience of passionate performance she discovers potentialities for participation rather than being satisfied with a life which allows no assertion of self. Earlier, appalled and wary, she had already discovered her own unsuspected prowess as an actor. She takes part, at M. Paul's peremptory insistence, in the 'vaudeville' he is preparing. 'It was a disagreeable part – a man's – an empty-headed fop's. One could put into it neither heart nor soul: I hated it. The play – a mere trifle – ran chiefly on the efforts of a brace of rivals to gain the hand of a fair coquette' (ch. XIV). M. Paul locks her in the attic, alone, to learn her part, then rushes her towards the audience and stage. The dreamlike alternations of movement, lights, and silence, find a stubborn halt when M. Paul insists that she dress as a man. She refuses: 'No. I would keep my own dress; come what might. M. Paul might storm, might rage. I would keep my own dress.' This passionate determination goes far beyond prudishness. It expresses Lucy's dread of being submerged in another, as well as her dread of submission. She has chosen her role early – that of the discreet spectator. This episode in the novel shows her painfully warming towards activity: 'It was not the crowd I feared so much as my own voice'. She becomes animated by a new exhilaration as she acts, wooing Ginevra, determined to outdo the honest lover whom she identifies with Dr John. She discovers the triumph of confident role playing, the speculative donning of another self for whom she need not bear the consequences: 'I recklessly altered the spirit of the role'. She exploits the role to pursue secret areas of her feelings towards Ginevra and Dr John. 'A keen relish for dramatic expression had revealed itself as part of my nature; to cherish and exercise this new-found faculty might gift me with a world of delight, but it would not do for a mere looker-on at life. . . . Withdrawing to a quiet nook, whence unobserved I could observe – the ball, its splendours and its pleasures, passed before me as a spectacle.' She will not venture out of hiding in her own person, but in disguise or in participation she begins to relish passion.

Her determination to shape life into 'scenes' set behind a proscenium arch while she sits safely in the body of the theatre is a persistent image throughout the book. She is to be interpreter and therefore controller. But towards the end of the book she experiences a false apocalypse when, under the influence of drugs, she wanders out into the streets of Villette at night and finds the whole town transformed into a great stage: The tense moves into the present: 'Villette is one blaze, one broad illumination; the whole world seems abroad; moonlight and heavens are banished; the town, by her own flambeaux, beholds her own splendour. . . . I see even scores of masks . . .' Alone, an unseen spectator, she interprets the groupings and wanderings of her friends. She feels that she is watching a series of cabbalistic happenings and allegories which unveil the truth of relationships to her eyes:

Somehow I felt, too, that the night's drama was but begun, that the prologue was scarce spoken: throughout this woody and turfy theatre reigned a shadow of mystery; actors and incidents unlooked-for, waited behind the scenes: I thought so: fore-boding told me as much.   (ch. XVIII)

The encounters between her friends persistently take on occult meanings engendered by their ignorance of her presence. She dreads being seen, because to her to be seen is to be possessed. So she haunts the fringes of the fête, watching, interpreting, organising the whole into a paranoid design. In her determination to hold to truth, not 'falsities and figments' she transforms contingent happenings into conspiracy: 'To see and know the worst is to take from Fear her worst advantage'. Lucy's passionate anxiety forces her to lend the properties of reversal, discovery and dénouement to the cheerful meeting of friends. The whole inordinate drama of the fête is directed against her happiness: it is *about* the spectator, because it is created by the spectator. She becomes convinced that M. Paul is in love with his ward, young Justine Marie, who is welcomed by her friends.

I leaned forward; I looked.
'She comes!' cried Josef Emanuel.

The circle opened as if opening to admit a new and welcome member.
At this instant a torch chanced to be carried past; its blaze aided the pale moon in doing justice to the crisis, in lighting to perfection the denouement pressing on . . .
The play was not yet, indeed, quite played out. I might have waited and watched longer that love scene under the trees, that sylvan courtship. (ch. XXXIX)

She flees homeward. In contrast to the Sotherton episode in *Mansfield Park* the climactic episode of the fête shows the spectator misled. The apparent vantage point offered by silence and inaction, the refusal to partake, or to foster and extend her social identity, misleads Lucy Snowe more rancorously than any role-playing. Her determination to be audience to a play has led her into falsehood, not truth. The truth is more spacious, sociable, physical: M. Paul loves Lucy.

Charlotte Brontë was the most introspective of all Victorian novelists. She invokes the theatre three times in this book. Lucy becomes first actor in M. Paul's vaudeville, then impassioned spectator of Vashti, and last dramaturge attempting to shape public spectacle into private tragedy. The presence of theatre in the book allows Charlotte Brontë to express the hazards of self-enclosure. She shows the way in which the inhibited inner world will demand vehement presence. She knows the dangers of being a spectator too long and sees that for her heroine to survive she must act, not only interpret. The carnival has meanings beyond those of first person narrative. The self atrophies without sufficient roles to play and begins to wizen the amplitude of the social world into false plots.

Despite the condescension with which Victorian literary figures discuss the theatre, some of the finest Victorian novelists draw upon the ideal of performance to give them access to areas of human needs and behaviour which will not yield themselves to the more meditative processes of narration.

Waiting for Prospero

JOHN NORTHAM

The collocation of two plays so dissimilar as *The Tempest* and *Waiting for Godot* may well appear an exercise in misplaced ingenuity. It cannot be justified by the indubitable evidence of Beckett's awareness of Shakespeare's play as he wrote his own (the near-quotation from Act I scene 2 in Lucky's speech) still less by the merely suggestive evidence that Caliban's character may be reflected in Gogo's (his coarse physicality, his greed, his flashes of poetry, his reluctant waking from a dream, his readiness to worship a man for his possessions), that Beckett's strategy of polarities (Gogo/Didi, Pozzo/Lucky) may owe something to Shakespeare's (Ariel/Caliban), or that Pozzo's reflections on the sky in Act I may be intended as a remote and reductive echo of 'our revels now are ended'. I hope merely to show how comparison based on different considerations has helped me clarify for myself the structure and meaning of a modern play which, while by its very nature it seems to refute any such analysis, deserves the same degree of attention as is paid to Shakespeare or Racine. Such comparison, extended to other modern plays but retaining *The Tempest* as the standard point of reference, might also help plot one or two points on a graph of a development in modern drama that would cut across the numerous sub-divisions from which the subject suffers.

Because limitations of space preclude a full analysis of *The Tempest* I have to concentrate, by way of short-hand, on the masque. Certainly it merits commentary by its remarkable formality which makes it stand out from the rest of the play. Or seems to; I would argue that the formality is what gives it its dramatic power. For its slow decorum exists in a play full of scenes of opposite character – episodes of drunkenness, violence, bestiality. It stands as an alternative to chaos.

Its poetry does the same. The nature it draws upon is overwhelmingly that of a Nature whose beauties are inseparable from cultivation, 'rich leas of wheat, rye, barley, vetches, oats and peas . . .' And this too in a play that contains another version of nature, 'fresh springs, brine-pits, barren place and fertile' and pig-nuts dug with Caliban's long nails. Cultivated nature is set against uncultivated by the poetry. The stately rhyming verse, the formal song, the graceful dance of nymphs and reapers, all gain point from their contrast with the vulgar prose, the drunken catches, the clod-hopping frenzy of Caliban and his mates.

The whole play is built around the fundamental oppositions indicated by the masque – love and lust, marriage and rape, service and mutiny, loyalty and treachery, Ariel and Caliban, crew discipline and passenger disorder, calm and tempest – but it is not a static opposition of virtue and its balancing vice. The play's dynamic comes from an urgent sense of the need to cultivate human nature, not merely in its vices but in its more attractive impulses too. All need discipline, Ariel as much as Caliban; even Ferdinand and Miranda must have their love tested by ordeal. Prospero represents and wields the necessary power. The play is a parable of discipline. Its implications are less simple than that description might suggest.

The skeleton of *The Tempest* is the triad, Prospero, Ariel, Caliban. No single terms are adequate to define what each 'stands' for; they declare themselves by the sum of their words and actions and by the words and actions referring to them. Yet each can be approximately defined. Ariel and Caliban represent polarities in human nature approximating to spirituality and sensuality; Prospero represents the exercise of discipline over both elements.

Shakespeare would not be Shakespeare if the play were merely an under-lining of the obvious assumptions that can be made about such a triad. He tests what he presents – Ariel, for all his attractiveness, is energy without purpose except that provided by Prospero; there is a kind of fragility in the characterisation; all the weight lies in those moments when he speaks as the mouthpiece of his master. Caliban, by contrast, shows sympathetic qualities that exempt him from outright condemnation. And the endearing qualities of both call in question the harshness of Prospero's authority. And yet Shakespeare would not be himself if he did not give clear indication of his ultimate assessment of the right relationship within the triad. The play is a vindication of discipline, and an elevation of the spiritual over the sensual by virtue of its acceptance of that discipline.

It would not be Shakespearean either if it worked at the level of abstract personification. Not only do the triadic characters possess dramatic identities of great vivacity and distinctness, but they, the skeleton, are clad in human flesh. Shakespeare does this by relating to each of them groups of characters out of 'real' life – Antonio and Sebastian as aristocratic 'Calibans', Stephano and Trinculo as plebeian; Ferdinand and Miranda as 'Ariels'; Alonso as a man who sloughs off the 'Caliban' to become an 'Ariel'. The linkage is delicate yet strong and structural. The Calibans are joined by one archetypal crime that threatens bestial anarchy; the Ariels by a readiness to accept discipline and thereby attain ultimate freedom in self-discipline. The groups are differentiated by constant reference to two versions of nature, one cultivated, the other wild; by formality (of speech, music, song, dance, pastime, masque) or travesty of formality. The play leaves no excuse for falling into the sentimentality (freedom is good, the primitive is better than the cultivated, the underdog necessarily superior to his exploiter) so dear to modern sensibilities. Such judgements it is possible from time to time to entertain but the play insists on modification and redress as it fulfills its structure.

The account is still too rigidly drawn. It omits the rigours of Shakespeare's vision which are not all subsumed in the harshness of Prospero's discipline. The play seems to imply a faith in Providence; it seems reasonable to say Christian providence. The language consistently gives it that character. Prospero strengthens the implication by being not merely a recipient of providential aid but by acting on the lives of others in a similar way. And he acts always with a moral purpose, to strengthen virtue and to reform or at least contain viciousness; the virtues are traditional: loyalty, obedience to ordained authority, chastity, self-restraint, love, faith, charity. Yet it is Providence seen imperfectly from the viewpoint of confused humanity. That it exists and operates is not apparent to those that suffer; and even the account rendered by Prospero leaves the identity and nature of Providence uncertain. His magic power, which enables him so to act, is given, not explained, and true Providence is something which is greater and more mysterious than he, since it has acted 'strangely' on his behalf. And though Providence may act in this way in the special circumstances of the play, it cannot be assumed to operate even with this degree of comprehensibility within the context of ordinary living; Prospero's magic powers are relinquished before the return to the world of social commitments. There man must live by his faith or lack of faith in Providence.

The emphasis is indeed not on the security Providence brings to human affairs, but on the responsibility of individuals to merit providential aid.

Prospero's magic solves no problems. It creates situations which amount to ordeals to which individuals respond with the force of their true natures. He may momentarily prevent an evil deed, but he cannot reform an evil man. Nor does he force virtue upon the indeterminate. Each character must find itself through its response to experience. Providence does not help there; indeed it may, for its own purposes, make experience dire and painful. Each man must, like Prospero himself, weather his own Tempest as best he can. Even Prospero can lapse into despair.

The tempest is internal. It is caused not by a simple incompatibility between spirit and sense (to employ shorthand, not to define) but by the danger inherent in both of anarchy. Love is an admirable sentiment; love at first sight may be mere infatuation; it becomes true love only when it has learnt self-discipline. Ariel must earn his freedom, not demand it.

Thus, for all the semblances of assured control and implied security, the play presents a vision of danger; it is strenuous and open-eyed. And yet it is, at the same time, a great positive affirmation.

It is a play that begins in storm and dispersal but ends in fair weather and in unity; begins with seemingly arbitrary rigour but ends in liberation and self-discipline. The keynote is unity – unity not just of people but of everything that makes human existence rich and truly human.

One of the incentives to misinterpret *The Tempest* is its emphasis on discipline. The concept has become discredited in our neo-Romantic age. Shakespeare presents a play which suggests otherwise. Prospero's discipline is recommended by the grim alternatives to it; without it man is a ludicrous, vicious beast. But there are more positive grounds. As presented, it enhances rather than represses vitality. Prospero himself, who is a superman by virtue of the self-discipline he has evolved for himself, has been transformed thereby from a weak and self-indulgent ruler to a man of iron self-control, but his self-discipline has not hardened him. He has decisive energy such as he lacked before, and it emerges, ultimately, in love and charity towards others; he uses it to make possible the restoration, through freely-willed repentance, of erring father to innocent son, to strengthen and confirm the newly-budded love between the children. The dramatic image of his influence is the nature celebrated in the masque; it, like human nature, is most rich and fecund when it has been cultivated. There is no antipathy between this kind of discipline and that kind of vitality and beauty.

Discipline also enhances community. The play ends in reunion and the promise of wider reunion through return to society. The discoveries of the action are not limited to private and cloistered virtues. The experiences have made those who have successfully undergone them not less but more fit to take their places as rulers, counsellors, husbands and wives in ordinary social life. The moral traffic is reciprocal: those who have profited from moral discipline return better equipped for social living; social living is based upon some, at least, of the virtues inherent in moral discipline. Thus the strong impression is conveyed that society itself is a moral structure; capable of distortion of course, of producing villains less pardonable than those whose viciousness is unsophisticated, but nonetheless a moral structure, and the only one, or so the conclusion implies, in which men and women can in any serious sense be said to live and have their significant being. Prospero's discipline, while not directly applied for this end, prepares men for return into a society whose structure reflects the moral values he has helped corroborate. There is no antipathy between his discipline and social living. Nor, one may add, between social living and vitality; the crown of love is not to be achieved until Naples is reached:

> And so to Naples,
> Where I may hope to see the nuptial
> Of these our dear-belov'd solemnized.

– the crown of love is the formal nuptial ceremony.

The Tempest is a play that probes and tests established certainties in the knowledge that they can stand. It embodies a vision that is immensely conservative yet alive; it offers to create no new values. It is Christian by unquestioned assumption, as the unselfconscious and undemonstrative use of language and imagery shows; aristocratic; it demonstrates the need to return to old proprieties temporarily obscured by events and emotions; it is, above all, structured and integrated. It may be an ideal vision rather than a statement of actuality, but it avoids sentimentality by its questioning; it also avoids sentimentality's complement, cynicism at the unattainability in full of the ideal. It portrays human life as potentially a splendid unity of all facets of existence: emotional, spiritual, social, political, religious. Personal joy and vitality, social fulfilment are both essential, and fully compatible, elements in the final harmony; and both are made possible only through the learning of discipline until it becomes self-discipline.

One fairly obvious link between *The Tempest* and *Waiting for Godot* is contained in the working method: Beckett's characters are conceived on much the same lines as Ariel and Caliban. His play opens with one, then two down-and-outs whose bowler hats relate them to the Chaplin tradition and symbolise the degradation of the once-respectable. Similar characters yet soon sharply distinguished: Gogo sensual and gross, impulsive, un-intellectual, greedy, Didi more thoughtful, more literate, more intellectual at least in ambition. The distinction is fixed and clarified by their dramatic emblems: a hat for Didi and boots for Gogo. They also serve to reinforce the feeling of decline. In the modern wasteland which Beckett seems to have introduced us to, thought is no more than an irritant and sensuality is disgusting.

If Gogo and Didi are thus distinguished as, in some terms, the higher and lower elements in modern man, they are also made indissolubly one by those same emblems. For together they make up the costume, suggest the nature, dimensions and way of life of one clownish specimen of humanity.

The relationship between this distinct yet inseparable couple is established in the dialogue and action, but their status in the structure of the play is defined with Beckett's typical economy of means in this passage:[1]

Estragon. (*feebly*) We're not tied? (*Pause*) We're not –
Vladimir. (*raising his hand*) Listen!
(*They listen, grotesquely rigid*)

Their train of thought disrupted, they drift off into inconsequence. Gogo cadges a carrot from Didi, and then the discussion resumes:

Estragon. (*his mouth full, vacuously*) We're not tied?
Vladimir. I don't hear a word you're saying.
Estragon. (*chews, swallows*) I'm asking you if we're tied.
Vladimir. Tied?
Estragon. Ti-ed.
Vladimir. How do you mean tied?
Estragon. Down.
Vladimir. But to whom? By whom?
Estragon. To your man.
Vladimir. To Godot? Tied to Godot? What an idea!... (pp. 19–20)

The emphasis is on 'tied'. It establishes them as creatures who are not tied, tied down, committed to anything or anybody – not even Godot. The word illuminates their relationship in which, although Didi is by and large the dominant personality, there is no fixed supremacy, just a fluctuating, confused partnership on roughly equal terms. A moment later and there is a '*terrible cry*' and Pozzo enters, driving Lucky by means of a rope passed round his neck. We are confronted by a totally opposite relationship; Pozzo and Lucky are tied.

Beckett goes on to amplify the new emblem. Pozzo is a man of material possessions and is committed to a philosophy to suit: class conscious, greedy, with a watch in place of a heart, he represents inhumane pursuit of progress; he is recognisably a visitant from the society in which Beckett's audience lives. Lucky is utterly dominated – the relationship is one of absolute servitude and tyranny. He conveys all that has been sacrificed to the way of life that Pozzo embodies. Once capable of fine speech, of poetry, of dance he is a ruin of intellect, a scarecrow remnant of past joy and alacrity.

Gogo gobbled a carrot, Pozzo guzzles a chicken, thus revealing the full horror of the new relationship. It is one where the Gogo principle is in total control, and the Didi principle in total subjection, where the higher is tyrannised by the lower. But the initial impression of complacent despotism does not survive for long; for Pozzo is as much tied to Lucky as Lucky is to him. He is made insecure by the very debility he has produced in his own slave. His weakness shows when he tries to display profundity of mind:

> Pozzo. . . . Will you look at the sky, pig! (*Lucky looks at the sky*) Good, that's enough. (*They stop looking at the sky*) What is there so extraordinary about it? Qua sky? It is pale and luminous like any sky at this hour of the day. (*Pause*) In these latitudes. (*Pause*) When the weather is fine. (*Lyrical*) An hour ago (*he looks at his watch, prosaic*) roughly (*lyrical*) after having poured forth ever since (*he hesitates, prosaic*) say, ten o'clock in the morning (*lyrical*) tirelessly torrents of red and white light it began to lose its effulgence, to grow pale (*gesture of the two hands lapsing by stages*) pale, ever a little paler, a little paler, until (*dramatic pause, ample gesture of the two hands flung wide apart*) pppfff! finished! it comes to rest. (*Silence*) But – (*hand raised in admonition*) – but – behind this veil of gentleness and peace (*he raises his eyes to the sky, the others imitate him, except Lucky*) night is charging (*vibrantly*) and will burst upon us (*he snaps his fingers*) pop! like that! (*his inspiration leaves him*) just when we least expect it. (*Silence. Gloomy*) That's how it is on this bitch of an earth.
>
> (p. 37)

It isn't just the appalling ineptitudes of style that convince us of the price to be paid for reducing mind to servility, it is the insecurity. Insecurity of tone, insecurity of feeling. Pozzo begins in complacency but ends in generalised melancholy. Being tied to society, being tied in the relationship where matter dominates mind, may produce wealth, power and progress, but also neurotic instability. And mental sterility – a point neatly made by contrasting Pozzo's baldness with Lucky's long white hair.

Meanwhile Beckett had been developing the contrast in other terms. If

Gogo asks for food, Didi gives generously the little he has; Pozzo shares his chicken with nobody. Throughout, Pozzo sustains a level of inhumanity that the others approach only intermittently. Gogo and Didi show sparks of something approaching generosity, compassion, friendship – each tiny manifestation followed by a lapse into its contrary but not cancelled or denied. At least the not-tied manage to retain vestiges of humaneness.

There is little doubt where our sympathies are expected to lie as between the two couples. The splendid curtain to Act I is evidence enough:

(*Estragon gets up and goes towards Vladimir, a boot in each hand. He puts them down at the edge of stage, straightens and contemplates the moon*)

Vladimir. What are you doing?

Estragon. Pale for weariness.

Vladimir. Eh!

Estragon. Of climbing heaven and gazing on the likes of us.

Vladimir. Your boots. What are you doing with your boots?

Estragon. (*turning to look at his boots*) I'm leaving them there. (*Pause*) Another will come, just as . . . as . . . as me, but with smaller feet, and they'll make him happy.

Vladimir. But you can't go barefoot.

Estragon. Christ did.

Vladimir. Christ! What's Christ got to do with it? You're not going to compare yourself to Christ!

Estragon. All my life I've compared myself to him. (p. 52)

We have seen and heard what came out of Pozzo's contemplation of the sky. Something quite different comes out of Gogo's. It is ludicrous, of course, this absurd gesture of generosity, this comparison with Christ; but in the poverty of his existence Gogo is sacrificing almost all he possesses; there is no ridiculous inflation of style; he is at least able to use the words of a true poet, Shelley, with genuine effect. The mood is sincere and it does not lapse into vague melancholy. Gogo is motivated by different feelings. He is responding, in his reference to the moon and to Christ, to a sense of there being something other whose superiority stands as a reproach to his base condition. Gogo, one of the not-tied, expresses what is potentially a fruitful discontent.

It is interesting that it emerges from the body, the senses, the lower of the two partners, not from the mind. Beckett seems to be justifying the near-equality between Gogo and Didi; neither has a monopoly of such impulses, and these, it is clear, are important to Beckett.

Act II elaborates and develops the contrasts established in Act I. If Pozzo yelled, in Act I, 'Coat!', Didi takes his off in Act II to keep the sleeping Gogo warm – and the distinction between inhumanity and humanity is reinforced. When Gogo cries 'God have pity on me!', he shows in more acute form the anguish that marked the ending of Act I, triggered by the same sense of inadequacy. When Gogo and Didi try to imitate Pozzo and Lucky they fail – the brutality is not in them.

Beckett resolutely inhibits any suggestion of progress in humaneness. As in Act I every positive indication is matched with its negative, every move towards possible significance drifts off into pointlessness. There is specifically no cumulation of experience in the not-tied couple; but equally there is no progressive degeneration. Boots hurt, cease to hurt and hurt again, fleas bite, cease to bite and bite again, Gogo and Didi stand and fall and stand again. Their condition fluctuates but remains static. Whereas Pozzo and Lucky have gone into irreversible decline. Lucky now dumb, Pozzo blind and shattered into terrible despair, they come on as a composite symbol of the price of commitment to modern society; they stagger off on a literally blind progress carrying the only wealth they have acquired, a bag of sand. Beckett has completed his contrast between the states of being tied and not-tied.

He seems, too, to have fulfilled a kind of vague promise hinted at in Act I. Near the beginning he dropped the reference to the two thieves on the Cross, in the most dubious of terms, emphasising the shakiness of evidence, the faintness of the possibility that one may, perhaps, have been saved. In my experience the reference resonates for various reasons: it comes out of the blue, without preparation; it is emphasised by Beckett's usual strategy of interruption and resumption; above all it sticks in the mind because the play itself, at that stage, does not supply the pattern it seems to require. Gogo and Didi, the only characters that we have met, do not seem separable in such absolute terms as salvation and damnation. But as Pozzo and Lucky leave in Act II, there can be little doubt that Beckett has provided the necessary pattern. There is no mistaking the damnation of the way of life represented by the tied pair, the one composite thief. We are left watching the other.

Damned or saved? Certainly not damned by Beckett as he damns the other. Yet in what sense could we even contemplate the thought that they might, somehow, be saved? Not in a Christian sense. In the modern wasteland the Bible provides ill-remembered tags, a vocabulary resorted to out of habit; prayer has become a vague supplication, and the image of

God reduced to a Godot, God seen as tycoon. Reference to Godot establishes neither the existence nor the non-existence of a god of any kind, merely this terrible debasement of concept. We are a generation that has inherited scraps, and only scraps, of a once-living faith.

Beckett is not suggesting that that faith was true and that Gogo and Didi may merit salvation by virtue of their obstinate fidelity however debased that may have become. He is merely demonstrating that in those who have not sold themselves into servitude to the modern way of life there can persist a vague, unfocused sense of need for something other than the existence they endure. And that in such people at least the vestiges of humanity have managed to survive. If there is hope, it resides there. Beckett does not commit himself to expressing hope, still less to defining how, if at all, salvation might come. Waiting in hope may itself be the final absurdity. All that is offered is the barest possibility of regeneration. Beckett's play is like a desert. If rain should fall, which is doubtful, dried seeds might flower – but that is doubtful too. One thief may, perhaps, in terms unspecified and unspecifiable, be saved. On the other hand, may not.

Beckett's world is, in every way, a reduction of Shakespeare's. The triad is diminished by the omission of Prospero, Ariel has become Lucky. There is no Ferdinand and no Miranda, no generations (the Boy is no substitute), no family, no marriage. Sex is reduced to orgasm on the gibbet, nature to four or five leaves on a dying tree. Superb poetic rhetoric has become minimal language, delicate lyric the skeletal poetry of leaves and ashes, dance the anguish of the Net.

Shakespeare's play moves from the island back into society. Beckett's play is static because movement can only be from bad to worse. Society is not a significant structure any more but a devastating force for evil. There are no ordinary people out of ordinary life because life has ceased to be ordinary, it has become a grotesque travesty of living. And there is nowhere else to go.

The only energy and power in Beckett's world is invested in Pozzo. In the absence of a principle of significant discipline, Caliban has inherited the earth from Prospero. Caliban stripped of everything that modified Shakespeare's portrait; Caliban turned modern aristocrat, selfish, brutal, without any sense of social or moral responsibility. His power leads not to eventual liberation but to the absolute suppression of human dignity, of all possibility of fulfilment in joy. There is no Prospero to unify Beckett's world because there is, in its presented state, nothing to unify.

Yet that cannot stand as the final word on the play. After all, something does seem to be taking its course. Pozzo fails to usurp power as Caliban did; in his collapse there is an appropriateness that suggests a logic of cause and effect underlying the apparent illogicality. If Beckett is able to identify as clearly as he does the greater attractiveness of one pair over the other, this implies reference to some kind of standard of value. There is something that makes it necessary for Gogo and Didi to go on waiting. And something that impels Beckett to write a play.

The famous preference for an art that would be 'the expression that there is nothing to express, nothing with which to express, nothing from which to express, no power to express, no desire to express, together with the obligation to express' cannot apply to *Waiting for Godot*. Beckett may depict the breakdown of language but he uses it with extraordinary felicity. He mocks bitterly the collapse of great systems of philosophy and religion yet not only has access to them himself but depends for full effect on his audience recognising Heraclitus, St Augustine, Berkeley and Swift. The remarkable symmetry of his play suggests that what is shaped has more significance than what is not shaped. The very act of publishing denotes a faith in communication and in the value of the thing communicated.

Beckett seems to deny these implied positives but they are there in his play. He may present a world that seems void of significance, yet it is not quite a void and it is perhaps not beyond reclamation. So long as Beckett responds to an obligation to express, even though he can give no explanation for the persistence of that obligation, he is in the position of Gogo and Didi, responding to the need to go on. Prospero does not exist in Beckett's play, but he, or a modern counterpart, remains a faint possibility. Beckett's acrid contempt for life, his bitterness and austere disgust may well be oblique indications that, like Gogo and Didi, he is waiting for Prospero.

For all its differences, Ibsen's *Rosmersholm* stands in relationship to both *The Tempest* and *Waiting for Godot*, as an early warning of the catastrophe recorded by Beckett. For in *Rosmersholm* a great crack begins to split the unity of Shakespeare's world. It can be identified through Prospero.

In *The Tempest* Prospero humanised Providence and showed it to be mindful of the individuality of those it worked upon. In *Rosmersholm* Prospero has become an institution, Rosmersholm itself; and this thing, supplanting that man, no longer concerns itself with the individual. It imposes itself upon its sons, demanding obedience without regard to aptitude or inclination – one must serve the State, another the Church, by rote, not by vocation. As a result its disciplinary force is inert and does not liberate, nor does it promote joy and vitality. It kills happiness.

It is true that Ibsen continues to see conjunction between this Christian tradition and society as Shakespeare did, but with a damaging shift of emphasis. In *The Tempest* society seemed to reflect the values that emanated from the divine origin of the universal structure; in *Rosmersholm* Christianity has come to reflect the values of society. Rosmer's religion in itself is of no concern to Kroll or Mortensgård; it matters only insofar as it serves as a weapon in the war of political parties, as a weighty expression of support for one social prejudice or another. In Shakespeare religion subsumed society, in *Rosmersholm* it has been reduced by assimilation into it. Thus religion and society work in unison but as a deathly alliance of frustrating power.

Ibsen's response to his own assessment is not to despair for liberation, for joy and vitality or for values by which life might take on dignity, purpose and meaning. If Prospero exerts power with a dead hand, and society cooperates, there is still Caliban. Ibsen exalts the primitive untouched nature over Nature. Since cultivation through the only disciplines available means death to vitality, he turns to a woman identified with flowers and birchtwigs, lonely bird-rocks and northern storms for an alternative. Rebekka West is Ibsen's Caliban – virtual murderess, incestuous, wildly passionate and subversive of the settled state of things – yet defined by imagery and action as the one source of free energy and thus of beauty in the play. And she has this quality by virtue of having grown up entirely outside the system.

There is the great fissure. Not only has Ibsen reversed Shakespeare's values but he has defined, as a prime characteristic of modern life, that unity is no longer a possibility. Men can no longer achieve their fullness as human beings within a society that reflects a universal structure. There is no structure; society must be fought against. The old values are dead and the individual must take up the burden of fighting endlessly to define new and living values out of his own creative moral imagination.

But even that process cannot, even in prospect, restore a sense of fullness to Ibsen's world, because for him energy and vitality, a capacity for joy, are not enough. Rebekka's qualities are superb but destructive. They need to be married to something which only society, for all its abominations, can generate – what might be called the social affections of love, gentleness, concern for others. Ibsen shows his respect for these in his sympathetic portrait of the social product, Rosmer. Fullness of life demands that these be joined to vitality; yet he demonstrates that they cannot be. Not, at least, in life. Thus where Shakespeare's play ends with a return from the isolation of the island to society, Ibsen's ends with departure from society into the ultimate isolation of an intensely private death. Only there can Rosmer and Rebekka achieve the essential union of their different virtues, the traditional and the individual.

The sense of loss and regret is strong in the play; it shows in comparison with *The Tempest* as sterility. Rosmer is listless and unfruitful, the last of a worn-out line, marriage is possible only in death with no hope of off-spring, the ending is not liberation but suicide, the messenger of Providence is not Ariel but the White Horse. Yet Ibsen retains much of Shakespeare's vision that Beckett has rejected. In his own terms he is as aristocratic in outlook, though it is aristocracy of spirit not of rank that he celebrates. He retains to the full a sense of the importance and dignity of human existence. His characters must inhabit a jarring world governed by a terrible process of inescapable cause and effect which threatens to destroy all autonomy. And yet, without the support of systems and structures, and without that common sense of value that systems can provide, they can still insist on shaping their own destinies on the assurance of no more than the impera-tives of their own moral promptings. Rosmer and Rebekka have no Prospero to guide them, but they guide themselves.

Ibsen's faith in individual vitality and its actions is a difficult one because the positives cannot be readily assessed against the unmistakeable negatives. Rosmer and Rebekka die; to understand what their decision means to them requires sympathetic understanding of evidence that must remain subjective. It is easy to see why Strindberg, so close in time to Ibsen, lost that faith.

Unlike *Rosmersholm*, Strindberg's *Ghost Sonata* can be directly linked to *The Tempest*. In his *Letters to the Intimate Theatre* he wrote:[2]

The Tempest is considered Shakespeare's last play . . . It is almost as if he had begun living on the other side, and has tried to depict a better world as man has conceived it in his dreams; He feels the end approaching; he is about to wake from the instructive dream that is called life . . . That is really how it is when one gets on in life; if one looks back at what one has lived through, it is so terrible one hardly believes it is real, and the best that had a sort of reality slowly dissolves as if it were smoke. Is it strange if one begins to doubt the reality of reality? In *The Tempest*, Shakespeare has in several places emphasized that life is a dream and has tried to dramatize this Buddhist idea . . . Shakespeare . . . ends his career with a regained certainty about the highest matters – that is faith! In this beautiful work of art Shakespeare as usual has not excluded what is ugly but on the contrary has given it a major place. That is Shakespeare's philosophy and poetics – one that I have followed. (pp. 202–5)

When Strindberg writes about himself, in private letters of about the same time (March and April 1907), he uses almost identical terms.

What has saved my soul from darkness during this work has been my religion (= Anschluss mit Jenseits). The hope of a better life to come; the firm conviction that we live in a world of madness and delusion (illusion) from which we must fight our way free. For me things have become brighter, and I have written with the feeling that this is my last sonata! . . . for a long time I have placed my hopes on 'the other side'.

And yet when Strindberg describes aspects of *The Tempest* (again in *Letters to the Intimate Theatre*) it is in a fashion that reveals the great gulf between his play and Shakespeare's, 'The gentle, conciliatory tone; the innocent love affair in which the young people are tested and resist temptation . . . Shakespeare's farewell to his public, in which he thanks them and ends with a prayer . . . The plot is, briefly, that Ferdinand meets Miranda and, after tests, gets her.' In Part II of *A Blue Book*, Strindberg describes Prospero as 'the old man who, grieving because he was helpless about doing anything for himself, wanted to teach his children how to win the sort of happiness he had thrown away'.[3] Strindberg's dependence on *The Tempest* is clear. *The Ghost Sonata* is about an innocent love affair between boy and girl and ends in a prayer; one of the key words in Strindberg's text is 'test'; Hummel is the old man seeking happiness for the younger generation. But Strindberg does not seem to recognise that he has inverted the play to which he responds so intimately. His tone is the opposite of gentle and conciliatory; the Young Student does not win the Young Lady; and the old man Hummel is not the hero but the villain.

Indeed the *Ghost Sonata* is as it were the photographic negative of Shakespeare's picture of life. The universe it depicts does not display a benign and providential, all-embracing system of discipline. Strindberg strews his stage with the corpses of Shakespeare's certainties. Society is no longer a significant structure. Even at the simplest, sociological level it is in a state of flux. Aristocrat depresses the working class, the working class takes its revenge on the aristocrat; the Colonel's household is tyrannised by the Cook, he himself is humiliated and disgraced by the *nouveau riche* Hummel. Worse than that, aristocracy itself is a mere sham: the Colonel is no Colonel, a Baron is no Baron, a daughter is no daughter, wealth is borrowed money. The institution of the family is no longer a microcosmic representation of universal order and decorum but of universal chaos: family life is a stagnation that rots and corrupts those imprisoned within it. Marriage is a mask for adultery. No wonder that Strindberg represents life in society as a dumb-show within a play, presented by a Mephisto-pheles/Hummel. Living in a society that offers no help to man for achieving a significant and dignified fulfilment of his best qualities, Strindberg's characters are ghosts of Shakespeare's. Miranda has dwindled into the sick Young Lady, Ariel into the dumb apparition of the Milkmaid, Ferdinand into the hectic yet oddly inactive Student. Trial and testing do not strengthen, they destroy; young lovers meet but the boy never gets his girl. Significantly the only characters who are enlarged in Strind-berg's conception are the Cook, a Stephano who defies all restraint, and Hummel.

Hummel represents Strindberg's sense of the one striking, not positive, product of modern society, its energy. *The Ghost Sonata* is not without its representative of discipline. Hummel is that. But it is a discipline founded upon materialistic and naturalistic assumptions: wealth, possessions, social influence, the inevitable and logical sequence of cause and effect constitute its apparent strength. Hummel represents discipline without any moral basis or moral end. His energy manifests itself in blackmail, coercion, murder of innocence, vindictiveness. He is Strindberg's great repre-sentative of the kind of power possible in his, as distinct from Shake-speare's, kind of world, but it is Caliban in the seat of authority, not Prospero, Satan not God. Small wonder that, where Shakespeare's play ends with the return from the island to life in full society, Strindberg's ends with the departure from society to the Island of the Dead.

Yet clearly this is not the whole of Strindberg's vision. As in *The Tempest*, so in *The Ghost Sonata*, there is evidence of the power of the spirit to surmount the awful condition of man. Hummel is not invincible; he is made to pay for his sins, the Milkmaid and the Mummy can destroy him; there is 'the other side' to be looked to, a heaven that is a haven. *The Ghost Sonata* is a statement of regained Christian faith as well as a state-ment of despair for life on earth.

It is precisely at this point that the most difficult questions arise in relation to this play. In *The Ghost Sonata* the power of the spirit is greatly circumscribed. As a dramatic presence the Milkmaid is, in comparison with Ariel, passive, pallid, intermittent and voiceless. She acts, but only to destroy, not to liberate. And the same is true of the Mummy. Towards the end of Act II, when she suddenly begins to speak in normal human tones, it looks as though Strindberg is presenting us with a person who has come through trial and tribulation to a restored human dignity. But Act III shows this not to be the case. There we see, in the inner room, the Mummy and the Colonel; they sit motionless; they do not converse. They are still ghosts; the Young Lady must still die; the great defeat of Hummel testifies only to the power of spirit to destroy evil, not to liberate joy and vitality. These remain impossibilities in the conditions of our terrible existence.

There is, however, still a heaven. It would be impertinent to question the sincerity of Strindberg's personal beliefs, but not to examine their dramatic presentation and its implications. In Shakespeare's play, characters become fit for society, which is the earthly embodiment of heavenly harmony, by virtue of their active response to ordeal. They have to prove themselves. The Young Lady is incapable of such active proof. She does not stand up to ordeal, she succumbs to it. She is admitted to Strindberg's heaven not because she has strenuously confronted trial but because she is young and beautiful. Her innocence is not a positive virtue forged in the knowledge of evil but the innocence of inexperience. Strindberg's heaven makes no demands; there is no indication of what we must do to be saved, no sign of an aiding grace extended towards struggling humanity. And if Strindberg cannot link his concept of heaven to a concept of a kind of life that might lead to heaven, equally he cannot define heaven itself in positive terms. It is significant that he describes it through privatives: it is a haven for a girl who is 'unhappy, guiltless, blameless'; it is a place where 'the sun does not burn', 'a home without dust', where one is greeted by 'friends without fault' and 'love without blemish'. Strindberg is defining heaven as simply that which the earth is not.

In terms of dramatic presentation the same thinness is perceptible. Heaven is created out of a white radiance, a humming harp, a picture, a hymn and an invocation, all at the very end of the play. The attempt is strenuous but sudden, unprepared.

In crude terms, Strindberg's heaven looks like a desperate assertion rather than a statement of secure faith. Though his play is shot through with references to the Bible and prayer-book, and though he conceives his young hero as a modern Christ, the emphasis is on Christ's suffering in this madhouse of a world, not on the triumph he wrung out of ordeal. Appropriately the symbol of spiritual power, of spiritual hope, that dominates Act III is the large figure of a Buddha. That is what Prospero has become in Strindberg's world; not an active, purposeful force for liberation, but a still, contemplative statue.

The Tempest, Rosmersholm, Ghost Sonata and *Waiting for Godot* are distinguishable in form, but such differences should not conceal the connections between them. Obviously changes in form indicate changes in vision, but not necessarily so. By his loss of Ibsen's faith, however qualified, in human autonomy, by the nightmare insignificance of his version of human life, modified by a slender belief in distant and doubtful salvation, by the slenderness of such implications as are conveyed by his writing a strictly organised play about a lunatic world, Strindberg represents a move further away from Shakespeare in Beckett's direction. It is a critical development not definable in terms of form alone. Chekhov shares his sense of listless impotence, Pirandello his scepticism about the status of reality. For all their external dissimilarities Ibsen and Strindberg between them help to define the point at which one kind of response to modern life begins to take shape in many forms, and Beckett provides what is to date its most fully developed expression. It is perhaps not inappropriate to define it as a feeling that, for us, the modern generation, 'Our revels now are ended'.

Social environment and theatrical environment: the case of English naturalism

RAYMOND WILLIAMS

THREE SENSES OF NATURALISM

There are three relevant senses of 'naturalism', and of the associated 'naturalist' and 'naturalistic'. The first, and most popular, indicates a method of 'accurate' or 'lifelike' reproduction. The second, and historically earliest, indicates a philosophical position allied to science, natural history and materialism. The third, and most significant in the history of drama, indicates a movement in which the method of accurate production and the specific philosophical position are organically and usually consciously fused.

The first sense began in English around 1850, mainly in relation to painting and especially landscape painting. Thus: 'the mannerism of the Italians, and the naturalism of the Flemish painters' (1852)[1]; 'the Gothic naturalism advancing gradually from the Byzantine severity' (1853)[2]; 'the Naturalist-landscape school, a group of painters who threw overboard the traditions of Turner' (1893)[3]. There was a common association of such a method with simplicity of attitude – 'a naturalism without afterthought' (1850)[4] – and, through the association with 'nature' and 'natural', of subject.

The second sense was already more generally established. It began in the late sixteenth century in a form of conscious opposition, or at least distinction, between revealed (divine) and observed (human) knowledge, and was used in close association with accusations of atheism: 'atheists or men . . . who will admit of nothing but Morality, but Naturalismes, and humane reason' (1641)[5]; 'those blasphemous truth-opposing Heretikes, and Atheisticall naturalists' (1612)[6]. With growing confidence from the seventeenth through to the nineteenth centuries it acquired the more positive associations of a method and practice and body of knowledge, in natural history and the natural sciences. 'Naturalist' in this sense became neutral, but 'naturalism' was still a doctrine in which there was appeal to and reliance on natural laws, forces and explanations, as distinct from and eventually consciously opposed to 'supernaturalism', and also in which, in matters of morality, there was appeal to and reliance on human reason and a (secular) natural law.

The third sense, in specific application to a particular kind of novel or play, and thence to a literary movement, appeared in French in the late 1860s and is common in English from the 1880s. Its relations with the two earlier senses are complex. On the one hand its conscious linkage of literary method with scientific method and with the laws of natural history was sharp, distinct and at times aggressive. On the other hand, in very general tendencies in fiction and drama before this period, many steps in this linkage had been practically taken. The link between painting and science had been made by Constable:

Painting is a science, and should be pursued as an inquiry into the laws of nature. Why, then, may not landscape painting be considered as a branch of natural philosophy, of which pictures are but the experiments?[7]

This was indeed the landscape-painting which had attracted the apparently simple technical term 'naturalist'. More generally, since the early eighteenth century, in plays and novels, there had been a practical reliance on a secular human dimension, in action, description and interpretation. Bourgeois literature, with increasing confidence, was in a distinguishing sense, by comparison with earlier literature, secular and social; an explicitly or implicitly metaphysical dimension was steadily and in the end without argument excluded. This is particularly evident in the drama, most clearly in bourgeois tragedy (from Lillo, *The London Merchant*, 1731), with its consciously secular, contemporary, social and socially extended emphasis, but it had many seventeenth-century precedents in prose comedy and in isolated examples of what would later be called 'domestic drama'. Within this powerful general movement towards a predominantly secular and social literature, many elements of 'naturalism' became habitual, but the conscious description awaited one further emphasis, in which the key term is 'environment'. It is one thing to present character and action in exclusively secular and social terms. It is or can be quite another to see and to show character and action as determined or profoundly influenced by environment, either natural or social. The novelty of the naturalist emphasis was its demonstration of the *production* of character or action by a powerful natural or social environment. This is radically distinct from exemplifications of 'permanent' human characteristics in an accurately reproduced natural or social 'setting'. The intellectual basis for the new emphasis is then a sense of historical production, both in the social sense that character is determined or profoundly influenced by its social environment, with the later and more penetrating observation that this social environment is itself historically produced, and in the wider sense of natural history, in the evolution of human nature itself within a natural world of which it is an interacting part. The theory of naturalism, in fiction and drama, is then a conscious presentation of human character and action *within* a natural and social environment. It is a specific culmination of a long tendency of bourgeois theory and practice. It only ceases to be bourgeois (and then, strictly, ceases to be naturalism) when, as in Marxist theory, action is seen not only within an environment but as itself, within certain limits and pressures, producing an environment.

Relations between the first and third senses of 'naturalism', in descriptions of works of art, are then inevitably complex. In popular and semi-professional usage naturalism means no more than accurate or lifelike reproduction of a character, an action or a scene. In a stricter historical use naturalism is an artistic method in which a particular environment is reproduced, of course as accurately and fully as possible, not because it is an observed feature but because it is a causal or symptomatic feature. Naturalism in the first sense is a general product of a bourgeois secular tendency, with its preference for a practical and recognisable everyday world. Naturalism in the third sense is the extension to art of the philosophical positions originally described as 'naturalism', in a conscious reliance on observed natural history and on human reason. Dramatic naturalism in the first sense can be plausibly related, but with complications that we shall notice, to developments in the means of production of physical theatrical effects. Dramatic naturalism in the third sense can never be so reduced, since it does not reproduce a physical feature or environment because it is technically available or interesting, but because such features and environments are integral parts of the dramatic action, indeed, in a true sense, are themselves actors and agencies.

It is a curiosity of dramatic history that naturalism, in the third sense, was relatively weak in England, by comparison with France, Scandinavia and Russia. Indeed, paradoxically, it was only after naturalism in the first sense had been modified that there were significant naturalist plays, in the third sense, in English. This is at first sight very surprising, since the intellectual movements which led to conscious naturalism were especially strong in England. The purest doctrine of the production of character by environment was that of Robert Owen, from as early as 1815. The most influential exponent of natural history as the production of human nature was, of course, Darwin. If anywhere, it might then seem, conscious naturalism would be developed it would be in England, and indeed the case can be positively argued in the development of English painting and the English novel. In the drama, however, the case is quite otherwise, and the specific reasons for this need careful examination.

PHYSICAL REPRODUCTION IN THE THEATRE

Limited to the first sense of naturalism, the history of 'lifelike' reproduction on the English stage has often been traced. It is worth looking at the main elements of this history, both for their own sake and for the light they throw on the limitations of any merely technical definition of naturalism.

'The modern stage affects reality infinitely beyond the proper objects of dramatic representations', complained an observer in 1827.[8] This was no sudden development. The indoor theatres, from the Restoration, had developed more and more complicated and effective types of painted scenery, but in the turn from the eighteenth to the nineteenth century there was a further decisive change. This can be summarised as the development of the 'set scene' from the system of scenic mobility which had dominated the eighteenth-century theatre. A crucial element in this was the steady reduction and eventual abolition of the apron-stage. This, together with the elaboration of backcloths and profiles as an alternative to moveable flats and wings, made the stage at once more integrated, more static and more enclosed. It was not until much later in the century, after prolonged controversy about the old kind of proscenium doors, that the fully enclosed picture-frame stage was established. The first was perhaps the Gaiety of 1869, but a description of the new Haymarket, in 1880, makes the point:

A rich and elaborate gold border, about two feet broad, after the pattern of a picture frame, is continued all round the proscenium, and carried even below the actor's feet. There can be no doubt the sense of illusion is increased, and for the reason just given; the actors seem cut off from the domain of prose; there is no borderland or platform in front; and, stranger still, the whole has the air of a picture projected on a surface.[9]

The whole development thus achieved points forward, certainly, to major features of the naturalist drama: in particular its specific central feature of the stage as a room. It points forward also, interestingly, to film and television drama: 'a picture projected on a surface'. Yet the dramatic intentions within this development have an ambiguous relation to naturalism. Vestris and Mathews, at the Olympic between 1831 and 1838, were perhaps the first to develop the drawing-room stage, and a reviewer noted that the 'more perfect enclosure gives the appearance of a private chamber, infinitely better than the old contrivance of wings'.[10] Moreover, in a further innovation, these rooms were fully furnished, including floors and 'walls'. But the plays performed in them, usually adapted French short comedies, were hardly concerned with the 'lifelike', and a sense of luxury rather than accuracy seems to have been the main staging motive. The wider development of technical means for more 'realistic' production is at an even greater distance from naturalism. Indeed, in all its early phases, technical innovation was primarily for spectacle. It is often asserted that naturalistic staging owed much to the introduction of gas-lighting, which was getting into theatres by 1820. Yet the main use of the new lighting was for new spectacular effects, such as sunrise dispersing early mist. Indeed one of its most powerful applications, burning lime in a gas-jet to produce limelight, became almost synonymous with a new kind of spectacle, and was extensively used in the development of melodrama. Perhaps the most interesting, because intermediate, case is the development of technical staging for historical productions and in particular for the staging of Shakespeare. Elsewhere the new means of production made for increased spectacle; here, while spectacle remained as an intention, there was also an emphasis on 'correctness' of setting. This is evident as early as Planché's work for Kemble in the 1820s and is best known from Kean's 'antiquarian' productions in the 1850s. The interest in 'historical accuracy', and its intended priority over what Kean distinguished as 'theatrical effect',[11] has something genuinely in common with elements of naturalism. What is intended is a *reconstructed* environment, and, as in the case of the historical novel, with its formative effects on the novel of social realism, this is a transitional phase towards the presentation of a specific physical environment as symptomatic or causal. Nevertheless, the very sense of historical reconstruction, looking backward, characteristically, to more splendidly clothed and furnished times, worked in the opposite direction, against the contemporary environment outside the theatre, which was to be a decisive influence in naturalism.

It was in the 1870s that the fully enclosed box-set began to be used to replace wings, flats and back-cloths, in close relation, of course, to the fully enclosed picture-frame stage. This provided a technical means for one of the central conventions of naturalism: the stage as an enclosed room. Yet even in this development, as in technical developments throughout the century, dramatic intentions remained variable. Spectacular illusion was as common as naturalistic illusion; or, to put it another way, even the motive for much naturalistic illusion was spectacular: the impressive reproduction of a 'real' environment, for its own sake rather than as an integral dramatic agency. This allows us to recall that in the theatre as in any other area of cultural technology, the doctrine of technological determinism – the creation of a form seen as determined by technical development; naturalism as the consequence of improvements in stage-carpentry – is false. And this in turn allows us to see the distinction, so decisive in the history of the drama, between naturalism as a technique among others, a particular staging effect among other varieties of spectacle, and naturalism as a dramatic form, in which the production or reproduction of a social environment, symptomatic or causal, is not just the setting for an action but is part of the action itself.

CHANGING SOCIAL RELATIONS IN DRAMA AND THEATRE

One dimension especially excluded by merely technical accounts of the development of naturalism is that of social relationships in the theatre. This is an especially significant exclusion in the case of English nineteenth-century theatre, where the changes in social relationships, in the course of the century, were radical.

We can distinguish three periods: that before 1830; from 1830 to 1860; and from 1860 to 1914. In the first period there was a completion of the long process, traceable from around 1700, in which the theatre moved back towards a more popular audience. This is not, in spite of some accounts, the entry of the 'mob' into the theatres. On the contrary it was the narrowing of the theatre audience which preceded this movement, from the 1620s to the 1690s and reaching a point of extreme class selectivity in the Restoration theatre, which was the novel phenomenon. In the course of the eighteenth century the audience broadened again, as well as increasing. In 1600 there had been some six successful theatres in London; in 1700, after the narrowing of the Restoration, there were only two. By 1750 there were again seven theatres in London, and a growing number of established theatres in the provinces. This process is usually summarised as the return of the middle class to the theatres. But social classes are not immortal, and the new eighteenth-century playgoers were in fact a new class: the greatly extended middle and lower-middle class of the developing cities: in a modern sense, a bourgeoisie. Until the end of the eighteenth century this was much more evident in London than elsewhere, for it was there that the explosive growth of a new kind of city had begun. By the beginning of the nineteenth century this urban bourgeoisie and petit-bourgeoisie had in effect taken over the London theatres, and a similarly 'popular' audience had become the mainstay of the multiplying provincial theatres. Many of the internal changes in theatre structure – the pit driving back the apron stage, the conversion of upper galleries to boxes – were directly related to this at once growing and changing audience. The Old Price riots at Covent Garden in 1809 are only the most striking among many manifestations of these class tensions and changes. 'Polite society', as it called itself, was in effect first invaded, then driven from the pit to boxes, then driven out altogether. This made the tension between the monopoly patent theatres, established under Restoration conditions to restrict serious drama to minority audiences, and the so-called 'minor theatres', pushing up every-where, using every device and exploiting every ambiguity of definition, very much more severe. In the period before 1830, 'minor theatres' such as the Lyceum, the Haymarket and the Adelphi were only nominally distinguishable from the old patent theatres, Covent Garden and Drury Lane, while south of the Thames, especially at Astley's and Surreyside, the 'transpontine theatre', more open, more popular and more spectacular in style, was serving new audiences.

The inevitable happened. A repeal of the monopoly legislation passed the House of Commons in that classic year of middle-class triumph, 1832, but was thrown out by the House of Lords. In 1843 the law was finally changed. Covent Garden, in 1847, became an opera house, with a more fashionable audience. Drury Lane became the centre of spectacles. The majority development of the English theatre went on in the middle-class theatres, which grew from seven in 1800 to nineteen in 1850. Astley's became the Royal, Surreyside the Olympic. In outlying districts new large theatres were opened, and from the 1840s the music-halls began their extraordinary development, both taking over variety from the minor theatres which had now moved up to drama and providing newly organised entertainment for the vastly growing population of the city. London had grown from just over a million to over two and a half millions in the first half of the century. The industrial cities now followed the same patterns.

In this period, between 1830 and 1860, the theatre, like the press and publishing, became open, varied and in its own forms vigorous. It could have gone in any of a number of ways.

What actually happened in the third period, after 1860, is again characteristic of general developments in the culture. There was an even faster rate of growth, but new dividing lines appeared between the 'respectable' and the 'popular', and at the respectable end there was an integration of middle-class and fashionable audiences and tastes. This integration, decisive in so many areas, had marked effects in the theatre. The 'popular' audience was now, in the new terms of an urban industrial society, largely working-class and lower middle-class, but on the whole they were not in the theatres, except on special occasions; they were in the music-halls. In the theatres what was happening was the process usually described as making theatre 'respectable' again: a process which included putting carpets and seats into the old pit; serving more discreet refreshments; altering times to fit with other social engagements. In the Restoration theatre there had been early afternoon performances, for the Court and its circle. Through the eighteenth century the time was steadily moved towards the evening, when people could attend after business and work. Early nineteenth-century performances usually began at six and went on four or five hours: an entire night out at the theatre. From the 1860s the time was moved to eight o'clock, and the performance ended at about eleven: largely to allow for dinner and supper engagements on either side. Matinées came in, for a new kind of leisured audience. What we now think of as West End theatre was established.

This social change must be remembered within the impressive statistics of growth. The whole point of the newly respectable integration was that it offered to be self-recruiting; it was socially inclusive, at a given level of price, taste and behaviour, rather than categorically exclusive, as in an older kind of society. London grew from the two and a half millions of mid-century to six and a half millions by 1900. Internal transport, in railways, omnibuses, and eventually the underground both increased possible audiences and permitted the physical concentration of theatres. From the 1860s an extraordinary wave of building, rebuilding and refurnishing began. In 1850 there had been nineteen theatres; in 1900 there were sixty-one, as well as some forty music-halls. What we think of as the modern theatre and its audience – though it is not modern, since it pre-dates cinema, radio and television which were to cut it back again – had been more centrally and more solidly established than at any other time, before or since.

MELODRAMA

It is in relation to these connected social factors – changes in audiences and physical changes in the theatres – that we can begin to consider the development of dramatic forms. The first important problem, in a way just because it seems to be at the opposite pole from naturalism, is the case of melodrama which, at least in the first half of the nineteenth century, can be reasonably claimed to be the only significant formal innovation. Yet melodrama is an especially difficult 'form' to define.

Some elements of its development are clear. The original 'melodrama' – mime to music in France, dialogue intermissions with music in opera in Germany – was not widely imitated in England, and where it was, usually passed under other names, connected with other precedents. By the time that it was recognised as a form in England its connection with music was little more than incidental or indeed tactical (one of the effects of the restriction of 'legitimate' drama to the patent theatres was to encourage the minor theatres to describe plays as anything but plays; if the inclusion of a song or a mime would do the trick with the Licensing Office – the Lord Chamberlain – then managers and authors would try it). What really came through, under this title, was a new kind of sensational drama, with close connections with the popularity of the Gothic novel. Monk Lewis's *The Castle Spectre* (1797) is an early English example, among a flood of similar imports from Germany (especially Kotzebue) and France. If we correlate this development with the changes of audience already noted, we can see connections between the replacement of sentimental comedy by melodrama and the replacement of a relatively restricted and 'polite' audience by a more open and more vigorous 'popular' audience. Yet within this, and also overriding it, are more complex elements. In France the melodrama, in the sense of sensational drama, had become overtly political during the Revolution, especially in the 'Bastille' plays (Pixérécourt). These sensational plays of prison, tyranny and liberation became popular in adaptation in England, but their political element was excluded, in the period of danger before 1830, when censorship of a conscious political kind was extensive. The English 'prison' melodrama then became more purely sensational. A certain radicalism, nevertheless, was inseparable from all English popular culture between about 1820 and 1850; a close correlate was the new kind of Sunday paper, combining sensation, scandal and radical politics. Much of the subsequent development of English social drama, with obvious effects on the case of English naturalism, was affected by this linkage and by its many contradictions and ambiguities. On the one hand, within the restrictions imposed by the status of the minor theatres, there was a constant pressure on authors to avoid more traditional dramatic forms, and the internal habits of these theatres, trained to action and to spectacle rather than to sustained dialogue, increased this. While it is still a question of the simple sensational drama there are no difficult analytic problems. Indeed in one sense this was the heir of Renaissance drama, in most of its external elements, but with the supernatural losing its metaphysical dimension, and the exploring moral and social energy declined to stereotypes: a process most evident in the reduction of dramatic language to rhetoric and stereotype, carriers of the shell of the action, the living body dead inside it. Yet from the 1820s onwards there was a discernible attempt to put new content into this sensational form. This is the attempt at once recognised and exaggerated by the description 'radical melodrama'.

The significant case is that of Douglas Jerrold. He had made his name in 1829 with *Black-Ey'd Susan*: melodrama in the simple transitional sense: a plot of innocence in danger, of miraculous rescue, tied, characteristically, to a ballad (Gay's), and with some marginal consciousness of the poor man (the sailor) as exposed and victimised. It is significant that then, in 1832, Jerrold wrote two plays, *The Rent Day* and *The Factory Girl*, which were quite open attempts to dramatise a new social consciousness. *The Rent Day*, which has survived, is again transitional. Based on a picture by David Wilkie, which the opening tableau directly reproduces, it is a 'domestic drama' in which a farm-tenant suffers from an absentee landlord and a cheating steward: in this sense radical but assimilated to an older consciousness and an older kind of play. The absentee landlord, initially taken as the representative figure gambling away his rents, has returned in disguise to see what is happening; he exposes the dishonest steward. Thus the actual social tension, which was especially acute in the period when the play was written, is at once displaced – the agent substituting for the landlord as villain – and sensationalised, in that through the magic of disguised and providential authority a happy ending to what had in fact no ending is contrived. *The Factory Girl*, which we know only by report, has many features in common, but what happened to it is, in its way, a significant moment in nineteenth-century culture. This account is taken from the contemporary *Figaro in London*:

Writers like Mr Jerrold deserve our gratitude as well as our admiration, for their aim is not merely to amuse, but to plead, through the medium of the stage, the cause of the poor and oppressed classes of society. Such is the author's object in *The Factory Girl*, in which he has drawn with lamentable truth the picture of a weaver's lot, which is to be the slave of the inhuman system of overworking in English factories, and too often a victim of the petty tyranny of those who are placed in authority over him . . . The story has interest and incident which would with the general good writing throughout the piece, and the quaint satirical humour of Harley's part, have carried off *The Factory Girl* triumphantly had it not been in some degree marred by the dénouement, in which letters were pulled out of bosoms, a labourer finds a brother in a rich merchant, and an extensive relationship is discovered among the principal characters. This comfortable arrangement for a happy ending naturally excited a smile which gave to the ill-natured a plea for sending forth their venomous breath in loud blackguard shouts of 'off'. . .¹²

This can be read in more than one way: as confirming the tendency, as in *The Rent Day*, to solve the insoluble by the devices of the sensational drama; as evidencing an audience which was becoming critical of this; or, with the specification of the 'ill-natured', as an example of the cross-pressures of the period. The play was taken off after two nights and never printed. There may be many reasons, but the contrived ending is not likely to be one of them, since it was, indeed, standard practice. Jerrold himself was sure that it was the new theme of the victimised industrial worker which made the play unpopular.

It is now some six years since the writer of this paper essayed a drama, the purpose of which was an appeal to public sympathy in the cause of the Factory Children: the drama was very summarily condemned . . . The subject of the piece 'was low, distressing'. The truth is, it was not then *la mode* to affect an interest for the 'coarse and vulgar' details of human life, and the author suffered because he was two or three years before the fashion.¹³

He refers to the subsequent success, in such subjects, of a 'lady writer', presumably Frances Trollope. The terms in which *The Factory Girl* was attacked may remind us of the arguments that raged around naturalism in the 1880s. Yet the history, again, is complex. There was nothing in the new naturalist or realist drama of the 1880s which, in terms of the vulgarity of low life or of the violence of events, was new to the English nineteenth-century theatre, and especially to the melodrama. There had been a long run of crime plays, from the stories of Maria Marten and Vidocq (both dramatised by Jerrold in the 1820s) through *The Factory Assassin* (Rayner, 1837), with a falsely accused mute, to the 'detective' plays beginning with Taylor's *The Ticket-of-Leave Man* – the appearance of the archetypical Hawkshaw – in 1863. Mayhew's *London Labour and London Poor* was dramatised, with the sub-title *Want and Vice*, at the Whitechapel Pavilion in 1860. Plays of city poverty and orphanage, including many adaptations of Dickens, were commonplace. In *Lost in London* (1867) a miner's wife was abducted by a wealthy Londoner, and there were scenes of contrast between Bleakmore Mine and a London champagne party. In Charles Reade's *It's Never Too Late To Mend* (1865) an actress dressed as a boy died on a meticulously staged treadmill (incidentally provoking a critic to get up in the theatre and shout 'Brutal realism' – one of the earliest examples of what was to become a standard phrase[14]). Sexual or at least marital scandals were common after the success of *East Lynne* (1861) and *Lady Audley's Secret* (1862), the latter including a scene of the wife hitting her husband with an iron bar and pushing him down a well, though he reappears in the final scene. Moreover, to look at it another way, there was a certain radicalism in many of the most popular melodrama plots: wicked landlords seduced the daughters of tenants, foreclosed mortgages, turned mothers and children into the snow; wicked officers and other wealthy young men did their best to emulate them. It is possible, from these examples, to speak of the radical melodrama, with close connections to other elements of the new urban popular culture. What has then to be observed is a paradox: that elements of the social and moral consciousness which was to inform serious naturalism went mainly, in England, into the melodrama, which at the same time preserved, as the foundation of its conventions, providential notions of the righting of wrongs, the exposure of villainy, and the triumph or else the apotheosis of innocence. At the same time, as we shall see, the more naturalistic presentation of scenes, characters and actions moved in general away from themes based in a radical consciousness. The result was a muddle. Melodrama touched every nerve of nineteenth-century society, but usually only to play on the nerves and to resolve crisis in an external and providential dramatic world. Its methods became a byword for sensational exaggeration, against which the more blurred and muted tones of English domestic naturalism made their way with the false reputation of a more essential truth. But this is not simply an internal history of the forms. The changes already noted in the social character of the theatre, after 1860, including especially the split between a 'respectable' drama and 'popular' entertainment, prevented, on either hand, the emergence of any sustainable adequate form. Melodrama, which in its own way had got nearest to the crises of that dislocated, turbulent and cruel society, became, in the end, no more than sensational presentation and then, inevitably, a mode to be patronised or mocked.

DOMESTIC NATURALISM

It is orthodox to date the appearance of English naturalism from Robertson's *Caste* (1867), or perhaps the earlier *Society* (1865). But it is again a matter of definition. It is indeed a world away from melodrama. A preliminary definition might be comedy of manners with a consciously social topic. But then this does not begin with Robertson. Bulwer Lytton's *Money* (1840) is an obvious earlier example. Its plot involves the familiar scheming for an inheritance, and the readjustments of all the finer feelings after it is known where all the money has gone. In fact to come to *Money* after *The Plain Dealer* or *The Way of the World* is to feel a certain continuity, though its language and incident are firmly contemporary. Or take Jerrold's *Retired from Business* (1851), in which a greengrocer retires to the country and is persuaded by his wife, as a matter of prestige, to change his name from Pennyweight to Fitzpennyweight. The anxious snobbery of this (suburban) country society is mocked in the character of Creepmouse, who at any mention of the actual world can exclaim:

Pumpkinfield is threatened with revolution. Retail marriage menaced at our firesides, and property barricaded with its own hearthstones.[15]

To go from Bulwer Lytton or Jerrold to Robertson's *Society* is hardly to feel the breeze of innovation. The plot is a standard account of the *nouveaux riches* trying to buy their way into fashionable society, and making the conventional coarse errors. In minor ways it is a nineteenth-century world: one of the Chodds' schemes, to acquire influence, is to start a newspaper, or rather two newspapers: the *Morning* and the *Evening Earthquake*. In the end, after scheming and counter-scheming, Chodd Junior rejects 'blue blood' and would 'rather have it the natural colour'.[16] But this does not prevent the play ending with the triumph of the impoverished barrister as Sir Sidney Daryl, Member of Parliament:

Countrymen, &c, wave hats – band plays, &c.[17]

Caste extends the social reference. An aristocratic officer courts the daughter of an unemployed and drunken workman; she is an actress. This outrages his mother, the Marquise. The girl, left with his child, becomes poor when he is reported killed in India and her father has spent the money left for her. But D'Alroy resurrects, the Marquise is reconciled, and the old workman, the only embarrassment, is pensioned off to drink himself to death in Jersey. Of course remarks are made about the silliness of 'caste' feeling when compared with the claims of true love, but to go from *Caste* or *Society* to the pushing world of mid-Victorian England, with its ready conversion of business fortunes into peerages, its movement of actresses into the old aristocracy, to say nothing of the general triumph of the new social integration of 'respectability', is to perceive a theatrical convention as impervious as anything in melodrama. It can then be said that the difference is the 'naturalness' of the dialogue, and it is true that the writing of *Society* and *Caste*, and for that matter of *Money* and *Retired from Business*, can be sharply contrasted with the exclamatory and incident-serving dialogue of, say, *Lady Audley's Secret*. In fact what is principally evident is a developed colloquialism at all but the critical points. Yet this again is not a novelty: *The Ticket-of-Leave Man*, slightly earlier, has more sustained colloquial speech, with less edge of caricature, within its 'melodramatic' plot. (Indeed it is an irony that the only words widely remembered from the play are the detective's, on emerging from disguise: 'Hawkshaw, the detective', which became a comic catch-phrase. The speech of most of the play is the most sustained 'naturalism', in the popular sense, in the English nineteenth-century theatre.)

What then is new in Robertson? It is naturalism in the most technical sense: that of the 'lifelike' stage. There were, as we have seen, precedents for this, in Vestris and Mathews and in the 'archaeological' productions. But Robertson fixed the form, in the new theatres and the new staging of the 1860s. The changes in the social character of the theatre helped him: single-play evenings, at the new later hours; longer runs. The technical means had only to be brought together, in an integrated production of an 'enclosed' play. It is in this exact sense that it is true to say that Robertson invented stage-management, and indeed invented the modern figure of the producer or director, impressing an overall atmosphere and effect. Styles of acting were modified to fit into this general effect, and the plays, in a real sense, are scripts for these productions, in a way that has since become very familiar. Robertson's detailed stage-directions are the most obvious evidence of this kind of integrated production, and the motive is undoubtedly, as in all technical definitions of naturalism, the 'appearance (illusion) of reality': 'the ivy to be real ivy, and the grass to be grass matting – not painted'.[18] In local ways these effects of environment are intended to be symptomatic: 'holding out kettle at arm's length. Hawtree looks at it through eyeglass', in a familiar contrast of social habits.[19] But the informing consciousness is always illustrative, and naturalism of this kind is properly described in terms of 'setting' or 'background'. The distinction that then matters can be explored by comparing this kind of reproduction of a known and recognisable environment with the superficially similar production of a symptomatic or causal environment in high naturalism: for example, the room and the garret beyond it in Ibsen's *The Wild Duck*; the trapped interior of Strindberg's *The Father*; or the social presence and social history of the orchard in Chekhov's *The Cherry Orchard*. It is not only, though it is also, a matter of dramatic reach and scale. It is a question of a way of perceiving physical and social environment, not as setting or background through which, by other conventions, of providence, goodwill, freedom from prejudice, the characters may find their own ways. In high naturalism the lives of the characters have soaked into their environment. Its detailed presentation, production, is thus an additional dramatic dimension, often a common dimension within which they are to an important extent defined. Moreover, the environment has soaked into the lives. The relations between men and things are at a deep level interactive, because what is there physically, as a space or a means for living, is a whole shaped and shaping social history. It is characteristic that the actions of high naturalism are often struggles against this environment, of attempted extrication from it, and more often than not these fail. The pre-naturalist conventions of providential escape or of resolution through recognition fall away in the face of this sombre assessment of the weight of the world: not a world which is a background, nor an illustrative setting; but one which has entwined itself in the deepest layers of the personality. It is this practice which makes sense of Strindberg's argument:

Naturalism is not a dramatic method like that of Becque, a simple photography which includes everything, even the speck of dust on the lens of the camera. That is realism; a method lately exalted to art, a tiny art which cannot see the wood for the trees. That is the false naturalism, which believes that art consists simply of sketching a piece of nature in a natural manner: but it is not the true naturalism, which seeks out those points in life where the great conflicts occur, which rejoices in seeing what cannot be seen every day.[20]

There is room for confusion, here, between 'naturalism' and 'realism', especially since later distinctions, of a comparable kind, have usually reversed the terms. But the central point is evident, and the reference to 'conflict' clarifies it. This view of a shaping physical environment and a shaping social environment is the intellectual legacy of the new natural history and the new sociology of the nineteenth century. Whatever the variations of subsequent attitude, among individual dramatists, this absolute sense of real limits and pressures – in physical inheritance, in types of family and social relationship, in social institutions and beliefs – is common and preoccupying. To produce these limits and pressures, in actually staged environments, was the common aim of the varied and brilliant period of dramatic experiment which this sombre consciousness provoked. Even where, eventually, the struggles and conflicts became internal, as in early expressionism, they were still between the physical limits and pressures of a shaped and shaping natural and social world, and the determined sense of a self, a possible self, which could try to get beyond them, though it usually failed.

It is hardly necessary to say that, set beside high naturalism, what became known as naturalism in the English theatre, after Robertson, is of another and much smaller dimension. But to follow the argument through we must look at what happened after Robertson, in the confident theatres of late Victorian and then Edwardian society.

NATURALISM AND THE PROBLEM PLAY

The key to an interpretation of the development of English drama between Robertson and the end of the century is the social character of the West End theatre, newly established in this form in the same period. Its audience, as we have seen, was not 'aristocratic' or even 'fashionable'; it was an integrated middle-class audience, in what was now at once a metropolitan and an imperial capital. But then, as in other areas of the culture of the period, and especially in those closely dependent on institutions (from parliament and education to the theatre) the dominant tones were those of an assumed and admired class: 'Society'. This is a radically different situation from theatres with a direct court or aristocratic linkage, notably the Restoration theatre, in which actions, audience and writers were, however narrowly, socially integrated. In the late Victorian theatre, to put it crudely, a largely middle class audience was spellbound by an image of 'fashionable Society'; the theatres were among the principal agencies for its display. Dramatists such as Henry Arthur Jones, originally a commercial traveller with a nonconformist upbringing, or Pinero, a legal apprentice and then an actor, were not of this displayed class but, like other theatre people, serving it and, as agents of the image, making their way into it. It is striking evidence of the prepotence of the display form that Jones and Pinero did not, as might have been supposed, succeed in writing bourgeois drama but what it was agreed to call 'Society drama'. It was not that they did not briefly try. Jones's *Saints and Sinners* (1884) grafted the problems of nonconformist dullness and respectability on to the old melodrama plot of the innocent girl seduced by a villainous officer and, though rescued, dying of a lost reputation. Pinero, in a late play, *The Thunderbolt* (1908) moved away from London society to a provincial (brewing) middle-class family; the play was found to be drab. In what was now overwhelmingly a bourgeois commercial society, the displacement represented by 'Society drama' would be almost incredible, were it not for the special character of the institutional cultural integration. It is instructive to go from Jones's *Saints and Sinners* to Stanley Houghton's *Hindle Wakes* (1912), not only because Houghton has moved into a bourgeois manufacturing world, but because Fanny Hawthorn, formal successor to the long line of compromised innocents (she has gone to Blackpool with the son of a rich manufacturer) refuses her conventional fate: he is not man enough for her to marry, she has had a good time and now she will make her own way. It is a generation later, of course, but the more significant difference is that the play developed and was produced outside the special atmosphere of the London theatre, in Miss Horniman's Repertory at Manchester. In its refreshing note of self-confidence it illuminates, by contrast, the extraordinary cultural subordination of the earlier bourgeois dramatists.

There is nothing difficult in the diagnosis of 'Society drama' as a form. It is the intrigue play moved up-stage, with strong scenes for display. What is more interesting is the interaction of this form with what became known as the 'problem play', for this is a crucial question in the matter of naturalism. Jones and Pinero, in their drawing-room plays, to some extent muted and blurred – or to put it another way, simplified and naturalised – the detail of the intrigue play. At the same time they developed characteristic intrigues to the status of 'problems': notably the old plot of the lady with a 'past'. The problem, here, was one of moral judgement, and there was an obvious loosening from the rigidities of, say, *Lady Audley's Secret*. The best-known example is Pinero's *The Second Mrs Tanqueray*, in which the problem is directly discussed. Tanqueray's first wife, a virtuous woman who also, it is suggested, 'kept a thermometer in her stays and always registered ten degrees below zero'[21] has insisted on a convent education for her daughter, before she dies. Tanqueray's second marriage is to a woman, Paula, whose 'past' is known to him: a succession of unmarried affairs. The problem of 'respectability' is then posed at two levels: the conventional prejudices of his circle against the second Mrs Tanqueray, including their fears about her influence on the daughter; second, the explosive situation in which the daughter falls in love with one of her stepmother's former men.

Paula tells the truth and kills herself. The daughter wishes she had 'only been merciful'.[22] It is a strongly emotional play, but it is the interaction of 'intrigue' and 'problem' that is significant, and that is significantly unresolved by the form. The sensational coincidence of the daughter falling in love with one of the stepmother's young men remains within the orbit of the intrigue drama, though one can easily see that, taken straight, it could lead directly to issues of relationship, including sexual rivalry and jealousy, which the major naturalist drama was exploring. It is not so taken, though the hint is there, and some of the ground has been laid for it, in the last scene of confrontation. On the other hand the generalised 'problem' is of a quite different kind. All the right questions are asked: do not men have 'pasts'; is not prejudice often hypocritical; even, are there not connections between respectability and frigidity? The points go to and fro, but of course that whole discussion is blown to pieces by the actual event, when the abstract question enters an intractable area of primary relationships. What happens is then a compromise, with neither the relationship nor the problem carried through.

Indeed the general character of the 'questioning' in the problem plays of Society drama is in the end strictly suggestive. The basic reason is that the conventions, alike of the structure of feeling and of the form, are restricted to the uneasy terms of the social integration. No sense of any life or any idea beyond the terms of this displayed society can be dramatically established; not even any strictly bourgeois viewpoint, since this is overlaid and compromised by the preoccupation with 'Society' (there is markedly less frankness about money, for example, than even earlier in the century). English naturalism, in this first phase, could then, inevitably, be no more than a technical matter.

Some breaks came. As in most other European situations, a new kind of drama needed a new kind of theatre audience. Virtually all the important new work in European drama of this period was done in breakaway independent theatres, based on a minority audience which separated itself at once from its own class and from the 'theatrical' integration. In England this minority was already large, in other fields, but in the theatre it was slow to organise: The Dramatic Students (1886), the Independent Theatre Society (1891), the Stage Society (1899). But it was through these organisations that different work came into the theatres: Shaw's *Widower's Houses* at the Independent Theatre in 1892; the *Plays Pleasant and Unpleasant*; and ultimately the Vedrenne-Barker régime at the Court Theatre between 1904 and 1907. By the last ten years before the war a different kind of

English drama had an independent base, though the West End continued to be dominated by Society drama (Sutro, Hankin, early Maugham) and, even more, by musical comedy.

Was this then, even if late, the period of English naturalism, in the most serious sense? In a way, yes. The plays of Galsworthy (*Strife*, 1909 and *Justice*, 1910) have a new breadth of reference and concern, and are specifically naturalist both in the technical sense and in the sense of a conscious correlation between character and environment. Barker's plays (*The Voysey Inheritance*, 1905, and *Waste*, 1907) are highly developed naturalism, in the technical sense, though their themes belong more to the anti-romantic, exposure-of-respectability, strain than to any positive naturalism. It is a significant but limited achievement, and the main reason for this is that Shaw, who most consciously adopted the naturalist philosophical standpoint, and indeed whose expositions of it are more conscious and explicit than those of any of the major naturalist dramatists, chose, for tactical reasons connected with the predominant styles of the orthodox theatre, to work mainly with old forms and then to alter them internally. In some plays, *Widowers' Houses*, *Mrs Warren's Profession* and the later *Heartbreak House*, the material is transformed; the last under the direct influence of a genuinely original naturalist form in Chekhov. But the main thrust of Shaw's drama is a sustained and brilliant polemic, in both plays and the significantly ancillary prefaces, within the terms of the established Society drama and the associated romantic intrigues, historical reconstructions and even the earlier melodrama and farce. It is unquestionably the most effective body of drama of the period, but it never attempted, in any sustained way, the specifically naturalist conjunction of philosophy and form, and it was supported in this by the reaction against naturalism which was already evident in the avant-garde theatre elsewhere. For of course high naturalism, as a form, itself broke down, under the tensions of its own central theme: the interaction of character and environment. To go more deeply into the experience of the self consciously trapped by environment the new subjective expressionism of Strindberg was already necessary. Also, to see environment actively – not as a passive determining force, but as a dynamic history and society – needed the new and more mobile conventions of social expressionism. Shaw has connections with the second of these tendencies, though significantly none with the first, and this must be seen as a reason for his actual development. But another reason is the prepotence of the theatrical forms then current within the special case of the English (London West End) theatre.

To trace the subsequent development of English naturalist drama is beyond the scope of this essay. We can only briefly note the extraordinary revival of naturalist drama in the theatre of the mid- and late-1950s, and its extensive and dominant transfer into television drama. We can also add that the persistence of a limited technical sense of naturalism has allowed many people, including especially directors and writers, to claim that they have abandoned, 'gone beyond', naturalism, when it is clear, on the one hand, that the great majority of plays now produced, in all media, are technically naturalist, and, on the other hand, that many 'non-naturalist' plays are evidently based on a naturalist philosophy: not only character and environment but the 'scientific' sense of natural history and especially physical inheritance. What remains to be emphasised is the special character of the social basis of theatre in England since the changes of the 1860s. It is significant that in centres other than London a different kind of drama has been evident. I have already given an example of the work at Manchester. Even more significant is the case of the Irish drama, which in spite of the very different preoccupations and influence of Yeats, produced in Synge's *Riders to the Sea* an especially pure naturalist tragedy, in his *Playboy of the Western World* a significantly localised naturalist comedy, and in O'Casey's early plays, for all their difficulties, work which belongs in the mainstream of European naturalist drama. A final example is of a negative kind: D. H. Lawrence, in his early writing years, worked consistently and sometimes successfully in a kind of naturalist drama, with a quite different social base and with a language significantly revitalised by contrast with the terms of the middle-class problem plays. *The Widowing of Mrs Holroyd*, in spite of limitations which he overcame when writing the same experience in the more flexible form of narrative, would also take its place in a European mainstream, and more work might have followed, but for the fact that, in the special conditions of the English theatre, he could not get his plays produced and so came to rely, as generations of English writers had done before him, on the more open medium of print.

CONCLUSION

The special conditions for the limitation and lateness of English naturalism are then reasonably clear. Some of these conditions indeed still exist in parts of the English theatre, though television has bypassed them. What remains for reflection is the very difficult question of the relations between naturalist method and what can still be distinguished, though the labels are often changed, as naturalist world-views and structures of feeling. The specific fusion of method and structure which we know historically as high naturalist drama has always to be seen in these terms, but it also, quite as much as the fashionable London theatre, had its specific historical conditions. The question about other forms of such a fusion, both actual and potential, remains central in the history of twentieth-century drama, and it is made very much harder to ask, let alone to answer, if, in loose ways, we go on describing naturalism as if it were only a set of techniques. English naturalism, in its very limitations, provides, in its real history, ample evidence against that. It also provides evidence for what is still the central inquiry: into the formation of forms and, which is another way of saying the same thing, into the relations between forms and social formations, crucial everywhere in art but in the drama always especially central and evident.

Notes

FOLK PLAY IN TUDOR INTERLUDES

1 C. R. Baskervill, 'Dramatic aspects of medieval folk festivals in England', *Studies in Philology* XVII (1920), 19–87; see also *Modern Philology* VIII (1908), 257–69; XIII (1916), 557–60; XXI (1924), 225–72. E. K. Chambers, *The Mediaeval Stage* (2 vols. Oxford, 1903), I, and *The English Folk Play* (Oxford, 1933 repr. 1969).

2 *Munimenta Academica*, ed. H. Anstey (2 vols. Oxford, 1868), I, 18.

3 See Keith Thomas, *Religion and the Decline of Magic* (London, 1971) chs 2 and 3; C. Phythian-Adams, 'Ceremony and the citizen: the communal year at Coventry, 1450–1550' in *Crisis and Order in English Towns 1500–1700*, ed. P. Clark and P. Slack (London, 1972), pp. 57–85.

4 Details from Chambers, *Med. Stage*, II, Appendix ; W. A. Mepham, 'Medieval drama in Essex', *Essex Review* LV (1945), 135–6; and from unpublished churchwarden's accounts for Bishop's Stortford, Saffron Walden and Great Dunmow.

5 Printed by Sydney Anglo, 'An early Tudor programme for plays and other demonstrations against the Pope', *Journal of the Warburg and Courtauld Institutes* XX (1957), 179.

6 *Rymes of Robin Hood*, ed. R. B. Dobson and J. Taylor (London, 1976), p. 4.

7 See *Norfolk Archaeology* IX (1884), 145–7.

8 George Gilpin, the Elder, *The Bee hiue of the Romishe Church* . . . (London, 1579) quoted in Karl Young, *The Drama of the Medieval Church* (2 vols. Oxford, 1933), II, 538.

9 See C. R. Baskervill, *The Elizabethan Jig* (Chicago, 1929, repr. New York, 1965), pp. 3–39.

10 H. M. Shire and K. Elliott, 'Pleugh song and plough play', *Saltire Review* II:6 (1955), 39–44. See also my discussion in *European Drama of the Early Middle Ages* (London, 1974), pp. 40–2.

11 *Itinerarium Cambriae* I:2, quoted in Chambers, *Med. Stage*, I, 189.

12 See Chambers, *Med. Stage*, I, 279; Axton, *European Drama*, p. 162.

13 Guidhall Letter-book I, fol. ccxxiii, quoted in *A Book of London English 1384–1425*, ed. R. W. Chambers and M. Daunt (Oxford, 1931), pp. 96–7.

14 See J. F. Szwed, 'The mask of friendship', in *Christmas Mummings in Newfoundland*, ed. H. Halpert and G. M. Story (Toronto, 1969).

15 p. 43. See also her 'Marlowe's *Dr Faustus* and the Eldritch tradition', in *Essays on Shakespeare and Elizabethan Drama in Honor of Hardin Craig*, ed. Richard Hosley (Univ. of Missouri, 1962), pp. 83–90.

16 *The Poems of William Dunbar*, ed. W. Mackay Mackenzie (London, 1932), pp. 170–4.

17 Mikhail Bakhtin, *Rabelais and his World*, trans. H. Iswolsky (Cambridge, Mass., 1968), pp. 257–63. See my discussion of the *Feuillée* in *European Drama*, pp. 144–58.

18 Seán Ó Súilleabháin, *Irish Wake Amusements* (Cork, 1967), p. 124.

19 On the place of these pieces in the earliest English drama see my 'Popular modes in the earliest plays', in *Medieval Drama*, ed. Neville Denny (Stratford-upon-Avon Studies 16, London, 1973), pp. 13–39.

20 Quotations from the Robin Hood plays are from W. W. Greg's texts in the Malone Society *Collections* 1:2 (Oxford, 1908), 117–36.

21 See P. Happé, 'The Vice and the folk-drama', *Folk-Lore* LXXV (1964), 161–93; Axton, *European Drama*, pp. 195–204.

22 I quote Copland's edition (*c.* 1560–62) from the Tudor Facsimile Text of *Youth*, ed. J. S. Farmer (London and Edinburgh, 1908).

23 *Fulgens and Lucres*, ed. F. S. Boas and A. W. Reed (Oxford, 1926). David Bevington makes a similar point in his 'Popular and courtly traditions on the early Tudor stage', in *Medieval Drama*, ed. Denny, pp. 99–101.

24 *Four Elements*, ed. J. S. Farmer (T.F.T., 1908).

25 *Thersites*, ed. J. S. Farmer (T.F.T., 1912).

26 The first extant play with prose seems to be Medwall's *Nature* (*c.* 1495? printed *c.* 1530). Among lost romantic plays (see Baskervill, *MP* XIV) is William Cornish's *Troilus and Pander* (1516).

27 Spanish quotations are from Fernando de Rojas, *La Celestina*, ed. D. S. Severin (Madrid, 1969). Early translations from the Spanish are reviewed by G. J. Brault in his *Celestine: a Critical Edition of the First French Translation (1527)* (Detroit, 1963). The author of the English interlude used a Spanish text (see H. D. Purcell, 'The *Celestina* and the *Interlude of Calisto and Melibea*', *Bulletin of Hispanic Studies* XLIV (1967), 1–15). Grüninger woodcuts for an early edition of Terence reappear as illustrations of the Toledo *Comedia de Calisto* in 1523. The interlude and Mabbe's complete prose translation of 1631 are conveniently printed together in H. Warner Allen, *Celestina, with an Interlude of Calisto and Melibea* (London, 1908).

28 See G. Ungerer, *Anglo-Spanish Relations in Tudor Literature* (Schweizer anglistische Arbeiten XXXVIII, Berne, 1956), 11.

29 Entries in the *Stationers Register* show that Elizabethan England knew play versions of the Spanish lovers. The debt in extant plays seems rather to its continental successors in romance than to *Celestina* itself.

30 *Calisto and Melebea* (MSR, Oxford, 1908).

31 *Early Middle English Verse and Prose*, ed. J. A. W. Bennett and G. V. Smithers, 2nd edition (Oxford, 1968), no. XV.

32 *Ibid.*, no. VI.

33 *European Drama*, pp. 22–30.

34 *Shakespeare's Festive Comedy* (Princeton, 1959), p. 12.

35 *The Sir Thomas More Circle* (Urbana, Illinois, 1959), p. 342.

36 *Calisto*, lines 129–36. This may be provocative humour at More's expense (it was

in 1528 that Bishop Tunstall licensed him to read heretical books). *Cf.* Thersites's 'vyage to olde purgatorye' (A4v).

37 Ed. J. S. Farmer (T.F.T., 1908).
38 Does Infidelity perhaps also have horns, goat-feet, and a phallus, like the dancing woodcut figure reproduced by M. Murray, *The God of the Witches* (London, 1931), Plate 11?

THE TUDOR MASK AND ELIZABETHAN COURT DRAMA

1 *Inigo Jones, the Theatre of the Stuart Court* (2 vols. London, 1973), I, 13.
2 *Old Arcadia* Bk 1; the text is from *The Poems* ed. William Ringler (Oxford, 1962), p. 20.
3 Sir Thomas Eliot, *Dictionary* (London, 1538), p. 111.
4 The challenge is in BM MS Harley 69 fol. 5v; a descriptive poem (STC 3543) survives: *Here begynneth the iustes of maye parfurnyssed & done by Charles Brandon*, [n.p. 1507].
5 Edward Hall, *The Union of the Two Noble & Illustre Famelies of Lancastre & Yorke* (London, 1550) b4. The 1548 first printing was issued without an index.
6 *The Great Chronicle*, ed. A. H. Thomas & I. D. Thornley (London, 1938), p. 372.
7 Hall, *The Union*, h5.
8 *Calendar of State Papers: Henry VIII*, ed. J. S. Brewer *et al.* (21 vols. London, 1864), II Pt 1, III, 117.
9 John E. Stevens, *Music & Poetry in the Early Tudor Court* (London, 1959), p. 411.
10 *Great Chronicle*, p. 371.
11 'The evolution of the early Tudor mask', *Renaissance Drama 1968*, ed. S. Schoenbaum (Evanston, 1968), pp. 7-8.
12 *Ibid.*, p. 7.
13 Polydor Vergil, *De rerum inventoribus* (London, 1546) k7v.
14 See my essay 'Robert Dudley & the Inner Temple revels', *Historical Journal* XIII (1970), 365-78.
15 'Drama as offering: the princely pleasures at Kenelworth', *Rice Institute Pamphlet* XLVI (1960), 59.
16 Unperformed masks for a cancelled meeting with Mary Stuart are edited by W. W. Greg in Malone Society *Collections* I:2 (Oxford, 1908), 144-8.
17 *Documents Relating to the Office of Revels in the Time of Queen Elizabeth*, ed. Albert Feuillerat (Louvain, 1908).
18 *Calendar of State Papers: Spanish 1558-67*, ed. Martin S. Hume (London, 1892), pp. 404-5.
19 Thomas Pound, Bodley MS Rawlinson Poet 108 fols. 33, 35.
20 *English Civic Pageantry* (London, 1971), p. 35.
21 John Nichols, *Progresses of Queen Elizabeth* (3 vols. London, 1823), I. Nichols reprints the two rare pamphlets: [Robert Laneham] *A Letter* [London] (1575); George Gascoigne, *The Princely Pleasures at Kenelworth* (1576).
22 R. Kimbrough & P. Murphy, 'The Helmingham Hall manuscript of Sidney's *The Lady of May*: a commentary & transcription', *Renaissance Drama 1968*, pp. 103-19; quotations are from this transcription.

23 Gilbert Talbot's letter to the Earl of Shrewsbury establishes the itinerary and the year of Dudley's Buxton letter. He writes from Charing Cross on 3 May 1578 that Elizabeth plans to visit Wanstead that month and alerts Shrewsbury that Dudley will visit Buxton later that summer; two letters dated '15 May 1578, Wanstead' confirm that Elizabeth, Dudley and Burghley were in residence that day; Dudley's letter dated '8 July, Buxton' confirms Talbot's information. See *Illustrations of British History* (2 vols. London, 1791), II, 171; *Calendar of State Papers, Foreign: Elizabeth (1577–83)*, ed. Arthur J. Butler (London, 1901), pp. 685–6, 689–90.

24 BM MS Additional 15891 fol. 53.

25 As Stephen Orgel suggests in *The Jonsonian Masque* (Cambridge, Mass., 1965), p. 50. Apart from this point, however, we differ in our interpretation of the entertainment.

26 Stevens, *Music and Poetry*, pp. 408–9.

27 (London, 1598), A1v.

28 trans. H. Rackham, Loeb Library (Cambridge, Mass., 1932), p. 13.

29 Feuillerat, *Elizabeth*, p. 287.

30 Henry Goldwell, *A Briefe Declaration of the Shews Performed Before the Queenes Maiestie and the French Ambassadours* [London, 1581].

31 *The Shepheardes Calender* in *The Works* ed. C. G. Osgood (8 vols. Baltimore, 1943), I, 74.

32 *Nugae Antiquae*, ed. Henry Harington (London, 1779) II, 136–7.

33 BM MS Additional 46367 fol. 103.

34 BM MS Harley 787 fol. 88.

35 BM MS Additional 15891 fol. 127v.

36 *The Complete Works*, ed. R. Warwick Bond (3 vols. Oxford, 1902), III.

COMIC FORM IN BEN JONSON

1 'To Ben Johnson uppon occasion of his Ode to Himself' in *Ben Jonson*, ed. C. H. Herford and Percy and Evelyn Simpson (11 vols, Oxford, 1925–52), XI, 335. All quotations from Jonson are taken from this edition, which is referred to in subsequent footnotes as 'HS'.

2 *Epistolae Ho-Elianae*, 1645, in HS XI, 417; (but see E. B. Partridge on Jonson's thought, in *The Elizabethan Theatre* IV, ed. G. R. Hibbard, 1974).

3 *Every Man out of his Humour*, III.vi.207; *Volpone*, Dedication to the Universities.

4 Ray L. Heffner, jr, 'Unifying symbols in the comedy of Ben Jonson' (1955), in *Ben Jonson*, ed. Jonas A. Barish (Englewood Cliffs, N.J., 1963).

5 Cf. L. C. Knights, *Drama and Society in the Age of Jonson* (1937).

6 See HS II, 89–93; *The Alchemist*, ed. F. H. Mares, (1967), pp. xxxi–xl; also: John Read, *The Alchemist in Life, Literature and Art*, (1947); E. J. Holmyard, *Alchemy*, (1957); and Lynn Thorndike, *A History of Magic and Experimental Science* V–VI (New York, 1941) (esp. V, 532ff., 617ff.; VI, 238ff.); Hiram Haydn, *The Counter-Renaissance* (New York, 1950); Marie Boas, *The Scientific Renaissance, 1450–1630* (1962).

7 *Every Man out of his Humour*, IV.viii.166–73; *The Magnetic Lady*, I.vii.5–16, IV.viii.27–31; cf. Marvin T. Herrick, *Comic Theory in the Sixteenth Century* (Urbana, 1964), ch. iv.

8 *Every Man out*, Induction, 256–9; *Discoveries*, 2643–53.

9 Heffner (n.4, above), p. 146.

10 *Plutus*, 123–97.

11 Cf. Coburn Gum, *The Aristophanic Comedies of Ben Jonson* (The Hague and Paris, 1969).

12 *Utopia*, Temple Classics, pp. 109–10; see Francis G. Allinson, *Lucian, Satirist and Artist*, (1927); H. A. Mason, *Humanism and Poetry in the Early Tudor Period*, (1959), pp. 59–73.

13 HS II, 50–3; cf. Mario Praz, 'Ben Jonson's Italy', in *The Flaming Heart* (New York, 1958).

14 *Timon*, 14 (in *Lucian* II, Loeb Library, trans. A. H. Harmon, 1915); Erasmus's trans. in *Luciani Opuscula* (Venice, 1516), fol. 65v.

15 Erasmus, fol. 64; *Timon* 8 (also 21, 42, 45, 54); see also HS IX, 687; Harry Levin, 'Jonson's Metempsychosis' (1943), in *Jonson: 'Volpone'*, ed. Jonas A. Barish (1972), p. 89.

16 Cf. M. C. Bradbrook, '*The Comedy of Timon*', in *Renaissance Drama* IX, 96–7.

17 See n. 15.

18 *The Jew of Malta*, III.v.4.

19 HS II, 58.

20 *Drama and Society*, p. 202.

21 *Utopia*, Temple Classics, pp. 155–61.

22 Henry Cornelius Agrippa, *Of the Vanitie and uncertaintie of Artes and Sciences* (1531), trans. J. Sanford (1575), fol. 157; see Thorndike, *History of Magic*, V, 127–38.

23 See *Dialogues of the Dead* V (Plutus and Hermes).

24 See HS X, 87–9; Edgar Hill Duncan, 'Jonson's *Alchemist* and the literature of alchemy', *PMLA* LXI, (1946); cf. Agrippa, *Vanitie*, pp. 158–159

25 E.g. *Love Restored*, 1612; *The Golden Age Restored*, 1615; *Mercury Vindicated from the Alchemists at Court*, 1616.

26 Bacon, *Works* (ed. Spedding, Ellis and Heath) III, 284–90; see HS XI, 273–4.

HE THAT PLAYS THE KING

1 John Ford, *The Chronicle History of Perkin Warbeck*, ed. Peter Ure, The Revels Plays (London 1968), p. 11. All subsequent quotations from the play refer to this edition. The dates given for all English plays are those suggested in *The Annals of English Drama*, ed. A. Harbage, revised by S. Schoenbaum (London 1964). Many are only approximate.

2 Thomas Dekker, *The Whore of Babylon*, in *The Dramatic Works of Thomas Dekker*, ed. Fredson Bowers (Cambridge 1955), II, 497, 499.

3 See my essay 'The king disguised: Shakespeare's *Henry V* and the comical history', in *The Triple Bond*, ed. Joseph G. Price (Pennsylvania and London, 1975), pp. 92–117.

4 Philip Massinger, *The Emperor of the East*, in *The Plays and Poems of Philip Massinger*, ed. Philip Edwards and Colin Gibson, (Oxford 1976), III. (1.1.18–22, 52–57, 64–78).

5 John Ford (?), *The Queen*, ed. W. Bang, *Materialien zur Kunde des älteren Englischen Dramas* (Louvain 1906), I, 257–9, 257.

6 All quotations from Shakespeare refer to *The Riverside Shakespeare*, ed. G. Blakemore Evans *et al.* (Boston 1974).

7 Thomas Middleton, *The Mayor of Queenborough*, in *Thomas Middleton*, ed. Havelock Ellis, The Mermaid Series (London 1890), II (1.2). *Nobody and Someody*, ed. J. S. Farmer, (Tudor Facsimile Texts) (London 1911) G1.

8 Dekker, *Sir Thomas Wyatt*, in Bowers, I (1.2.13–18, 31–2).

9 C. V. Wedgwood, *Oliver Cromwell and the Elizabethan Inheritance*, (London 1970).

10 Sir Anthony Weldon, quoted in *Portraits in Prose*, ed. Hugh Macdonald (London 1946), pp. 20–4.

11 Jonas Barish, '*Perkin Warbeck* as anti-history', in *Essays in Criticism* XX, 168.

12 Philip Edwards, 'The royal pretenders in Massinger and Ford', in *Essays and Studies* (1974), p. 34, 25.

13 See Ure, p. lxxvii. There is also a perceptive account of Ford's complex handling of audience expectations in the chapter on *Perkin Warbeck*, in Tucker Orbison's *The Tragic Vision of John Ford*, Salzburg Studies in English Literature (Salzburg 1974).

14 Massinger, *Believe As You List*, ed. Edwards and Gibson, (IV.4. 74–5).

15 K. M. Lea, 'Sir Aston Cokayne and the "Commedia dell' Arte"', *Modern Language Review*, XXIII (1928), 48.

16 Sir Aston Cokayne, *Trappolin Supposed a Prince*, in *The Dramatic Works of Sir Aston Cokayne*, ed. J. Maidment and W. H. Logan (Edinburgh 1874), pp. 151, 173.

17 J. W. (Gent.) *The Valiant Scot* (London 1637) E4v.

18 William Cartwright, *The Royal Slave* (London 1639) B2v, B4, G3v, D3v.

19 Compare the incident at E2v with Clarendon's account of the character of Charles I in *The History of the Rebellion*, 695–8. (World's Classics selected edition, ed. G. Huehns, Oxford 1955, p. 318).

20 Quoted in Leslie Hotson, *The Restoration and Commonwealth Stage* (Cambridge, Mass. 1928), p. 40.

MEDICINABLE TRAGEDY

1 The most recent studies of *Samson Agonistes* have not confirmed the speculative dating of the drama in the period 1647–53. See Anthony Low, *The Blaze of Noon* (New York, 1974), pp. 222–7; William Kerrigan, *The Prophetic Milton* (Charlottesville, 1974), pp. 201–2; Edward LeComte, *Milton's Unchanging Mind* (Port Washington, 1973), pp. 37, 45–7; Hugh M. Richmond, *The Christian Revolutionary: John Milton* (Berkeley, 1974), pp. 189–92; Balachandra Rajan, *The Lofty Rhyme* (London, 1970), pp. 128–30.

2 See William Riley Parker, *Milton, a Biography* (Oxford, 1968), II, 843; John Arthos, *Milton and the Italian Cities* (London, 1968), p. 146.

3 All the quotations from the passage discussing Milton's plans in poetry may be found in *The Reason of Church Government urg'd against Prelaty*, I, *Complete Prose Works of John Milton* (New Haven, Yale University Press), 1953, pp. 812–23. All

quotations from Milton's poetry are made from *The Works of John Milton*, ed. Frank Patterson *et al.* (New York, 1931–40).

4 See Barbara Lewalski, '*Samson Agonistes* and the "Tragedy of the Apocalypse"', *PMLA* LXXXV (1970), 1050–62.

5 In a forthcoming book entitled *Toward 'Samson Agonistes': The Growth of Milton's Mind*, Princeton University Press.

6 M. C. Bradbrook, *English Dramatic Form: A History of its Development* (London, 1965), pp. 22–33.

7 See John M. Steadman, '"Passions well imitated": Rhetoric and poetics in the Preface to *Samson Agonistes*' in *Calm of Mind*, ed. J. A. Wittreich (Cleveland, 1970).

8 William Riley Parker in *Milton's Debt to Greek Tragedy* (Baltimore, 1937), found Milton's eclecticism and transformation of Greek sources more striking than any specific indebtedness. See also Northrop Frye, *Five Essays on Milton's Epics* (London, 1966), 94–7, for a discussion of Milton's formal radicalism.

9 For a discussion of Milton's place in the critical war of the ancients and moderns, see Morris Freedman, 'Milton and Dryden on rhyme', *Huntington Library Quarterly*, XXIV (1961), 337–42. Wherever possible in the ensuing discussion for the convenience of readers my quotations from critics will be taken from Allan H. Gilbert, *Literary Criticism: Plato to Dryden* (New York, 1940). Other sources will be specified. See John Dryden, *Of Dramatic Poesy and Other Critical Essays*, ed. George Watson, 2 vols (London, 1962), II, 202.

10 See Paul Sellin, 'Sources of Milton's catharsis: A reconsideration', *Journal of English and Germanic Philology* LX (1961), 712–30; Martin Mueller, 'Sixteenth century Italian criticism and Milton's theory of catharsis', *Studies in English Literature* VI (1966), 139–50; Raymond B. Waddington, '"Melancholy against Melancholy": *Samson Agonistes* as Renaissance Tragedy' in *Calm of Mind*; John Arthos, 'Milton and the passions: A study of *Samson Agonistes*', *Modern Philology* LXIX (1972), 209–21; Annette C. Flower, 'The critical context of the Preface to *Samson Agonistes*', *Studies in English Literature* X (1970), 409–23; Steadman 'Passions well imitated'; and Low, *Blaze of Noon*, p. 161.

11 See Flower, 'critical context', p. 411; Sellin, 'Sources of Milton's catharsis', p. 716; Steadman, 'Passions well imitated', pp. 185–6.

12 Gilbert, *Literary Criticism*, p. 620; *The Works of John Dryden* (Berkeley, 1965), XVII, 35, 189.

13 See the discussion in Robert D. Hume, *The Development of English Drama in the Late Seventeenth Century* (Oxford, 1976), who quotes Rapin, p. 160; see also Eric Rothstein, *Restoration Tragedy* (Madison, 1967), pp. 22–3, 113.

14 Gilbert, *Literary Criticism*, pp. 421, 426, 430, 432. Scaliger is quoted on the same point in *Neo-classical Dramatic Criticism 1560–1770*, Thora Burnley Jones and Bernard De Beer Nicol (Cambridge, 1976), p. 24. See also Minturno in Gilbert, *Literary Criticism*, p. 289.

15 Dryden affirms 'for the learned Mr. Rymer has well observed, that in all punishments we are to regulate ourselves by Poetical justice', and his view is confirmed by Dennis, Blackmore, Collier and a host of others. See Hume, *Development of English Drama*, p. 156.

16 Gilbert, *Literary Criticism*, pp. 616, 620; *Of Dramatic Poesy and Other Critical Essays*,

II, 194; see Earl R. Wasserman, 'The Pleasures of Tragedy', *ELH* XIV (1947), 283–307, and Hume, *Development of English Drama*, p. 175. Hume quotes supporting passages from Dennis, Rhymer and Rowe.

17 See Steadman, 'Passions well imitated', pp. 183–5.

18 Quoted in Rothstein, *Restoration Tragedy*, pp. 17–18, and in Jones and Nicol, *Neoclassical Criticism*, pp. 107–8.

19 *Of Education, Complete Prose Works*, II, 405. See for example Cinthio in Gilbert, *Literary Criticism*, pp. 272–3; and Puttenham, Sidney and 'E.K.' in G. Gregory Smith, ed., *Elizabethan Critical Essays* (London, 1950), II, 173; I, 199; and II, 178.

20 In Gilbert, *Literary Criticism*, see Minturno. Castelvetro and Tasso, pp. 276, 319, 480; see Mazzoni and Sidney, pp. 387, 412.

21 *Ibid.*, pp. 621, 653.

22 Quoted in Eugene M. Waith, *The Herculean Hero in Marlowe, Chapman, Shakespeare and Dryden* (London, 1962), pp. 152–3.

23 See Anne Davidson Ferry, *Milton and the Miltonic Dryden* (Cambridge, 1968), pp. 127–218; E. S. LeComte, '*Samson Agonistes* and *Aureng-Zebe*', *Etudes Anglaises* XI (1958), 18–22; and Waith, *Herculean Hero*, p. 192.

24 All quotations taken from *The Dramatic Works of John Dryden*, ed. George Saintsbury (Edinburgh, 1882), VI, 120–240.

25 See *A Variorum Commentary on the Poems of John Milton*, II, i, *The Minor English Poems*, ed. A. S. P. Woodhouse and Douglas Bush (London, 1972), pp. 233–41. See also Rosalie L. Colie, *Shakespeare's Living Art*, (Princeton, 1974), pp. 208–42; Bridget Gellert Lyons, *Voices of Melancholy* (London, 1971); and Robert S. Kinsman, ed., *The Darker Vision of the Renaissance* (Berkeley, 1974).

26 See R. Klibansky *et al. Saturn and Melancholy* (London, 1964), pp. 228ff. See S. K. Heninger, 'Sidney and Milton' in *Milton and the Line of Vision*, ed. Joseph Anthony Wittreich (Madison, 1975), pp. 72–83, for a study of the relationship of the companion poems to Spenser's *Shepheardes Calender*.

27 See Robert Burton, *The Anatomy of Melancholy* (London, 1948), III, 3, 55, 153, 205; I, 192, 275, 298, 439; II, 157; I, 117.

28 The shift has been studied for the continent by Michel Foucault, *Madness and Civilization: A History of Insanity in the Age of Reason* (London, 1967), pp. 117–58.

29 Burton, *Anatomy of Melancholy*, III, 417, 401.

30 See Kester Svendsen, *Milton and Science* (Cambridge, Mass. 1956), pp. 174–210; see also Lee Sheridan Cox, 'Natural science and figurative design in *Samson Agonistes*', *ELH* XXXV, 1968.

EXOTICK BUT RATIONAL ENTERTAINMENTS: THE ENGLISH DRAMATICK OPERAS

1 The fullest discussion is provided by K. G. Ruttkay, 'The critical reception of Italian opera in England in the early eighteenth century', *Studies in English and American Philology* I (1971), 93–169.

2 *Roger North on Music*, ed. John Wilson (London, 1959), p. 307

3 *Albion and Albanius*, as originally planned, was merely the all-sung prologue to a dramatick opera (*King Arthur*); thus the original intention was to produce another work directly in the English tradition of opera.

4 Gerard Langbaine (continued by Charles Gildon), *The Lives and Characters of the English Dramatick Poets* (London, [1699]), p. 75.

5 Downes's *Roscius Anglicanus* (London, 1708) is notoriously unreliable about dates, whilst in this century there has been fierce controversy over almost every aspect of the earlier dramatick operas. My abstract of Downes is necessarily arbitrary; in preparing it I have paid particular attention to E. J. Dent, *Foundations of English Opera* (Cambridge, 1928); Allardyce Nicoll, *Restoration Drama, 1660–1700* (Cambridge, 1952); *The London Stage, A Calendar of Plays, Entertainments . . .* (Carbondale, 1960–8).

6 The post-Restoration history of *The Siege of Rhodes* remains uncertain and needs clarifying: I have taken as my starting point the edition by Ann-Mari Hedbäck (Uppsala, 1973).

7 S.P. 29.99 Item 26; English was not Gascoyne's native tongue.

8 S.P. 44.23 p. 29 (Entry Book).

9 *North on Music* pp. 350–1.

10 For Evelyn the word 'Italian' indicated the *manner* of performance rather than the *language* of performance; see *The Diary*, ed. E. S. de Beer (Oxford, 1955), III, 144; IV, 220. In this instance it probably meant no more than 'all sung'.

11 See Lionel Salter, 'Strauss to Monteverdi's Wagner', *The Listener* 11 May 1967, p. 632; Winton Dean, *The Musical Times* July 1967, p. 636.

12 There is a full discussion in Eugene Haun, *But Hark! More Harmony : The Libretti of Restoration Opera in English* (Ypsilanti, Michigan, 1971).

13 The best examination of French opera in Restoration London is by Dennis Arundell, *The Critic at the Opera* (London, 1957).

14 I know of a single copy of Grabu's *Pastoralle* in the Pepys Library, Magdalene College, Cambridge (Day and Murrie, *English Song-Books, 1651–1702* no. 71); for the St Evremond pieces see *The Letters*, ed. John Hayward (London, 1930), p. 206, n.; p. 309. The dedication of the *Pastoralle* to Louise de Queroalle, Duchess of Portsmouth, suggests a performance under her auspices.

15 The disbandment of the French music may be traced through the pathetic appeals in the State Papers (e.g. S.P. 29.237 Item 135; S.P. 29.281 Item 225). For the employment of French musicians on the English establishment see H. C. de Lafontaine, *The King's Musick* (London, 1909), particularly the roll for *Calisto* (pp. 280–1).

16 *Ariane* was sung in French. Bi-lingual opera books are by no means a modern innovation, and exist for several of the early London Italian operas (e.g. Scarlatti's *Pirro e Demetrio*) as well as for some of Handel's operas. They demonstrate that the problem of intelligibility was not wholly ignored by operatic managements; unfortunately the survival rate of these fragile and ephemeral books is poor, and it is hard to know how many works received the benefit of such translations.

17 *Letters of Sir George Etherege* ed. Frederick Bracher (Berkeley, 1974), pp. 119–20.

18 Only one song by Lully appears in any English song-book published before 1700. It is worth noting that the *Collection of New Songs* by 'Mr. Gillier' published in 1698 is thoroughly anglicised.

19 See *Historia Histrionica*, ed. R. W. Lowe in his edition of *An Apology for the Life of Colley Cibber* (2 vols. London, 1889), I, xxxii.

20 Eleanore Boswell, *The Restoration Court Stage* (London, 1932), p. 136.
21 This copy of Raguenet's *Comparison* is in the Cambridge University Library, MR. 700.c.70.1.
22 *North on Music* p. 307, n.
23 Mrs Phillips originally obtained settings of the songs from friends, and servants of friends; presumably these, in conjunction with John Ogilby's tunes for the dances, were used in the Dublin performance (1663).
24 St Evremond, *Letters*, p. 162.
25 *Miscellanea: or Various Discourses . . . Written Originally By the Sieur de Saint Euvremont. And made English By Ferrand Spence* (London, 1686) C5v.
26 Betterton's activities are no more than hinted at by Judith Milhous, 'Thomas Betterton's playwriting', *Bulletin of the New York Public Library* Summer 1974, pp. 375–92. The problem of Betterton's collaboration with Dryden in dramatick opera has still to be adequately treated; I believe, despite the obvious objections, that Dryden had a hand in *Dioclesian*, and am impressed by the fact that Tonson chose to advertise Dryden's works on the title-page of *The Fairy Queen*, in which a number of details could be taken to show the influence of Dryden, if not his direct intervention. At several points the interpolated material relates to episodes and lyrics in Benserade's *Ballet de la nuit*.
27 Dennis commented, in the *Essay on the Opera's after the Italian Manner* (1706) that 'Operas . . . which are Dramatical may be partly defended by the Examples of the Antients'. The annotator of the Cambridge copy of Raguenet, however, thought it 'very Likely' that 'the Antient tragedys were all sung' and 'the Contrary hard to bee proved'. Modern scholarship bears out this last assertion.
28 Roger Savage, 'The Shakespeare–Purcell *Fairy Queen*', *Early Music* I (1973), 201–21; despite some powerful advocacy Robert Etheridge Moore (*Henry Purcell and the Restoration Theatre*, London, 1961) believes that Purcell's theatre 'was not yet ready for opera in the fullest sense', and this regret restricts his approach.
29 A reasoned guess may at least give a direction to future enquiries. William Corbett, the composer and violinist (d. 1748) was in the right places at the right times, and the hand could be his, but I have no conclusive evidence.

THE SIGNIFICANCE OF GAY'S DRAMA

1 Mr P. E. Lewis has written: 'Another look at John Gay's *The Mohocks*', *Modern Language Review*, LXIII (1968), 790–3; 'Gay's burlesque method in *The What D'Ye Call It*', and 'Dramatic burlesque in *Three Hours After Marriage*', *Durham University Journal*, LX (1967–8), 232–9 and LXIV (1971–2), 13–25. These are helpful studies. I differ from them in thinking that the category of literary burlesque alone is insufficient for the explication and appreciation of Gay's drama. Mr. Lewis's very well judged critical study of *The Beggar's Opera* (1976), published by Edward Arnold appeared too late for inclusion in my discussion.
2 I am speaking of the lifetime of Gay (1685–1732). This is not yet the period of Richardson and Fielding, but it may be thought that the fictions of Defoe merit the term 'realism'. Without doubt certain scenes in Defoe evoke the word 'realistic' but it is doubtful if the same is true of his fictions as a whole. Where they reach beyond

a limited subjectivity (Crusoe or Moll) it is in the direction of a providential and ultimately metaphysical order. Restoration comedy, on the other hand, offers something of a secular and objective scrutiny of a number of different individuals in a social pattern, which I take to be a requisite of realism.

3 With the exception of *The Beggar's Opera* and perhaps of *Three Hours After Marriage* none of Gay's plays has been satisfactorily edited. In quotation I have: (i) used John Gay, *The Beggar's Opera*, ed. P. E. Lewis (Edinburgh, 1973), the best modern edition of the *Opera*; (ii) cited the accessible *Poetical Works of John Gay*, ed. G. C. Faber (Oxford, 1926) for all other plays whose complete texts are included in that volume; and (iii) in the case of the plays not so included (*The Wife of Bath*, *Three Hours After Marriage*, *The Distress'd Wife* and *The Rehearsal at Goatham*) cited the first editions, giving page references. I have sometimes reversed the founts in Gay's use of Italic, and regularised abbreviations of characters' names.

4 The debt to *Much Ado About Nothing* has been noted by W. H. Irving, *John Gay: Favorite of the Wits* (Durham, North Carolina, 1940), p. 66 and F. S. Boas, *An Introduction to Eighteenth-Century Drama, 1700–1780* (Oxford, 1953), p. 169.

5 Gay and Pope were both working in the aftermath of Dryden's revival of interest in Chaucer. See Irving, *John Gay*, pp. 77–8 for the immediate context of the comedy.

6 The play exists in two versions, 1713 and 1730; it is radically revised in the later version. F. W. Bateson, *English Comic Drama, 1700–1750* (Oxford, 1929), p. 82 and P. M. Spacks, *John Gay* (New York, 1965), pp. 131–2, are especially contemptuous.

7 The judgement of Irving, *John Gay*, p. 79, who is, however, much the most interesting critic on this play.

8 Bateson, *English Comic Drama*, p. 83, has well said that 'the parody itself becomes creative and develops into a miniature comedy of sentiment of singular attraction' – though this oversimplifies – and Boas, *Eighteenth-century Drama*, p. 173, notes that Kitty's grief finds 'moving expression' in the ballad.

9 *The Letters of John Gay*, ed. C. F. Burgess (Oxford, 1966), pp. 17–18.

10 Pope to Caryll, 3 March 1715; *Letters of John Gay*, p. 19.

11 Benjamin Griffin and Lewis Theobald, *A Complete Key to the Last New Farce The What D'Ye Call It* (London, 1715); Pope to Caryll (see n. 10 above).

12 Gay to Parnell, 29 January 1715 (see n. 9 above).

13 George Sherburn, 'The fortunes and misfortunes of *Three Hours After Marriage*', *Modern Philology*, XXIV (1926–7), 102–5; this essay is an admirable account of the play's performance and reception.

14 Gay to Parnell (see n. 9 above) and the title-page of *Three Hours After Marriage*.

15 Ian Donaldson, *The World Upside-Down: Comedy from Jonson to Fielding* (Oxford, 1970), pp. 185–6. Donaldson's chapter on Gay in this book is much to be recommended.

16 Bateson, *English Comic Drama*, p. 87.

17 Sherburn, '*Three Hours After Marriage*', p. 102.

18 B. H. Bronson, '*The Beggar's Opera*', first published in *Studies in the Comic* (Berkeley, 1941); reprinted in *Restoration Drama: Modern Essays in Criticism*, ed. John Loftis (New York, 1966), pp. 298–327; see p. 314. As Bronson observes, the significance of Gay's having written the libretto for Handel's *Acis and Galatea* cannot be forgotten.

19 This is observed by William Empson, *Some Versions of Pastoral* (London, 1950), pp. 241–2.

20 This is clear from the suspicious/hostile attitude of Griffin and Theobald in *A Key . . . to The What D'Ye Call It*, and from the appreciative attitude of a paper on *The Beggar's Opera* submitted to *The Craftsman* on 23 April ?1728, by 'W.B.' The whole paper is of great interest for the contemporary reception of the *Opera*, and especially its recognition that an allusion to another author is not necessarily a mockery of him. W.B. writes of 'pleasant Parrallells with some of our most celebrated Dramatic Authors, who at ye same Time must not be understood to suffer by this jocular Treatment, no more than ye great Virgil by Cotton's Travesty, or the mightiest Homer by Dr Swift's exquisite pleasantry in his Battel of Books . . . At ye Quarrelling Scene of Peachum and Lockit, I could not help thinking on Brutus and Cassius, but without lessening my Respect for those Ancient Heroes, or the incomparable Shakespear, and Porcia must likewise excuse me, if I remembered her, when Polly sends Filch to the Old Bailey to learn what he coud of Macheath.

The Rival Queens seem Rivald again in Polly & Lucy who contend as earnestly for their little Robbr as Statira & Roxana did for the Great Plunderer of the World'. (Cholmondeley (Houghton) MSS. 74. 48. These are the papers of Sir Robert Walpole at present deposited in the Cambridge University Library.) *The Craftsman* was close to the Scriblerus Club writers, and such literary criticism as was submitted to it may be thought to have some authority.

21 Nathaniel Lee, *The Rival Queens, Or The Death of Alexander The Great* (London, 1677), alluded to in the *Craftsman* MS. cited above.

22 Bronson, '*The Beggar's Opera*', p. 309.

23 I am indebted for this valuable insight to Mr J. S. Bull, of the Department of English Literature, University of Sheffield.

24 Arthur Sherbo, 'John Gay: lightweight or heavyweight?', *The Scriblerian* (November 1975).

25 Gay's standard, though plausible, affirmation to Swift concerning the moral seriousness of *Polly* (Gay to Swift, 18 March 1729; *Letters*, p. 78) is interestingly endorsed by what his patroness, the Duchess of Queensberry, told Mrs Larpent on the occasion of the opera's first performance on 19 June 1777. Mrs Larpent, described by one who has studied her papers as 'a rather dull, puritanical young lady' noted in her journal that she was 'extremely pleased to go with the Duchess of Queensberry to see this Opera, which from the protection she gave its author Gay, & from the spirit of those times, occasioned her dismission from Court . . . the moral [of the opera] is nothing remarkably pointed, altho' the Duchess told me, that on Gay's being accused of immorality in the end of ye Beggar's Opera, some Nobleman (I really think Lord Bath but I am not certain) said "Why Gay you have only *transported* him pursue him, & bring him to punishment –" & see says she "how finely he has wrought out the tale".' (L. W. Conolly, 'Anna Margaretta Larpent, The Duchess of Queensberry and Gay's *Polly* in 1777', *Philological Quarterly*, LI.4 (October 1972), p. 956).

26 Most critics consider it so; see especially Irving, *John Gay*, pp. 270–1 and Spacks, pp. 159–61. The trouble is that, because *Polly* is a narrative continuation of the *Opera*, it has been assumed that Gay wished to write a formally similar work, and

that since *Polly* is not formally similar it must be a failure.

27 Irving, *John Gay*, pp. 78–80 offers some comparative remarks.

28 *A History of Early Eighteenth-Century Drama* (Cambridge, 1925), pp. 157–8. In half a sentence, however, Nicoll considers it 'a good comedy'.

29 For this theme in the attack on Walpole, see my book, *The Social Milieu of Alexander Pope* (London, 1975), pp. 243–59, especially p. 244.

30 The phrase is the title of the study by Sven Armens (New York, 1954).

31 Thomas Mann, *Doctor Faustus*, translated from the German by H. T. Lowe-Porter (London, 1949), pp. 151–2.

32 *Brecht on Theatre*, edited and translated by John Willett (London, 1964), p. 46.

'COMING WONDERS': USES OF THEATRE IN VICTORIAN NOVEL

1 Henry Mayhew, *London Labour and the London Poor*, (4 vols. New York, 1968), III, 151. First published 1851. The boy described how during a period when he was bound to sea he was brutally misused by the ship's mate: 'He used to beat me with the rope's end – sometimes the lead-rope – that was his usual weapon, and he used to leave marks on me. I took the part of Hamlet, and instead of complaining, I thought of that part where he says,

> "And make us rather bear those ills we have,
> Than fly to others that we know not of."

That's the best play of Shakespeare; he outdoes himself there.' Q. D. Leavis in F. R. and Q. D. Leavis, *Dickens the Novelist* (1970), pp. 111–17 discusses Dickens's use of Tartuffe; my *Meredith: A Change of Masks* (1970), pp. 122–4, indicates the influence of Molière on *The Egoist*.

2 Edward Bulwer Lytton, *England and the English* (1874), p. 266. First publ. 1833.

3 G. H. Lewes, 'Foreign actors and the art of acting' in *On Actors and the Art of Acting* (1878), p. 113. This collection of essays spans the period of the 1850s and 60s.

4 p. 134. Lewes comments: 'About three hundred plays are every season sent in to each patent theatre – about three or four plays are produced'. And he adds a note: 'It must be remembered that this was written five years ago, now there is not one patent theatre in which the legitimate drama is performed'.

5 *The George Eliot Letters*, ed. Gordon Haight (New Haven, Conn. 1954), II, 18.

6 'The drama in Paris, 1865' in *On Actors and the Art of Acting* (1878), p. 154.

7 Hippolyte Taine, *Notes on England*, trans. E. Hyams (1957), p. 214. First published 1872.

8 *Household Words*, (30 April 1850).

9 Henry James, *A Small Boy and Others*, F. W. Dupee (1956), p. 64. 'It was the age of the arrangements of Dickens for the stage, vamped-up promptly on every scene. Dire of course for all temperance in these connections was the need to conform to the illustrations of Phiz, himself already an improvising parodist and happy only so long as not imitated, not literally reproduced. Strange enough the "aesthetic" of artists who could desire but literally to reproduce.' pp. 65–6.

Sally Vernon in 'The London theatre and the English novel, 1830–65' unpublished Ph.D. dissertation, Cambridge (1975), gives a thorough and intelligent account of the interplay between novels and stage in terms of adaptation, stage-craft and themes.

10 In Winifred Gérin, *Charlotte Brontë The Evolution of Genius* (Oxford, 1967), p. 481.
11 *Dickens the Novelist* (1970), pp. 111–17.
12 *Household Words* (17 January 1852).
13 *The Examiner*, 26 January 1817, quoted in Michael Booth's introduction to *English Plays of the Nineteenth Century* (Oxford 1976), v, 5.
14 For example, William F. Axton, *Circle of Fire : Dickens's Vision and Style and the Popular Victorian Theatre* (Lexington, Ky., 1966), J. B. van Amerongen, *The Actor in Dickens* (1926), Earle Davis, *The Flint and the Flame; The Artistry of Charles Dickens* (1964), Robert Garis, *The Dickens Theatre* (Oxford 1965), George Rowell, *The Victorian Theatre : A Survey* (Oxford, 1956).
15 Jonas A. Barish, 'The anti-theatrical prejudice', *Critical Quarterly*, VIII (1966), 329–48; 'Exhibitionism and the anti-theatrical prejudice', *ELH*, XXXVI (1969), 1–29; 'Anti-theatrical prejudice in the nineteenth century', *University of Toronto Quarterly*, XL (1971), 277–99.
16 Mrs E. J. Burbury, *Florence Sackville* (1851), II, 247; George Herbert, *Gerald Fitzgerald* (1858), II, 93. Both novels are cited in Myron Brightfield, *Victorian England in its Novels: 1840–70* (Los Angeles, 1968). See the section on actors and opera, II, 308–18.
17 I. J. Wise & J. A. Symington, *The Brontës: Their Lives, Friendships & Correspondance*, (4 vols. Oxford, 1932), III, 253, 251.
18 Gérin, 481–2.

WAITING FOR PROSPERO

1 Samuel Beckett, *Waiting for Godot*, (1956).
2 trans. Walter Johnson (1967).
3 *En blå bok* (Stockholm, 1907).

SOCIAL ENVIRONMENT AND THEATRICAL ENVIRONMENT

1 *Naturalism*, 3,b in *A New English Dictionary on Historical Principles* (*OED*) (13 vols, Oxford, 1933).
2 *OED Naturalism*, 3,b
3 *OED, Naturalist*, 6,B.
4 *OED, Naturalism*, 3,a.
5 *OED, Naturalism*, 1.
6 *OED, Naturalist*, 1.
7 John Constable, *Fourth Lecture at the Royal Institution* (1836), in *John Constable's Discourses*, ed. R. B. Beckett (Ipswich, 1970), p. 69.
8 J. Boaden, *Memoirs of Mrs Siddons*, (2 vols. London, 1827), II, 355.
9 P. Fitzgerald, *The World Behind the Scenes* (London, 1881), pp. 20–1.
10 Cit. G. Rowell, *The Victorian Theatre* (Oxford, 1956), p. 18.
11 J. W. Cole, *The Life and Theatrical Times of Charles Kean* (London, 1835), II, 382.
12 Cit. W. Jerrold, *Douglas Jerrold, Dramatist and Wit* (2 vols. London, 1914), I, 211.
13 *Ibid.*, I, 214.
14 Cit. M. Willson Disher, *Melodrama* (London, 1954), p. 70.

15 *The Writings of Douglas Jerrold* (Collected Edition, 7 vols., London, 1853), VII, 286.

16 T. W. Robertson, *Society*, Act III, in *Great English Plays*, ed. H. F. Rubinstein (London, 1928), p. 1060.

17 *Ibid.*, p. 1061.

18 T. W. Robertson, *Birth*, Act III, Sc.i, cit. Rowell, *Victorian Theatre*, p. 79.

19 T. W. Robertson, *Caste*, Act I, in *Nineteenth Century Plays*, ed. G. Rowell (2nd edition, Oxford, 1972), p. 354.

20 A Strindberg, *On Modern Drama and Modern Theatre* (1889) in *Samlade Skrifter*, (55 vols. Stockholm, 1912–19). XVII, 288–9.

21 A. W. Pinero, *The Second Mrs Tanqueray*, Act I, in *Late Victorian Plays, 1890–1914*, ed. G. Rowell (2nd edition Oxford, 1972), p. 13.

22 *Ibid.*, p. 79.

See also:

Nicoll, A. *A History of Late Nineteenth Century Drama* (2 vols. Cambridge, 1946).

Rowell, G. *A Bibliography of the English Theatre, 1792–1914* in *The Victorian Theatre* (Oxford, 1956), 159–96.

Disher, M. Willson, *Winkles and Champagne : Comedies and Tragedies of the Music Hall* (repr. Bath, 1974).

The books and essays of
Muriel C. Bradbrook
and a selection of her book reviews

COMPILED BY PATRICIA RIGNOLD

Muriel Bradbrook is a regular or occasional reviewer for the following journals:

Financial Times 1971–75
Modern Language Review 1951–65
New Statesman 1951–76
Review of English Studies 1952–59
Shakespeare Quarterly 1952–67
Sunday Telegraph 1963–71
Times Literary Supplement 1960–76
Year's Work in English Studies 1950–54

1932

Elizabethan Stage Conditions (Harness Prize, 1931), Cambridge University Press.
'Notes on the style of Mrs Woolf' *Scrutiny* I, 33–8.
review: J. Dover Wilson, *The Essential Shakespeare. Scrutiny* I, 182.

1933

'*Hero & Leander*' *Scrutiny* II, 59–64.
'The criticism of William Empson' *Scrutiny* II, 253–7.
'Milton & the masque: a correlation' *Cambridge Review* LV, 47–8.
review: G. Wilson Knight, *Shakespearean Tempest. Scrutiny* I, 396–8.
      W. B. Yeats, *Words for Music Perhaps. Scrutiny* II, 77–8.

1934

'Coleridge's "Waste Land"' *Cambridge Review* LV, 383–5.

1935

Themes & Conventions of Elizabethan Tragedy, Cambridge University Press.

1936

The School of Night: a study in the literary relationships of Sir Walter Ralegh, Cambridge University Press.

1937

review: *Letters of Hartley Coleridge*, ed. G. E. Griggs & E. L. Griggs, *Cambridge Review*
LVIII, 288–9.

1939

'Marvell & the concept of metamorphosis' (M. G. Lloyd Thomas & M. C. B.) *Criterion*
XVIII, 236–54.

1940

Andrew Marvell (M. G. Lloyd Thomas & M. C. B.), Cambridge University Press.
"'*Tis Pity She's a Whore*' *Cambridge Review* LXI, 401–2.
review: M. M. Knappen, *Tudor Puritanism*. *MLR* XXXV, 229–30.

1941

Joseph Conrad: Poland's English genius, Cambridge University Press.
'Authority, truth & justice in *Measure for Measure*' *RES* XVII, 385–99.
'Marvell & the poetry of rural solitude' *RES* XVII, 37–46.

1942

'The liturgical tradition in English verse' *Theology* XLIV, 13–23.
'The latest verse of T. S. Eliot' *Theology* XLIV, 81–90.

1943

'*Little Gidding*' *Theology* XLVI, 58–62.

1946

Ibsen the Norwegian: a revaluation, Chatto & Windus (revised 1966).
review: G. F. Sensabaugh, *The Tragic Muse of John Ford*. *RES* XXII, 235–6.

1947

'Two notes upon Webster' *MLR* XLII, 281–94.
review: John C. F. Hood *Icelandic Church Saga*. *Theology* L, 151–3.

1948

'The good pagan's achievement: the religious writing of W. B. Yeats' *Christian Drama* I,
1–6.

review: *Ben Jonson: the poems, the prose works* VIII, ed. C. H. Herford, P. & E. Simpson
MLR XXXV, 229–30.

1949

'The elegant eccentrics' *MLR* XLIV, 184–98.

review: Richard D. Altick, *The Cowden Clarkes. MLR* XLIV, 272–3.
P. F. D. Tennant, *Ibsen's Dramatic Technique. Cambridge Journal* II, 248.

1950

T. S. Eliot. Writers & their Work, Longman for the British Council (revised 1968).

'Virtue is the true nobility: a study of the structure of *All's Well that Ends Well' RES*
n.s. I, 289–301.

review: 'Shakespeare' *YWES* XXXI, 108–24.

1951

Shakespeare & Elizabethan Poetry, Chatto & Windus.

'The sources of *Macbeth', SS* IV, 35–48.

review: *The Permanence of Yeats*: selected criticism, ed. James Hall & Martin Stein-
mann, *MLR* XLVI, 498–9.
Shakespeare Survey III, ed. Allardyce Nicoll, *MLR* XLVI, 262–3.

1952

'Shakespeare & the use of disguise in Elizabethan drama' *Essays in Criticism* II, 159–68.

review: Wolfgang Clemen, *Development of Shakespeare's Imagery. SQ* III, 125–6.
Bergliot Ibsen. *The Three Ibsens*: memoirs of Henrik, Susannah & Sigurd Ibsen.
NS (5 January).
Edward J. H. Green, *T. S. Eliot et la France. MLR* XLVII, 583–4.

1953

The Queen's Garland: verses made by her subjects for Elizabeth I . . . now collected in
honour of H. M. Queen Elizabeth II, Oxford University Press.

'*The Phoenix & the Turtle' SQ* VI, 356–8.

review: *Ben Jonson* XI, ed. C. H. Herford, P. & E. Simpson *MLR* XLVIII, 460.

1954

'Fifty years of the criticism of Shakespeare's style: a retrospect' *SS* VII, 1–11.

review: *A Hopkins Reader*, ed. John Pick; *Selected Poems of Gerard Manley Hopkins*, ed.
James Reeves, *MLR* XLIX, 370.
The Oxford Book of English Talk, ed. J. Sutherland, *MLR* XLIX, 488–9.

1955

The Growth & Structure of Elizabethan Comedy, Chatto & Windus (revised 1973).
'A note on Fanny Price' *Essays in Criticism* V, 289–92.
'Young barbarians at play' *Time & Tide* XXXVI, 1288–9.
review: Madeleine Doran, *Endeavours of Art*: a study of form in Elizabethan drama.
   MLR L, 68–70.
   John E. Hankins, *Shakespeare's Derived Imagery*, *RES* VI, 313–14.
   Marchette Chute, *Ben Jonson of Westminster*. *Cambridge Review* LXXVI, 393.

1956

review: Wolfgang Clemen, *Die Tragödie vor Shakespeare: Ihre Entwicklung im Spiegel
   der dramatischen Rede SQ* VII, 434.
   Thomas H. Johnson, *Emily Dickinson*: an interpretive biography; *Poems oj
   Emily Dickinson*, ed. Thomas H. Johnson, *MLR* LI, 592–4.
   Guiliano Pelligrini, *Il Teatro di John Marston; Barocco Inglese*, *RES* VII, 198–9.
   Lewis Leary, *Motive & Method in The Cantos of Ezra Pound*. *RES* VII, 440.

1958

Sir Thomas Malory, Writers & their Work, Longman for the British Council (revised
   1967).
'What Shakespeare did to Chaucer's *Troilus & Criseyde*' *SQ* IX, 311–19.
'An *Ecce Homo* of the sixteenth century & the pageants & street theatres of the Low
   Countries' *SQ* IX, 424–6.
'Dramatic rôle as social image: a study of *The Taming of the Shrew*' *Shakespeare Jahrbuch*
   XCIV, 132–50.
'Conrad & the tragic imagination' *Joseph Conrad Korzeniowski* Essays & Studies, Polska
   Akademia Nauk (Warsaw) 7–10.
review: *Narrative & Dramatic Sources of Shakespeare*, I, ed. Geoffrey Bullough, *Cam-
   bridge Review* LXXIX, 369.

1959

'Ibsen' *Indian Literature* (New Delhi) II, 45–9.
review: *The Letters of Emily Dickinson*, ed. T. H. Johnson, *MLR* LIV, 269–70.
   The Wakefield Pageants of the Towneley Cycle, ed. A. C. Cawley; Richard B.
   Young *et al.*, *Three Studies in the Renaissance MLR* LIV, 583–5.
   William Shakespeare: the comedies, the histories, the tragedies, ed. Peter Alex-
   ander, *SQ* X, 229.
   Thomas Moser, *Joseph Conrad: achievement & decline*; Robert F. Haugh,
   Joseph Conrad: discovery in design. *RES* X, 209–11.

1960

'No room at the top: Spenser's pursuit of Fame' *Elizabethan Poetry*, ed. John Russell
   Brown, Stratford upon Avon Studies II.

'Drama as offering: *The Princely Pleasures at Kenelworth*' Rice Institute Pamphlet XLVI, 57–70.

'The old lad of the castle' *SQ* XI, 382–5.

'The image of the delinquent in literature 1955–1960' *Metaphor & Symbol*, ed. L. C. Knights, Proceedings of the 12th symposium of Colston Research Soc., 24–34.

review: Hugh Kenner, *The Invisible Poet : T. S. Eliot. Cambridge Review* LXXXI, 346–9. J. W. McFarlane, *Ibsen & the Temper of Norwegian Literature ; Brand*, trans. James Forsyth; Ibsen *Plays*, I, trans. Michael Meyer: *The Oxford Ibsen*, VI trans. J. W. McFarlane, *TLS* (19 August) 521–2.

1961

review: Don Cameron Allen, *Image & Meaning, Metaphoric Traditions in Renaissance Poetry. Renaissance News* XIV, 297–9. F. W. Dillistone, *The Novelist & the Passion Story. Frontier* IV, 143–4.

1962

The Rise of the Common Player, Chatto & Windus.

'Marlowe's *Dr Faustus* & the Eldritch tradition' *Essays on Shakespeare & Elizabethan Drama in honour of Hardin Craig*, ed. Richard Hosley.

'Beasts & gods: Greene's *Groats-worth of Witte* & the social purpose of *Venus & Adonis*' *SS* XV, 62–71.

'Peele's *Old Wives Tale*: a play of enchantment' *English Studies* (Amsterdam) XLIII, 323–30.

review: Edith Sitwell, *The Queens & the Hive ; Fanfare for Elizabeth. NS* (7 September) 292–3. Charles R. Anderson, *Emily Dickinson's Poetry*; Theodora Ward, *The Capsule of the Mind*: chapters in the life of Emily Dickinson. *MLR* LVII, 599–60. J. G. Ritz, *Robert Bridges & Gerard Hopkins 1863–1889. MLR* LVII, 254–5. Martin Turnell, *Modern Literature & Christian Faith*; Martin Jarrett-Kerr, *D. H. Lawrence. Frontier* V, 449–50.

1963

'The drama of T. S. Eliot' *Notes on Literature* XXVII, British Council.

review: Hilda M. Hulme, *Explorations in Shakespeare's Language. MLR* LVIII, 404–5. P. J. Yarrow, *Corneille NS* (1 November) 622. G. Wilson Knight, *Ibsen. Scandinavica*, II, 57. *The Penguin Book of Religious Verse*, ed. R. S. Thomas, *Theology* LXVI, 420–2.

1964

'St George for spelling reform!' *SQ* XV, 129–41.

'The inheritance of Christopher Marlowe' *Theology* LXVII, 298–305, 347–53.

'Some Shakespearean recollections' *Library Chronicle* XXX, 58–61.

'A new reading of Sonnets 85 & 86' *Filološki Pregled* (Belgrade) I–II, 155–7.

'Shakespeare & the Elizabethan theatre' *English Language & Literature* (Korea) XV, 3–34.
'An interpretation of Hamlet' *Hiroshima Studies in English Language & Literature* XI, 27–9.
'Shakespeare in Elizabethan England' *English Literature & Language*, Sofia Univ. (Tokyo) 1–16.
review: C. S. Lewis, *The Discarded Image*; Morris Bishop, *Petrarch & his World*. *NS* (7 August) 188.
   Wolfgang Clemen, *Chaucer's Early Poetry*; Derek Brewer, *Chaucer in his Time*; T. W. Craik, *Comic Tales of Chaucer*. *NS* (27 March) 494–5.
   'Some recent books on Shakespeare' Pt I *British Book News* CCLXXXIII, 167–71; Pt II CCXXXIV, 249–54.

1965

English Dramatic Form: a history of its development, Chatto & Windus.
'Shakespeare's primitive art' *Proceedings of the British Academy* LI, 215–34.
'T. S. Eliot' *Notes on Literature* XLIV, British Council.
'Yeats & Elizabethan love poetry' *Dublin Magazine* IV, 40–55.
'Eliot's course' *Theology* LXVIII, 506–14.
review: *Conrad's Polish Background*: letters to & from Polish friends, ed. Z. Najdar, trans. H. Carroll, *MLR* LX, 267–8.

1966

'*The Comedy of Timon*: a reveling play of the Inner Temple' *Renaissance Drama* IX ed. Samuel Schoenbaum.

1967

review: Irving Ribner, *The English History Play in the Age of Shakespeare* (revised edition 1965) *SQ* XVIII, 188–9.

1968

'The Merry Wives of Windsor' *The Stratford Scene 1958–68*, ed. B. A. W. Jackson (Toronto).

1969

Shakespeare the Craftsman (Clark Lectures 1968), Chatto & Windus.
That Infidel Place: a short history of Girton College 1869–1969, Chatto & Windus.
'King Henry IV' *Manner & Meaning in Shakespeare*, ed. B. A. W. Jackson, Stratford Papers 1965–7 (Shannon, McMaster University Library Press).
'The Girton centenary' *Cambridge Review* XC, 203–4.

1971

review: Samuel Schoenbaum, *Shakespeare's Lives*. *Sunday Telegraph* (10 January) 10.
   Halvdan Koht, *Life of Ibsen*; Michael Meyer, *Henrik Ibsen* II, III; Orley I. Holtan, *Mythic Patterns in Ibsen's Last Plays*. *TLS* (10 August) 1091.

1972

Literature in Action: studies in continental & Commonwealth society, Chatto & Windus.
T. S. Eliot: the making of THE WASTE LAND, Writers & their Work, Longman for the British Council.

1973

'I. A. Richards in Cambridge' *I. A. Richards*, ed. Reuben Brower *et al.*
'John Donne' *Dome* x, 4–9.
review: Peter J. French, *John Dee. Listener* (18 January) 88–9.

1974

Malcolm Lowry: his art and early life, Cambridge University Press.
'The ambiguity of William Empson' *William Empson*, ed. Roma Gill.
'A new Jacobean play from the Inns of Court' *Shakespearean Research & Opportunities*, ed. W. R. Elton, VII & VIII, 1–5.
review: Douglas Day, *Malcolm Lowry*; Tony Kilgallin, *Lowry. NS* (5 April) 481.

1975

Barbara Bodichon, George Eliot and the limits of Feminism (James Bryce Memorial Lecture) Holywell Press Oxford for Somerville College.
'Some futures of English literature' *Poetica* (Tokyo) III, 72–84.
'Women in Cambridge, 1975' *Cambridge Review* XCVII, 33–6.
review: Rosalie Colie, *Shakespeare's Living Art. MLR* LXX, 603–5.

1976

The Living Monument: Shakespeare & the theatres of his time, Cambridge University Press.
'Conrad & Lowry' *Joseph Conrad: A commemoration*, ed. N. Sherry.
'A dream within a dream: Yeats & the legend of Ireland' *Mosaic* x, 85–96
review: James McAuley. *A Map of Australian Verse. TLS* (9 April) 422.
     'Dame Edith Evans 1888–1976'. *NS* (23 October).

1977

'My Cambridge 1927–1977' in *My Cambridge*, ed. Ronald Hayman.

Forthcoming

George Chapman, Writers & their Work, Longman for the British Council.
'Marvell & the masque' *Andrew Marvell* 1678–1978, ed. K. Friedenreich.

Index of Plays, Operas and Entertainments

General Index